APPLIED STATISTICS FOR
MANAGEMENT STUDIES

APPLIED STATISTICS
FOR MANAGEMENT
STUDIES

DAVID CROFT

M.A., B.Sc., M.I.S.

Principal Lecturer in Management Statistics and Operational Research,
Management Department, Slough College of Higher Education (Constituent
of Thames Valley Regional Management Centre)

THIRD EDITION

MACDONALD AND EVANS

Macdonald & Evans Ltd.
Estover, Plymouth PL6 7PZ

First published 1969
Second edition 1976
Reprinted 1979
Third edition 1983
Reprinted 1984

ISBN: 0 7121 0182 9

Printed in Great Britain by
J. W. Arrowsmith Ltd, Bristol

PREFACE TO THIRD EDITION

THIS book is intended to give an introduction to the ideas and methods of statistics to students on courses such as the Post-Graduate Diploma in Management Studies and the Work Study and Industrial Engineering Diploma. To this end I have not felt it necessary to introduce any mathematical proofs or derivations of the standard statistical formulae, and have concentrated on indicating the application rather than the theory of statistics. Experience suggests that Chapter Two in particular will be welcomed by many students, and I have tried to avoid excessive use of mathematical notation whenever possible.

I would like to express my thanks for permission to use copyright material from the Publications Board of the United Nations and the Controller of Her Majesty's Stationery Office.

I would also like to acknowledge permission to use statistical tables from the literary executor of the late Professor R. A. Fisher and Oliver & Boyd Ltd., Professor G. W. Snedecor and the Iowa State University Press and Professor A. Hald and John Wiley & Co. Inc.

Opportunity has been taken to revise and bring up to date those sections of the book dealing with current statistical practice in the United Kingdom. Some calculations have been modified to reflect the use of electronic calculators and mention has been made of the use of microcomputers in this area.

I would like to thank those colleagues and students who have made helpful comments on the earlier editions and who have encouraged me to believe that this book is meeting the need for which it was designed.

December 1982   D. C.

seemed helpful. Lastly, worked answers are now provided for many of the numerical questions set at the end of each chapter. It is hoped that these will meet the need of those students who learn best by practice.

July 1974   D. C.

CONTENTS

LIST OF ILLUSTRATIONS

LIST OF TABLES

CHAPTER ONE

INTRODUCTION TO STATISTICS

The task of statistics

Development of statistics as an analytical tool

THE techniques of preparing, analysing and presenting data which are now included under the title of "Statistics" have been developed in many different fields of study. This has had the advantage of bringing to the subject a variety of approach which has prevented any over-formalisation, but has unfortunately led to a multiplicity of different terms and symbols having the same meaning. Stemming from this varied background is the characteristic of statistics that the methods pioneered in one field of application are often developed and standardised in another.

Some of the main contributions to statistics may be indicated by a short history of the subject. The word "statistics" appears to have been first used in the late eighteenth century, to refer to the verbal description of the resources and political organisation of European states then being published. The word gradually transferred to numerical data of this type, and in the form of "official" or "government" statistics is still very important. At the same time, information was being collected on the behaviour of prices, and measures such as "index numbers" were developed. These were the subject of considerable theoretical discussion in the late nineteenth century, and again in the 1920s and are still capable of arousing controversy.

Another line of statistical development started with the discussions on gambling in the seventeenth century which led to the basic ideas of probability. With the growth of measurement as a tool of scientific inquiry, the results of probability problems were applied to the study of errors in measurements and so to the formulation of the theoretical distributions of measurements. In the exact sciences, where careful control of experimental procedure was leading to a high degree of reproducibility of results, these statistical results were little used, but by the late nineteenth century the study of agriculture and biology by experiment and measurement was producing a mass of variable results, and these could only be dealt with by statistical methods.

Much that is still of great value in statistics was developed at this stage and the association of statistics with agricultural science led to the establishment by the 1920s of many of the major methods of statistical analysis. It was also becoming realised that the same methods were suitable, with slight modifications, for the analysis of any measurement showing a mixture of controlled and uncontrolled variability, and statistical results began to be used in sociology, psychology and economic studies, and in industrial and commercial applications. Typical of this was the development of sampling for opinion polls and market research just prior to the Second World War.

The late 1920s saw the development of a purely industrial statistical technique, that of "statistical quality control," but the major advances in this field came under the impetus of the mass-production of armaments during the Second World War. Since 1950 it has become more and more obvious that industrial and commercial data are well suited to analysis by statistical methods, and new methods and applications are continually being reported. Certain fields such as market research are by now largely based on the use of statistical methods. Similarly in a recent survey of operational research scientists in which they were asked which analytical techniques they made use of regularly, only statistical analysis was named by more than 50%.

The latest development has been the increasing availability of electronic computers and calculating machines to handle computational work. This has led to a renewed interest in methods which were known theoretically, but were not thought feasible because of the amount of computation they required. Some of these are particularly interesting in the study of industrial and commercial problems involving many uncontrolled variables. Even the simpler techniques become much easier to handle, and the growth of the hand-held electronic calculator industry is providing tools which allow "on the spot" analysis and will give a further boost to the use of statistical methods as a routine procedure in business.

Modern uses of statistics

Statistics in the modern world have an application in any situation in which numerical information is handled, and especially where the data is of a variable nature. Statistical results and procedures are used at all stages of the processing of data. When the data is to be collected, statistics help in identifying the most efficient methods to use, whether experiment or survey. When the data is to be analysed, statistical measures summarise the information collected, and statistical tests examine it for significance. When the results are reported, statistical statements present the conclusions unambiguously and statistical diagrams display them in visual form.

It is important to realise that the use of good statistical methodology can lead to a considerable increase in the value of numerical information, and that its absence is often an indication that the information may be poor or even misleading.

Statistics and management

Statistics and scientific management

The art of management is the art of taking decisions, and the basic necessity for correct decision-taking is good information. It is becoming increasingly recognised that the more information there is available the better the decision taken. What is termed "scientific management" is basically management on the basis of precise numerical information, and to try to use such numerical information without using statistics to aid in its preparation is to fail to use one of the major tools of efficient management. In fact even when not recognised in its own right statistics is an essential part of most modern management services. In market research, in work study, in production control and planning, in quality control, in stock control, in sales analysis and forecasting, in project planning and in operational research there is a core of statistical methodology. Increasingly, also, the nature of decision-taking and the inherent element of probability is becoming recognised, and statistics is providing a vocabulary in which risks and confidence can be recognised and measured.

The statistician in management

Given this picture of management as a profession increasingly concerned with numerical information and analysis, the statistician has an important place as an adviser. The fear is often expressed that the "experts" in measurement and numerical manipulation will supplant the manager by presenting results which remove doubt and the need for decision-taking. This is far from true, and as more information becomes available in any situation, then the critical decisions become more clearly focused and often more difficult to make. Where information is incomplete or inaccurate an incorrect decision can often escape notice, and an inadequate manager fails to realise his inadequacies. The role of the manager is likely to grow more important and more demanding as he is able to draw on more and more expert information.

In this situation the statistician appears as a provider of information and advice, but not as a taker of decisions. He should be consulted at the early stages of the collection of data to ensure that the most efficient methods are used. He will, of course, be mainly concerned with the analysis of the information collected, and he will present the results in such a way that their content and significance is clear. He may indicate the implications of the results, but taking action to avoid or realise these implications is the responsibility of the manager.

Statistics in management education

As the emphasis on scientific management increases, so does the demand for management education, and the interested manager is told to study a wide and increasing range of subjects. Of these, statistics is usually regarded as a basic necessity and there are two main reasons why this is so.

First, the manager will be taking decisions and assessing probabilities, whether consciously or not. Statistical method can often provide some degree of measurability in an apparently unmeasurable situation. The manager will sometimes also have to reduce numerical data to a pattern of information suiting his particular needs, and again statistical methods are appropriate. The need to use statistical method is likely to grow with the expansion of the facilities available for computation on large computers via remote terminals, and on programmable desk calculators. These facilities will include libraries of standard calculations, and their very ease of use places more importance on the correct choice of data to feed into them and the correct interpretation of the results obtained.

Secondly, the manager will wish to know when the statistician can make a useful contribution to the analysis of a situation, and what limitations there are on the use of statistical methods. He may also need to assess the validity of conclusions presented to him and to argue with their originator.

From this it follows that there is a dual requirement in the statistical education of a manager. He should be able to use those methods which are appropriate to non-expert use, and he should appreciate the power and basis of statistics and should know when to call in a more expert analyst. There is no better way to achieve the first of these requirements than the actual practical use of statistical methods, and some arithmetical labour is well rewarded by a better knowledge of the methods involved.

CHAPTER TWO

INTRODUCTION TO STATISTICAL SYMBOLS AND SOME MATHEMATICAL REMINDERS

Symbols

Use of symbols

THE use of symbols instead of words in statistical formulae produces a considerable saving in space and time, and there seems little point in trying to avoid the use of such convenient aids to understanding. The symbols used in this book have been chosen in an attempt to avoid confusion, and their meaning will be described when they are introduced in the text. The symbols used correspond as far as possible to those in general use in the United Kingdom and the U.S.A. Unfortunately there is no universal set of symbols in statistics, and the reader is advised to check if similar symbols have similar meanings when referring to other statistical literature.

Special conventions

Two particular conventions will be adhered to throughout this book.

(*a*) Original quantities will be symbolised by capital letters, *e.g.* X, while derived quantities will be symbolised by the corresponding small letter, *e.g.* x. If the distinction is not necessary, then the small letters only are used.

(*b*) Statistics derived from samples will be symbolised by English letters, *e.g.* m, s, while the corresponding population statistics will be symbolised by the equivalent Greek letter, *e.g.* μ, σ. The use of these conventions will be further explained as they are required.

Suffixes

Suffixes will be used to distinguish between quantities of a similar type, such as repeated measurements of the same quantity:

e.g. $x_1, x_2, x_3, \ldots x_i, \ldots x_n.$

Here there are n measurements of type x and x_i is the general form of x. Where there is little chance of confusion the suffix will not be used, *e.g.* "n measurements of x" will be written instead of x_i where $(i = 1$ to $n)$.

Mathematical notation

In addition to the mathematical notations in everyday use, certain other less-common notations will be used; a short description of these is now given for reference.

Multiplication

As well as $\times$ a stop . will be used to indicate that two or more items must be multiplied together:

e.g. $x \cdot log. x = x \times log. x.$

Two symbols placed together, *e.g.* *ab*, will also have the same significance, *e.g.* $ab = a \times b$.

Inequalities

The inequality signs are used with the following meanings:

$x > y$, x is greater than y;
$x \geqslant y$, x is greater than or equal to y;
$x < y$, x is less than y;
$x \leqslant y$, x is less than or equal to y.

The sense of the inequality may be remembered by the fact that the open end of the sign is always placed towards the larger item. A common use of the inequality signs is $5 < x < 10$, meaning that x has a value between 5 and 10, or $5 \leqslant x \leqslant 10$, where the values 5 and 10 are also included.

Approximations

$x \simeq y$, x is approximately equal to y. This occurs when approximations are used in calculations where less accuracy is required than has previously been kept in the calculation. It implies that the values of x and y can be regarded as equal on the particular occasion being considered, although they may be distinguished on other occasions.

Limits

An arrow will indicate that a quantity tends to a certain value, and under the described conditions approaches closer and closer to it, *e.g.* $x \to 5$, x tends to 5, implies that x becomes close to 5, but not that x ever equals 5. We can imagine that $(5 - x)$ is less than any real amount, however small it may be. In particular $x \to 0$, x tends to zero, implies that x becomes very small; $x \to \infty$, x tends to infinity, implies x becomes very large. Note that $x \to 0$ does not imply that x ever becomes zero, and the size of x implied by $x \to \infty$ will depend on the circumstances.

Modulus

The sign $| \ |$ implies: take the numerical value of the quantity inside the sign and make it positive:

e.g. $|2| = 2, \ |-2| = 2, \ |(5 - 10)| = 5.$

Factorials

$r!$ is read as "r factorial" and is the product of all the integers from 1 to r, *i.e.* $5! = 5 \times 4 \times 3 \times 2 \times 1$. Note that by definition $0! = 1$.

Summation

We will often require the sum of a number of similar quantities,

e.g. $x_1 + x_2 + x_3 \ldots + x_n$

where n quantities of type x are added together. This operation of summation is symbolised by the use of the Greek capital letter Σ. The full notation for the above sum would be:

$$\sum_{i=1}^{i=n} x_i = x_1 + x_2 + x_3 \ldots + x_n.$$

The symbols above and below the Σ show the limits of the summation. If all the possible values of x are to summed then these may be omitted and the simpler form Σx used.

To avoid confusion with the use of the small letter σ, the name sigma is reserved for the small letter, and Σx is read as "sum of x."

The summation sign is known as an *operator*, because it is an instruction and cannot stand by itself.

When a compound quantity is summed, *e.g.* Σxy, then the expression after the summation sign must be calculated before the summation is made. Note especially the difference between:

$$\Sigma x^2 \text{ "square then add," and}$$
$$(\Sigma x)^2 \text{ "add then square."}$$

Combinations

In sampling theory the number of ways in which a particular sample may be obtained is often required, *e.g.* "how many ways can n items be chosen including r of a particular distinguishable type?" This is given by $\binom{n}{r}$, read "the combinations of r items from n where:

$$\binom{n}{r} = \frac{n!}{r!\,(n-r)!}."$$

In writing out an expression of this type a simple procedure may be followed. Write for the top line of the fraction $n\,.\,(n-1)\,.\,(n-2)\ldots$ for r terms, the bottom line is then $r!$:

e.g.
$$\binom{10}{3} = \frac{10 \times 9 \times 8}{3 \times 2 \times 1} = 120.$$

Note
$$\binom{10}{8} = \binom{10}{10-8} = \binom{10}{2} = \frac{10 \times 9}{2 \times 1} = 45.$$

Choose the form with the lowest figures for calculation:

e.g.
$$\binom{40}{38} = \binom{40}{2} = \frac{40 \times 39}{2 \times 1} = 780.$$

Calculation

Accuracy

It is impossible to study statistics without some arithmetic work. Although many statistical results are not required to a high degree of accuracy, there is often a risk of considerable loss of accuracy during a calculation. As a working rule two more significant figures should be used in a calculation than are required in the final answer. This means that answers derived using four-figure logarithm tables should only be quoted to two significant figures.

Most of the inexpensive electronic calculators on sale now will work to a minimum of six significant figures, and these are excellent for statistical work. The danger here is that the user is so impressed by the string of numbers so easily obtained that their significance is not sufficiently critically examined. The rounding off of final figures to show the true precision with which they are known is important and should not be forgotten.

Significant figures

By significant figures we mean those figures in a number which give information other than its magnitude. The following numbers are all given to four significant figures:

$$548\cdot6, \; 41\cdot29, \; 432\,900, \; 0\cdot001\,592.$$

When a final zero is shown in a decimal fraction such as $0\cdot04190$ it must be taken as a significant figure. In the case of large figures these may have to be indicated by a note $4\,100\,000$ (4 *sig. figs.*).

Certain arithmetic operations may rob us of a large number of significant figures:

e.g. $$458\,978 - 457\,987 = 991$$

The first two numbers were given to six significant figures, but their difference has only three significant figures. The standard routines given later have been designed with this danger in mind, and it is always wise to follow them.

Rounding off

When it is required to express figures to a smaller number of significant figures than are available they must be rounded off. The figure following the last significant figure is examined. If it is less than 5 then the last significant figure stands as it is, *e.g.* 423 becomes 420. If it is greater than 5 or 5 followed by any further figures it is increased by 1, *e.g.* 423·6 becomes 424 and 423·502 becomes 424. When this figure is exactly 5 there is a problem. Any rule such as "round 5's down," or "round 5's up" must introduce bias, so the following rule is preferred. Round off the 5 so that the last significant figures become even, *e.g.* 1975 becomes 1980 and 1965 becomes 1960. This rule should produce as many roundings up as roundings down and so avoid bias. Where rounding off of figures is known to have occurred it is wise to try to find what rule was used, so that the possible presence of bias is known.

Computation of square roots

Square roots are frequently required in statistical calculations and can cause problems. If there is any doubt about a value it is always simply verified by multiplying it by itself. This must return the original number.

Most electronic calculators now have a key giving square roots directly; if this is not available then the following routine can be used.

(*a*) Guess a figure for the square root.

(*b*) Divide the number whose square root is required by the guess.

(*c*) The square root is approximated by half the sum of the guess and the quotient in (*b*), *e.g.* find $\sqrt{2957}$.

This method may be applied as follows:

(*a*) Guess $=$ bigger than 50, say 54.

(*b*)
$$
54)\overline{2957}\ (54{\cdot}76
$$
$$
\begin{array}{r}
270 \\ \hline
257 \\
216 \\ \hline
410 \\
378 \\ \hline
320
\end{array}
$$

(*c*) $\sqrt{2957} \simeq \dfrac{54 + 54{\cdot}76}{2} = 54{\cdot}38.$

Note as a rough guide, as many figures can be added as are common to the guess and the quotient, *e.g.* 54 and 54·76 have two in common, so two can be added.

If greater accuracy is required repeat the calculation, this time dividing by the result of (c). The accuracy of the determination increases rapidly. Those who possess even the simplest electronic calculator will find this method extremely easy with a little practice and its use is recommended. (The method is sometimes referred to as the *Newton–Raphson Iterative Method*.)

Microcomputers

The compact and relatively inexpensive small computers, usually known as microcomputers, represent a new and very flexible tool for the statistician. These machines combine the calculating power of the older, or mainframe, computers with a more "user friendly" mode of usage and cheap means of storing data.

The simplest of these machines will have a keyboard used for the entry of data and programs, a visual display unit in the form of a small T.V. screen on which all the instructions or data entered are shown as well as the results, and a cassette unit which allows the storage of programs and data on compact cassettes. This form of storage is very cheap but rather slow in operation. Much faster storage with a much greater capacity is obtained on disc storage units. These are built into the more elaborate micro-computers and can be connected into the simpler machines. In addition a printer which allows us to output results onto paper can also be connected.

BASIC

In order to instruct a computer to perform the calculations we require, it is necessary to supply it with a program. These may be bought or can be written by the user. Almost all microcomputers can be programmed in the language called BASIC, and it is not difficult for a complete beginner to learn how to use this language.

All the calculations described in this book can be programmed in BASIC without great difficulty. Anyone who intends to make extensive use of a microcomputer should become proficient in a language such as BASIC, not least because the commercially available programs may not be precisely what you require, and are not always fault free.

Questions

1. If $x = 35, y = 20$ and $z = 5$, find the value of:

(a) $x . y + z$ (b) $|x - y|$
(c) $|y - x|$ (d) $z!$

2. If $x = 4, y = 7$, what is the maximum value z can take if:

(a) $x + z \leqslant 10$?   (b) $y/z > 1\cdot4$?
(c) $y - z \geqslant x$?

3. If $n = 20$, calculate the value of $\binom{n}{r}$ when:

(a) $r = 0$ (b) $r = 3$
(c) $r = 5$ (d) $r = 17$

4. The following corresponding values of x and y have been obtained:

$$x, \quad 1, \ 3, \ 4, \ 5, 7, \ 9, \ 12, \ 14$$
$$y, \quad 12, \ 10, \ 6, \ 9, \ 4, \ 0, \ -1, \ -5$$

Calculate:

(a) Σx and Σy (b) Σx^2 and $(\Sigma x)^2$
(c) Σxy and $\Sigma x . \Sigma y$ (d) $\Sigma |x - y|$

5. Use tables to find:

(a) $\sqrt{41\cdot97}$ (b) $\sqrt{3\cdot930}$
(c) $\sqrt{0\cdot00442}$ (d) $\sqrt{0\cdot1039}$
(e) $\sqrt{63\cdot580}$

6. Round the following numbers off to three significant figures:

(a) $429\cdot7$ (b) 3042
(c) $0\cdot005901$ (d) $0\cdot005805$
(e) 3875 (f) $3905\cdot1$
(g) 2997 (h) $4\cdot315$

7. Calculate, accurate to six significant figures:

(a) $\sqrt{70}$ (b) $\sqrt{0\cdot00049}$ (c) $\sqrt{340}$

8. Given the values of Σx, Σx^2 found in Question 4, and $N = 8$, calculate:

$$(a) \ \sqrt{\frac{1}{N}\left[\Sigma x^2 - \frac{(\Sigma x)^2}{N}\right]}$$

$$(b) \ \sqrt{\frac{1}{N-1}\left[\Sigma x^2 - \frac{(\Sigma x)^2}{N}\right]}$$

9. Given $n = 10, p = 0\cdot3$

use $P(r) = \binom{n}{r} p^r . (1 - p)^{n-r}$

to calculate:

(a) P(o)
(b) P(3)

10. Given $P(r) = \dfrac{e^{-m} \cdot m^r}{r!}$

use tables of e^{-x} to find:

(a) P(2) when m = 1·0
(b) P(1) when m = 1·4
(c) P(0) when m = 2·0

CHAPTER THREE

THE COLLECTION OF DATA

Collection

Reason for collection

BEFORE deciding how to collect data we should first enquire as to the purpose of collecting the data. Depending on this, the criteria we use in selecting our method of collection may include speed, precision, cost, wide usefulness as well as other factors. There is a main division into data which will be collected on a *regular* basis (and hence involve considerations of staffing, filing and circulation of the data), and data which is required for a *one-off* study only. In both cases we should think carefully as to the likelihood of the data being referred to in future. Data which will have a continuing value tends to require more ancillary inform-ation than ephemeral data. A mere suspicion that some data may be useful in future is not a good motive for its storage, as it will usually be found to be lacking in some essential when it is looked at again. In contrast, the storage of data with a definite purpose and to meet planned analytical needs may be most valuable. Forethought and planning are always repaid in full by the in-creased value of the results subsequently obtained.

What to collect

A part of the planning for data collection which must never be omitted is the consideration of what should be collected. This will be controlled by the purpose but we must also ask:

(*a*) does the data *exist already*?
(*b*) can it be *obtained easily*?
(*c*) can *measurements* be made easily?
(*d*) would the *addition of some extra data* make the study more valuable?
(*e*) are we going to *satisfy the purpose*?

The last question reminds us that in considering the various restraints on data collection we must beware of doing what is easy rather than what is necessary. Eventually we must consider the value of the information to be produced, and set this against the cost of our proposed methods. Experience suggests that it is always easier to initiate the regular collection of data than it is to stop the collection of redundant data, and a cost-conscious attitude is as necessary here as in other aspects of management.

Primary and secondary data

It should not be forgotten that much data has already been collected, both within the particular organisation and by agencies such as the government. The value of this data compared to that the firm collects itself is variable and a useful distinction can be made between primary and secondary data.

Primary data refers to data collected either by or under the direct supervision and instruction of the investigator. Such data usually implies considerable knowledge of the conditions under which the data are collected, and so of the limitations which must be placed on their use. This familiarity of the investigator with the background of data is valuable and can often prevent errors arising which would otherwise be undetected.

Secondary data refers to all other data where a lesser degree of control by the investigator exists. Here the possibility of misinterpretation increases as the degree of control decreases.

Validity of data

The usefulness of data depends on its reliability and suitability for the analysis intended, and care must be taken in assessing the value of any data. It is useful to ask several questions of all data. In the case of primary data these should all have a reasonable answer, in the case of secondary data any inadequate answers should serve as an indication of where trouble may lie when using the data.

The questions are:
 (a) what was measured?
 (b) who measured it?
 (c) how was it measured?
 (d) in what units?
 (e) when was it measured?
 (f) is it stable?

The relevance of the first five questions should be obvious, but it is surprising how often the information required to answer these questions is not available. Question (f) is required to establish if repeat measurements or observations will produce similar results. If not, then a series of repeat measurements or observations is necessary in order to determine the limits of the variability.

For most official statistics reasonable answers to these questions can be obtained, although the relevant information may not be easy to find. Many other sources of published data are not so satisfactory. Often when authorities are quoted, *e.g.* "according to 'A' . . .," it is found that the figures involved are in fact being quoted at third hand. The possibility of errors in such a transmission of data is very great and such data must be examined very carefully before use. Statements such as "it is well known that" and "it is accepted that" are also often indications that the data following them have *not* been checked by the person quoting them, and so must be treated with caution.

The following example clearly illustrates the dangers of uncritical adoption of data. Early 1973 saw considerable interest in, and public discussion of, the "energy crisis," and many competing sets of data were made public, and future scenarios based on them. A survey of published major studies revealed some fifteen to sixteen apparent sources of data, but a critical examination showed that these were all secondary, and in fact derived from not more than four primary sources. It was fascinating that the same original data was used to support different arguments and was presented so as to appear at odds with itself. The greatest care was needed to obtain data which was not already coloured by personal opinion.

The problems arising from defining terms and checking the validity of data are always highlighted in negotiations on pay and productivity. Careful reading of competing claims made in accounts of negotiations will often reveal that there is disagreement as to the facts of the situation which are at the heart of the conflict. When international comparisons are also attempted, then the statistician is faced with a major problem, which is inevitably further confused by emotional judgments on the part of many of the persons involved. The same considerations will be present to some degree in many data-collection operations and serve to emphasise the need to examine all secondary data with the greatest care.

Sample surveys

Experiments

Returning to the practical collection of primary data, we may distinguish two situations. In the first we set up a situation and observe its behaviour in response to various stimuli. This is an experiment. Alternatively we observe an existing situation and its response to factors not necessarily under our control. The use of experiments is typical of the classical sciences, and is possible in some industrial and commercial studies. The design of statistical experiments so as to make best use of the resources used is outside the scope of this book, but is a major contribution of statistics to applied research. More frequently the exigencies of company operations rule out experiments, and data has to be collected by direct or indirect observation of the real-life system, that is by surveys.

Surveys and censuses

A large amount of the data studied by a statistician is collected by means of a survey of the relevant population. This applies in market research, opinion sampling, work sampling, the sampling of clerical records, demographic studies and many other fields. When a survey is made in which all members of the population are surveyed, then the survey is described as a *census*. Surveys in which only part of the population is surveyed are described as *sample surveys*. The comments made in this chapter concerning the planning of a survey apply equally well to a census or a sample survey.

The principal problem in using a survey rather than a census is that of ensuring that the sample taken is truly representative of the population sampled. The methods of doing this and of estimating the accuracy of the information obtained will be indicated later, and it may be noted that only by the use of statistical sampling schemes can unbiased information be obtained and its accuracy assessed.

The use of samples

The widespread use of samples is often criticised by non-statisticians as an inaccurate second-best. In fact it is in many cases the census which is more likely to be faulty. This arises from the perfection needed in a census. If we aim at 100%, then less than this will produce inaccuracy, but the inaccuracy produced cannot be judged if we do not know which items are not covered. Very often this is precisely the information lacking, and the degree of inaccuracy present cannot be estimated without making checks additional to the survey.

In a correctly-taken sample a much higher response can be obtained, as more effort per member of the population can be expended. As will be shown, the errors involved in expanding sample results to represent a population are known before the sample is taken. It is preferable to have a result of known accuracy than one in which the size of errors is a variable quantity, and except where the population to be surveyed is small enough for a census of high precision to be taken, a sample survey is to be preferred to a census.

In addition, there is the practical advantage of dealing with a small rather than a large inquiry. Without the resources available to a government, a census is not feasible in many cases simply because of the amount of work required. When a small number of inquiries only are made, then each inquiry may be more exhaustive and expensive, and yet despite this the time taken to complete the survey may be reduced considerably. This last factor is of great importance in many market research inquiries, where the data sought may be ephemeral, and hence useless if delayed. Here speed and lack of bias may be more desirable than high accuracy.

Lastly the cost of a survey will in general be less than that of a census, and the type of survey carried out can be designed to a given cost. This cost can be balanced against the value of the information required so that the minimum expenditure is made for any given purpose.

Practical sampling

Planning

Much of the trouble experienced in sampling investigations is the result of inadequate planning. Only if the planning is complete and thorough before a sample survey is made will the results be of the standard desired. The planning should cover the choice of sampling method, questions and all administrative details, as well as the analysis intended. If such decisions have to be taken during the course of a survey then there is always a possibility of a bias entering into the results. Equally, if it is not possible to answer the questions which will be raised during planning such as the precision required in the results and the analytical resources available, then the whole exercise should be postponed until these points have been resolved.

Pilot surveys

It is quite possible that there does not exist sufficient information and experience to allow initially of satisfactory planning for a complete survey, and a pilot survey may be undertaken to supply this information. A pilot survey can also be of great use in training personnel in survey methods, to try out the questionnaire and to test the administrative arrangements. If the pilot survey is satisfactory and no changes have to be made for the main survey, then the results of the pilot survey can be combined with those of the main survey. However this should not be done if any doubts are expressed, particularly if there is any evidence of time-dependence.

Questionnaires

Assuming we have reached agreement on the data required then a questionnaire can be drawn up. This involves several considerations. First, the questions themselves. Where factual information is required this should be trouble-free, but even so we must be careful to ask for the exact information required, and if necessary to indicate the way in which the data should be obtained by the person completing the questionnaire. If we require exact rather than estimated figures, we must say so, and where alternative measurement techniques are possible we must indicate the exact routine to be followed. When opinions are being sought we have to be extremely careful not to influence the respondents' answers. In general people give the answers they think are wanted. The problem for the survey-taker is to so present his questions that it is not obvious what the "correct" response is. Many costly and complex inquiries have been invalidated by lack of attention to this point. If the results are very important, then a follow-up survey which checks a proportion of the main survey may be needed to double check the replies for possible bias caused by "helpful" respondents.

The second consideration is the physical design of the questionnaire. This depends on who is to complete it, and on the data processing to be employed. If the questionnaire is to be posted or delivered in some way to the respondent, who is to complete it unsupervised, then to ensure accuracy and a good response rate the form used should be laid out clearly and not give any impression of complexity. Adequate notes and instructions must be given, possibly on an attached sheet, and the whole should be double-checked for completeness in itself. If a trained person is to fill in the form, then a simpler format is possible, but we should never forget that error rate is always linked to design of the form. Complexity on a questionnaire produced by trying to put too much on one sheet so as to save stationery costs is likely to prove expensive later. Forms which are to be completed on a regular basis, but perhaps by different people, must also be carefully thought out. Care should be taken that the stationery used is appropriate to its use. A form to be used on a factory floor must be robust enough to resist rough handling, a postal questionnaire must be attractive and give a good impression if a reasonable response is wanted.

Lastly we should be aware of the data processing required. Much data is now handled by electronic methods, both for transfer from one location to another and for analysis by the various forms of computer now available. If our form is to be a punching document for transfer to punched cards or punched or magnetic tape it should be laid out to facilitate this transfer. The possible responses to the questions may be pre-coded by unobtrusive symbols to aid the punching staff, and prevent transposition of data. This can be taken too far, and it is likely that the appearance of a form which has a multitude of squares laid out in the data fields to be filled in, accompanied by a variety of unexplained symbols, will not be acceptable to many people, who will complete such a document with reluctance. Even when they are compelled to complete such a questionnaire the risk of errors is increased considerably. If mechanical data handling is to be used then similar considerations apply, and particularly when the hand-transfer of information is needed the various systems of aligning documents to simplify the work are worth looking into.

A wealth of good advice and information is contained in the Stationery Office publication, "The Design of Forms," and anyone likely to be involved in this type of work should possess a copy of the latest edition.

The purpose of the survey

The first item in the planning list is to decide on the purpose of the survey. This may appear to be an obvious item, as the person controlling the survey is usually presented with a statement of aims by the "customer." If this is accepted without question until after the survey is completed, then misunderstandings of what was required can invalidate the whole of the work carried out. A discussion of the purpose with all interested parties is a sound precaution, and the statistician should be consulted at this stage to prevent the formulation of impossible demands.

A common result of such a study is to find that a slight expansion of the survey would provide results of value to persons other than the initiator of the survey. There is obviously scope for savings by the avoidance of duplication in such a situation, and a feasibility study designed to show what extra information would cover the subsidiary purpose should be carried out. The results of this study must now be subjected to the questions:

(*a*) can this extra information be obtained,
(*b*) are we making the survey too large?

Judicious pruning, followed by a check to see that the original purpose will still be satisfied, should produce the optimum inquiry in terms of economical use of available resources.

Population and sampling frames

When the purpose of the survey has been established then the population to be sampled should also be clear. This population must be unambiguously defined, even if it is known that it cannot be sampled in its entirety. By so doing the inadequacies of any practical survey can be judged against the theoretically desirable survey. The actual list of members of a population from which a sample is chosen is known as the sampling frame. This may be a list prepared by the person conducting the survey, a published list, or an ordered collection of items such as invoices in a file.

Ideally a sampling frame should include all possible members of a population; in practice this is rarely achieved. When using published lists care must be taken to establish the exact relationship between the sampling frame and the population, and to anticipate bias when this is present.

For in-company surveys, both for commercial and industrial applications, company records should supply suitable lists. Such lists as pay-rolls, customer files, stock records, accident reports and equipment registers should be close to being complete lists. Even so, never assume that everything is "according to the book." Over a period of time even the most carefully controlled procedures "drift" and omissions and duplications creep in.

Published lists used in market research and opinion polls include: for business concerns, trade directories and telephone directories; for households, large-scale plans, rating lists, street directories; for individual persons, telephone directories and the Electoral Register. Of these the Electoral Register is the most commonly used in political opinion polls and in consumer inquiries.

Where a particular profession is to be sampled then suitable lists are often available such as lists of members of professional associations, the *Law List*, the Armed Forces lists and *Crockford's Clerical Directory*.

If the population to be sampled forms part of a larger population which is adequately listed, then it is a time- and money-consuming procedure to abstract the special list from the full list. Instead the situation may be dealt with at the sampling stage, as described later.

The electoral register

The Electoral Register is a list of all those entitled to vote at general and local elections. It should contain the names of all persons over the age of eighteen (and those attaining this age during its currency) who are not debarred in some way. In fact it is at best about 95% complete and may include duplications and incorrect entries, although omissions are the most common defect. The register is compiled in October of each year by a combination of a canvass by the registration officer for each constituency and an inquiry form sent to householders and the managers and wardens of residential hotels and hostels. A provisional register is available for inspection in November and errors and omissions can be notified for correction at this stage. A final register is published in February and remains in force without further alteration for twelve months. It should be noted that the register is effectively four months old when introduced and sixteen months old when it is superseded by a new one.

The register is published in sections containing up to about 5000 names, representing polling districts. These are sub-divisions of administrative areas and represent lists of persons who will vote at a given polling station. For obvious reasons the districts in rural areas contain less names than urban polling districts. The separate sections may be purchased, and this ease of availability is an important factor in making the register a useful sampling frame. In each section the names of electors are given in order of address, street by street in urban areas, and alphabetically in dispersed rural areas. The names are numbered serially through the section, again a useful feature.

Certain electors are distinguished in the register; those who are only entitled to vote in local authority elections by reason of business qualification, service voters and merchant seamen who are absent from home, and young voters whose eighteenth birthday occurs during the currency of the register. Unfortunately the register does not indicate the relationship between the persons listed as resident at any one address and in particular does not indicate the marital status of the females listed.

It has been estimated by independent surveys that the accuracy of the register is about 95% complete when it is new and as little as 85% when it dies. There may be bias through certain classes of person deliberately avoiding registration, and as the register is not revised during the year removals create further errors. Despite this the register is widely used for market-research surveys, and is of course the natural frame, being almost coextensive with the population, for political opinion surveys.

Sampling methods

Types of sample

The types of sample available fall into two principal groups: judgment samples and random or probability samples. Of these the probability samples are the more important as they are unbiased and allow estimation of the size of error involved. In both judgment and probability sampling, multi-stage and stratified sampling may be used; the distinction is that in a probability sample a random selection method is employed in the final stage of sampling. In a judgment sample, the final items are chosen to be representative of the group being sampled, and this choice may lead to unbiased estimates, but relies on the skill and knowledge of the person choosing the sample.

Multi-stage sampling

When a survey covers a large population a concentration of effort is very desirable. A survey of 1800 electors over the whole of England, Wales and Scotland would lead to about three interviews in each constituency. This would require either a large number of interviewers or a similar number with a large amount of travelling; either way a large amount of administrative work would be required and costs would rise. By taking a sample of, say, twenty constituencies which are representative of the whole, and taking about ninety interviews in each constituency, the administrative work and cost can be reduced. Fewer interviewers are required and each interviewer is involved in less travelling between interviews. The system can be extended, *e.g.* within each constituency a further stage may be introduced by taking a sample of the polling districts and concentrating the sampling effort in these.

Similar methods apply in other circumstances. In sampling expensive clerical records it would be very inconvenient to have to take a sample which is thinly spread through several files or ledgers. By taking a sample of the larger units the sampling can be concentrated, with a great saving of time and effort.

Multi-stage sampling, with a random selection of units at each stage, should lead to unbiased estimates, but will tend to increase the variability of the results. The exact size of the increase is difficult to predict, but a figure of twice the existing variability has been suggested when multi-stage sampling replaces simple sampling. This loss of precision is by far offset by the savings made in using multi-stage sampling, and can often be compensated for by taking a larger sample without increasing the cost beyond that of a comparable simple sample.

Stratified samples

When the population to be sampled can be classified in such a way that the responses to the questions asked in the survey are more consistent within the classes than between the classes, then the technique of stratified sampling may be used. This consists in taking random samples within each class and combining these samples proportionally to their size to ensure that the sample is representative of the population. This procedure can considerably reduce the size of the errors of sampling. This can be extended to make use of stratification with respect to several features of the population, and in practice is carried as far as possible. We are effectively removing a source of variability from the final results, and this must be reflected in increased precision.

To make use of concepts introduced later (pp. 190–193): In terms of the analysis of variance we are removing the "between classes" variability and leaving only the "within classes," variability. The greater the variability between classes compared to the variability within classes the greater the reduction in the variability of the final results.

The use of stratification has an intuitive appeal as well as ensuring that the sample, in some respects at least, is a model of the population being sampled. The optimal sampling situation is obtained when we allocate our sampling effort to take account of the varying variability of responses within strata by taking larger samples of the more variable sets of items. The student who wishes to pursue these techniques is referred to more advanced texts where a well developed theory of sampling is available.

Cluster sampling

When parts of a population are known to be locally homogeneous then the method known as cluster sampling may be used. In this, a series of starting-points within the population is chosen by a random method, and a number of members of the population close to the starting-point are taken into the sample by following some pre-assigned rule. This gives a cluster of items and since in a homogeneous area there is little difference between adjacent items, it is hoped that the arbitrary cluster will adequately replace a random selection.

It is difficult to assess the errors involved in cluster sampling, and the method is often regarded with disfavour despite its administrative attractions.

As an example of cluster sampling, an interviewer might be instructed to start at a given address, and then to sample every fifth house he came to. He would be given rules to obey for use at road junctions, in cul-de-sacs and other interruptions to straightforward sequences of houses.

Quota sampling

The previous methods have involved random selection at some, if not all, stages of the sampling process. In quota sampling the members of the sample are chosen by a non-random process and thus it is not possible to estimate the accuracy of results obtained from the sample.

The method is to stratify the population by several factors and then to specify the number of members of the sample required from each of the classes which have been defined by given combinations of factors, so that the sample is a microcosm of the population. As in cluster sampling, the method depends on the assumption that the members within each class are homogeneous, so that replacement of one member by another makes little difference to the results.

When carried out by a competent organisation with accurate stratification and correct placing of the sample into classes, the method can yield excellent results. This depends, especially for the last requirement, on the calibre of interviewers available, as they may be required to carry out judgments as to age and social class. It is attractive in that the required sample size is always reached, and call-backs to specified desired members of the sample are not needed as in many random sampling schemes. It is also attractive in that it is easily justified to laymen, as there is an inherent reasonableness in selecting a sample which is a miniature of the population. The refinement of adding a random final stage is often difficult to explain.

Quota sampling can be misleading when the homogeneity of members within classes is not high, especially if this is not anticipated. In general, quota sampling is attractive to the amateur, but best left to the expert.

Random selection methods

Mechanical selection

A random selection method is one in which each item is selected completely independently of any previous choices. When the whole sampling frame is sampled at one time, then this implies that each member of the frame has an equal chance of being chosen. Note that this "equal chance" property is a consequence of random selection, not a definition of it as is often suggested.

It seems reasonable that if all the items to be sampled are represented by identical objects and a "blind" choice made from these, then the resultant sample will be random. This is the philosophy behind the selection of winners in raffles and tombolas. Unfortunately in practice it appears, firstly that the mixing methods used are rarely as good as supposed, and secondly that unsuspected differences arise in the objects sampled which lead to non-random selection. In one case it turned out that a series of balls, identical dimensionally and differing only in colour, gave biased samples. Eventually it was found that minute differences in the slipperiness of the paint surface existed for different colours.

The possibility of achieving perfect conditions is so remote that mechanical sampling is rarely if ever used in statistical sampling schemes.

Random numbers

Random numbers are sets of digits such that the occurrence of any digit is unaffected by which digits precede it. This means that the digits 0 to 9 should be equally represented in a long series of digits, that all the doubles 00 to 99 should be equally represented and that all the trebles 000 to 999 should be represented, etc. They are derived by generating digits by a process which it is hoped will produce digits in a random order, and then testing the combination digits obtained to see if their relative frequencies observe the conditions given above. Several published sets of random numbers are available and known to be reliable; an extract from such a set is given in Appendix II (Table F).

A sophisticated electronic device for generating such numbers has been constructed to choose prize-winners in the Premium

Bond lottery. This is ERNIE, the Electronic Random Number Indicating Equipment.

Random numbers are used by assigning a number to each member of the frame, and then taking suitable size combinations of the random numbers. When a number is selected which corresponds to a member of the frame that member is selected as part of the sample. It does not matter how many redundant numbers are chosen as this does not affect the randomisation.

Most computer software libraries now contain random number generating programs. As these are preprogrammed the sequences produced from any starting-point are predictable. From this aspect the sequences produced are not random. However the sequences are sufficiently extensive, and the starting-points sufficiently numerous, for the sequences produced to be regarded as random for all practical purposes.

The standard function $RND(A)$ is used in the BASIC programming language. The exact effect of using this function depends on the dialect of BASIC in use, but the following is typical. If the variable A used is less than 0 then a negative random number between 0 and -1 is produced. If the variable is 0 a fixed sequence of random numbers is obtained with values between 0 and 1. If A is greater than 0 a different sequence of random numbers is obtained each time RND is used.

Systematic sampling

A simpler selection method is to decide on what fraction of the frame is required in the sample, i.e. $k = n/N$ where n is the sample size and N the size of the frame. This is known as the *sampling fraction*. If members are selected serially at intervals of $1/k$ in the frame, then a sample of the correct size will be obtained. This is known as a systematic sample. The first member selected is usually chosen by a random selection method from the first $1/k$ members.

When the members in the frame are arranged in a random order a systematic sample becomes a random sample, and if they are arranged in order of some factor such as would be used in stratification, then the sample obtained is automatically stratified. This provides a very convenient method of dealing with stratification by a continuous measurement. For example, if employees are given a number on a serial basis as they join a company, and if the numbers are not used again when employees leave, then a systematic sample of employees taken from a list in number order is stratified with respect to length of service. Many document series, such as invoices, can also be treated in this way.

The danger in systematically sampled sampling is that there may be periodicity in the arrangement of items in the frame. If this corresponds to the sampling interval, then bias is inevitable. Care should be taken that this is not so, and once again the importance of full information about the data being studied must be emphasised.

Sampling errors and sample size

For random samples it is possible to estimate the errors likely in the results obtained. These are always proportional to the sample size and so we can decide on the sample size needed for any given precision required in the results. To do this requires the use of statistical theory which will be developed later, and reference should be made to the Index for examples.

A general rule may, however, be stated now. Except when the sample size is more than a tenth of the frame size, the precision with which results are obtained is independent of the frame size. Thus the sampling fraction is irrelevant, only the absolute sample size is important. A rule such as "take a sample of 1 in 100 items" means that a different precision will be obtained for each size of frame sampled, and is usually an indication that the sampling procedure was not set up with proper regard to good statistical principles.

Questions

1. Discuss the problems likely to occur when using data for which you have no background information. Illustrate your answer by reference to the following statement: "The working population of Littlebourne is 3801."

2. What supplementary information would you like to have available to enable you to assess the validity of, and apply, data which you have not yourself been concerned with collecting?

3. "Desk research" often consists of the assembly of the data relevant to a problem from various technical data books and similar publications. Discuss the likely sources of error in such a method of examining a problem.

What information would we wish to know regarding any data obtained in this way?

4. Distinguish carefully between a probability sample and a judgment sample. Explain in what circumstances a systematic sample could be regarded as a probability sample.

5. Explain the use of stratified and multi-stage sampling, and comment on the advantages to be gained by using these methods.

6. A television company wishes to measure the extent to which its advertisements are remembered by the public in the London area. Suggest a suitable sampling method to obtain this information, and indicate some of the steps that might be taken to avoid bias in the results.

7. Discuss the initial planning of a sample survey, and explain the importance of the choice of sampling frame.

8. What is meant by a sampling frame? Suggest suitable sampling frames for use in surveys of:

(a) purchasers of a brand of coffee,
(b) orders in a wholesale drapers, and
(c) retail pharmacists.

9. Justify the use of a sample survey instead of a census, indicating the points of advantage of the survey.

10. Discuss the circumstances in which quota sampling might be preferred to some form of random sampling.

CHAPTER FOUR

CLASSIFICATION AND TABULATION

Classification

Types of classification

The first step in most examinations of data is to put the data into a table. It is not possible to appreciate the implications of a large body of data until this is done. The results of a market research inquiry may consist of several hundred inquiry forms, each with a score or more figures or answers on it, and the reduction of this to a series of tabulations may be the major part of the analysis.

Data which is to be tabulated must first be classified. Classification may be by a numerical criterion or by some qualitative feature or attribute. In the latter case the division into classes may be obvious, *e.g.* male/female, but often requires arbitrary decisions and the use of standards for comparisons. Whatever system is used any classification must meet certain conditions as given below.

A body of data may be classified with respect to more than one attribute at a time, giving rise to two-way, three-way or even more complex classifications. The presentation of such multiple classifications becomes difficult for more than two-way classifications and such analyses are best carried out in sections.

Rules for classifications

A good classification should satisfy two conditions.

(*a*) It should cover all possibilities. There must be a class into which every item of data can be placed—even if only "others."

(*b*) It must be unambiguous. There must be only one class for each item of data.

Occasionally it is desirable to have overlapping classes—but where this is so it must be clearly shown or confusion may arise.

This does not apply to composite or "totals" classes which are often required.

Numerical classifications

Where numerical data is involved the classes may consist of measurements having particular values, but in general the number of possible values will be very large and each class must consist of a range of possible measurements. It is important to define classes so that the assignment of measurements to classes may be made unambiguously. Rules such as placing half a unit in each of two classes which have a common boundary when a measurement falls on the boundary are not very satisfactory.

Class boundaries

If the measurements are discrete, taking only a series of special values, then the classes are adequately defined by quoting the least and the greatest value to be placed in each class, as shown in Table I.

Table I—Class Boundaries for Discrete Data

(a) Counts of individual items	(b) Measurements of height to the nearest $\frac{1}{2}''$
0– 9	$50''$–$51\frac{1}{2}''$
10–19	$52''$–$53\frac{1}{2}''$
20–29	$54''$–$55\frac{1}{2}''$
30–39	$56''$–$57\frac{1}{2}''$
40–49	$58''$–$59\frac{1}{2}''$

Note that the actual boundaries between classes are $51\frac{3}{4}''$, $53\frac{3}{4}''$ and so on, similar boundaries are often used even when they may not correspond to real measurements, *e.g.* in (a) we may imagine the boundaries as $9\frac{1}{2}$, $19\frac{1}{2}$ and so on. Where measurements are continuous, taking any value within the possible range, then more care is necessary. The preferred method is shown in Table II.

Table II—Class Boundaries for Continuous Data

5″ up to but less than 10″	OR 5″ →
10″ up to but less than 15″	10″ →
15″ up to but less than 20″	15″ →
20″ up to 25″	20″ → 25″

The boundaries in this case are 5″, 10″, 15″ and so on. For any real method of measurement there is only a finite series of measurements possible, so it is possible to regard all measurements as being discrete. In practice when the minimum unit of measurement is less than one-twentieth of the class interval little error will result in treating the measurements as continuous.

Care should be taken where figures are rounded up or down, as the class boundaries will be different from those suggested above, *e.g.* ages are almost always quoted to the number of completed years, and so classes:

> 5 years–10 years
> 11 years–15 years

would in fact represent:

> 5 years up to but less than 11 years
> 11 years up to but less than 16 years

with the boundaries at 5 years, 11 years, 16 years and so on.

Two measurements required when working with classified data are the class interval and the class mid-point.

Class intervals

The class interval is the difference between the lower boundary of the class, or the least measurement in it, and the lower boundary or least measurement of the next higher class. The method of calculation should be obvious from Table III. Alternatively the highest measurements may be used.

Table III—Calculation of Class Intervals

Class	Interval	Class	Interval
0–9	10	0 →	25
10–15	6	25 →	10
16–20	5	35 →	10
21–30	10	45 → 60	15

Class mid-points

The class mid-point is taken as being half-way between the least and the greatest measurement in the class. In the case of continuous data, the greatest measurement in one class is taken as indistinguishable from the least measurement in the next higher class. Examples are shown in Table IV.

Table IV—Calculation of Class Mid-points

Class	Mid–point	Class	Mid–point
0–9	4·5	0 →	12·5
10–15	12·5	25 →	30
16–20	18	35 →	40
21–30	25·5	45 → 60	52·5

Choice of classes

The choice of classes for numerical data should be made so that as far as possible equal interval classes are used, as this simplifies subsequent calculations. When it is necessary to use unequal classes to avoid many classes with very few members, as tends to occur when a set of data contains extreme values, it is best to make the larger classes simple multiples of the smaller classes. Unequal classes are also desirable when the measurements being classified are bunched rather than dispersed. Here it is preferable to try to place the class boundaries between the "bunches." Since the mid-point of the class will be used to represent the whole class the least loss of accuracy occurs when the members of a class are grouped near the mid-point.

There is always a loss of information when measurements are classified, as individual measurements cannot be distinguished after classification. This loss has to be balanced by the increase in speed and ease of calculation when using classified data and by the greater ease with which classified data can be understood. At least seven classes and not more than twenty probably indicates the preferred range with ten to twelve as the most popular numbers of classes.

Tabulation

The need for tabulation

After classification, data is usually tabulated. This is nearly always necessary before calculations may be started on the data. and often represents a useful method of examining the data itself. The opportunity should be taken of starting the analysis of the data by placing the various classes so that comparisons may be made between them. The form which the subsequent analysis takes may well be suggested by observations made at this stage. By grouping related classes, group totals may be calculated and given in the tabulation.

Construction of tables

It is not possible to illustrate all the types of tabulations which may be required, and it is suggested that the subject may best be studied by reference to examples in government and similar publications. The *Monthly Digest of Statistics* and the *Department of Employment Gazette* should provide a range of suitable examples. Certain points may be noted; all tables should:

(*a*) have a clear title;
(*b*) have clear headings and sub-headings;
(*c*) indicate all units used;
(*d*) indicate the source of data;
(*e*) be easy to read.

The last point is essential in a good table. The aim of tabulation is clarification and if this is not achieved then the table should be redesigned. Often two simple tables are to be preferred to one complex one.

Ratios

A table is often made more useful by the conversion of some or all of the figures in it into ratios, or more often percentages. These may be shown in a column next to the original data, or in a separate table. (See Table V.)

Table V—Use of Percentages in Tables

INDUSTRIAL STOPPAGES BEGINNING IN NOVEMBER 1981

Principal cause	Number of stoppages	Number of workers involved	% of total workers involved
Wages:			
rates	34	73 500	63·9
other reasons	3	200	0·2
Hours of work	10	34 000	29·5
Redundancy questions	5	2400	2·1
Trade union matters	4	500	0·4
Working conditions	10	1500	1·3
Money and work allocation	14	1300	1·1
Dismissals	8	1600	1·4
Total	88	115 100	100·0

Questions

1. Suggest a suitable classification for:
   (*a*) hair colour,
   (*b*) eye colour,
   (*c*) physical build.
How would you ensure that a given person was correctly assigned to the classes you have chosen?

2. Obtain a list of parliamentary constituencies in England giving their size, and suggest a suitable classification into not more than eight classes. What other characteristics could be used to classify these areas?

3. How can the way in which a set of similar measurements is classified into a small number of classes affect the subsequent analysis of the data?

4. A researcher uses the following questionnaire and has obtained 300 replies. Draw up some tables he could use to help in his analysis of the data.

Survey into Ice–cream Eating

Respondent's sex   male ☐   female ☐

Respondent's age   up to 7yrs ☐   7 up to 11 ☐   11 up to 16 ☐

16 up to 21 ☐   21 up to 40 ☐   over 40 ☐

Q1. Do you eat ice–cream

never ☐   once a month ☐   once a week ☐   every day ☐

Q2 Do you buy from

ice–cream van or kiosk ☐   ice–cream shop ☐

grocer ☐   supermarket ☐   other shop ☐

Q3 Do you prefer

cornets ☐   wafers ☐   tubs ☐   blocks ☐

Q4 Do you prefer

plain vanilla ☐   cornish ☐   other flavours ☐

---

5. The number of items ordered per invoice for a sample of invoices are as follows. Classify the numbers into a suitable series of classes

which you feel will best simplify the data, without losing too much information: 48, 72, 54, 36, 36, 30, 72, 42, 18, 54, 66, 12, 24, 30, 36, 24, 12, 48, 42, 48, 36, 48, 42, 12, 66, 36, 30, 30, 24, 60, 72, 48, 48, 36, 12, 30, 48, 36, 18, 72, 60, 48, 18, 54, 36, 30, 36, 36, 24, 54, 24, 72, 60, 24, 24, 30, 36, 48, 60, 30, 66, 24, 24, 48, 42, 42, 36, 60, 36, 24, 24, 42, 48, 30, 36, 48, 24, 36.

6. The sample of households co-operating in the 1980 Family Expenditure Survey contained 18900 persons. Of these 4800 were children under 16 years of age, 2600 were retired and 2100 were housewives or not working.

Of those above 16 years of age, there were 5700 males between 17 and 65 years of age and 900 males of 65 and older, with 5900 and 1600 females in these ranges respectively. Of the children 2500 were males.

Draw up tables showing the distribution of the sample by work status and by age and sex. Use percentages to help in making comparisons.

7. The monthly rainfall for the period 1941–1970 and for 1979 and 1980 is shown below. Draw up a table of percentages to help in comparisons between the rainfall in recent years and the average figures given.

MONTHLY RAINFALL IN ENGLAND AND WALES (mm)

	Average 1941–1970	1979	1980
January	86	86	78
February	65	66	93
March	59	125	104
April	58	68	18
May	67	124	32
June	61	42	128
July	73	33	74
August	90	94	96
September	83	38	67
October	83	78	131
November	97	87	87
December	90	161	71

Source : *Monthly Digest of Statistics*

CHAPTER FIVE

THE PRESENTATION OF STATISTICS IN DIAGRAMMATIC FORM

Introduction

The place of diagrams in statistics

Most people do not find it easy to look at a number of figures and appreciate their content without considerable study, so it is desirable to present data in such a way that its salient characteristics are quickly and easily seen. This is often best accomplished by presenting the data in a pictorial or graphical form.

Such representations are of common use and of great value if carefully prepared without intent to deceive. The reader is invited to examine the examples to be found in newspapers, periodicals, company reports and on television and to examine them for suitability and unbiased presentation of the parent data. It will be found that not all examples are as unbiased as might be wished, and hence contribute to the opinion that "statistics can prove anything." However, many examples should be found which do lead to greater clarity and understanding.

Limitations of diagrams

Before describing the common types of diagram and graph it must be emphasised that they can never replace original data. It is inevitable that detail will be lost. The aim of a diagram is not to provide quantitative information, but to give a qualitative appreciation of a set of data. The person interested in further information should be able to obtain the original data on which the diagram or graph is based, and not have to rely only on what is shown. An important part of the use of diagrams is to arouse interest, so that the data on which the diagram is based are examined, when they might otherwise be disregarded as just another set of figures.

Types of diagram

The number of possible types of diagram which can be used to illustrate statistics is limited mainly by the ingenuity of the person drawing the diagrams. Certain types in common use will be described and illustrated. The names used to describe these diagrams differ between various authors, but it should be obvious which is referred to.

The main groups of diagrams are:

(*a*) pictograms and pie charts;
(*b*) bar charts;
(*c*) time graphs;
(*d*) maps;
(*e*) planning charts;
(*f*) analytical graphs.

The discussion of the last two categories will be deferred to the next chapter, as they represent the active use of diagrams, as more than illustrations.

Pictograms and pie charts

Pictograms

In a pictogram the magnitude of the figures referring to a particular item is shown by a number of identical simplified pic-

Fig. 1(a).—*A pictogram—misleading version*

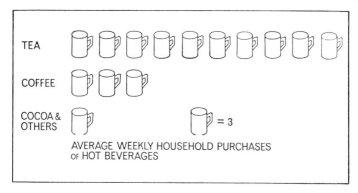

FIG. 1(b).—*A pictogram—preferred version*

tures of the item. The use of multiple symbols is much to be preferred to varying the size of symbols, as it may not be obvious
whether the height, area or volume of the symbol is being compared. As the aim of such a diagram is to give a general impression
of the data there seems little point in the careful construction of
fractional symbols. If a finer measure is required, use smaller
symbols and more of them.

This form of diagram is of great use for popular publications
and many good examples may be found in both the daily and
periodical press.

Pie charts

These are a popular form of diagram in which a sector of a
circle represents each item of a total. They are commonly used
for depicting the breakdown of expenditure, or revenue, from
several sources. Since the area of a sector of a circle is directly
proportional to the arc of the circle bounding it, the diagram may
be drawn by dividing the circumference of the circle in proportion
to the size of the various components to be represented. Special
chart paper with circles whose circumference is divided into
100 parts is available and allows the direct use of percentages. If
the total area of the pie is made proportional to the total sum
depicted then two or more pies of differing sizes may be used, to
show the varying quantities for differing years, or areas. Note
that the area, not the radii, should be made proportional to the
total figures being illustrated.

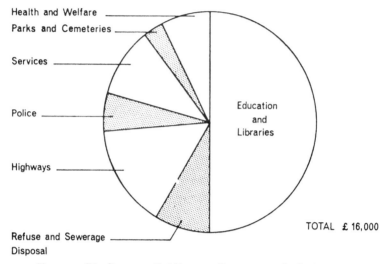

FIG. 2.—*Pie diagrams. Public expenditure 1982, Canley District*

Pie diagrams are usefully employed in the preparation of statistical maps, as described later.

Bar charts

Simple bar charts

If instead of the rows or columns of pictures used in the pictogram we represent our data by columns of varying length then we have a bar diagram. Bar diagrams are constructed with the bars drawn proportional in length to the size of the measurements they represent, and the bars may be placed either horizontally or vertically. The horizontal format makes it possible to place longer titles against each bar, and enables more bars to be used in one diagram. The choice of format depends on the data to be illustrated; as in all statistical diagrams clarity and informative layout should take precedence over any preconceived ideas of what is correct. The use of colour when possible is desirable to add impact.

Construction of bar charts

Some general guidance on the construction of bar charts may be found useful.

(*a*) Choose a scale so that convenient dimensions are obtained. It is not necessary to fit the graph paper available—make the graph paper fit the data! Scales such as 1 cm = 1 unit, 2 units, 5 units or multiples of these will be found easiest to work with. Wherever possible include the zero in the scale to avoid distorting relative effects. If the zero is omitted make this clear by "breaking" the scale.

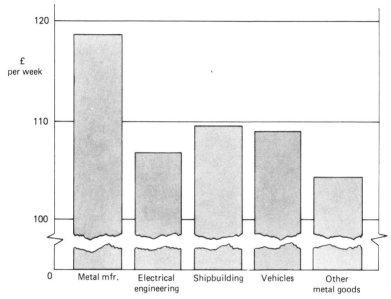

FIG. 3.—*Bar charts. The indication of a broken scale. Average earnings in metal working industries*

(*b*) Make the width of a bar about one-fifth to one-tenth of the longest bars. This may need modification if there is a large number of bars on the graph.

(*c*) Allow half-bar width between bars and at each end.

(*d*) Show a few scale lines only. It is not necessary for accurate measurements to be taken from the graph. For accuracy the original data must be consulted. Too many scale lines, or a full graph grid are merely distracting.

(*e*) Label clearly all scales and bars, and give a clear general heading to the graph. Quote the source of information briefly at the foot of the diagram.

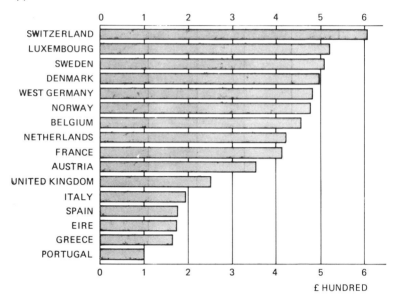

FIG. 4.—*Horizontal bar chart.   Gross domestic product per head of population,
western Europe 1965*

Multiple bar charts

Information of similar nature, but from various sources or
years; may be combined on a multiple bar chart. Two or more
bars are drawn side by side, and the different series of bars must

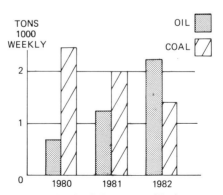

FIG. 5.—*Multiple bar chart. Fuel usage*

be clearly distinguished by colour or shading and a key shown. The total width of the multiple bars should be made 1 to 1¼ times that of a simple bar, and it will be found best not to exceed 3 series of bars to avoid a confusing effect.

Component bar charts

Where the bar represents a total, then the contributions of the component parts may be shown by a suitable division of the bar and colouring or shading. As it is easiest to judge the size of the component which starts from the base line, the most important component should be placed here, but the same relative order of components should be given in all the bars. Again a key to shadings or colourings should be given. In all the bar charts where shading is necessary thought should be given to the effect produced. The eye distinguishes different areas best by the density of shading. Shadings having the same spacing of lines and differing only in the direction of lines should be avoided. Black is best reserved for small but important components (*see* Fig. 6).

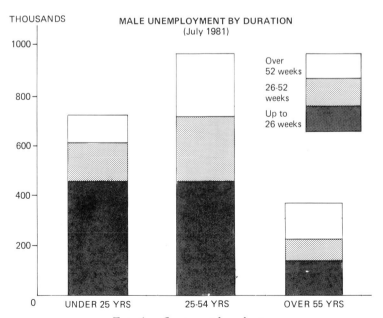

FIG. 6.—*Component bar chart*

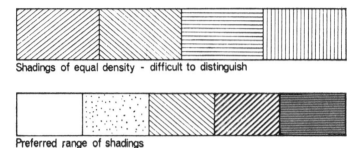

Shadings of equal density - difficult to distinguish

Preferred range of shadings

FIG. 7.—*The choice of shadings for diagrams*

Percentage component bar charts

When the relative proportions of the components are more important than their absolute values then each bar can be made the same size to represent 100%. The bar is then divided up in proportion to the size of the components. In this case both the top and bottom components can be judged by reference to fixed base lines of 100% and 0% respectively, and these proportions should be reserved for the more important components.

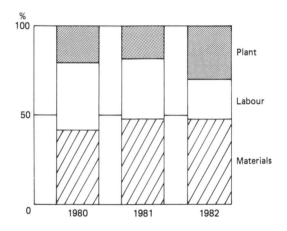

FIG. 8.—*Percentage component bar chart. Production costs*

Floating bar charts

When there is an obvious base from which measurements are made in both a positive and negative direction, *e.g.* £0 for profits and losses, bars may be drawn away from the line in both directions to give a floating bar chart. This type of diagram is also useful for showing performances against a target, which need not be constant for every bar.

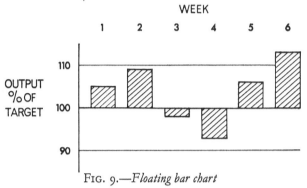

FIG. 9.—*Floating bar chart*

Comparison bar charts

Where similar figures are to be compared, then two bar charts may be placed back to back. This may be done with the bars placed horizontally. Do not attempt to compare bar charts by placing one over another, the effect will be confusing. If it is desirable to compare two or more bar charts and the comparison bar chart method is not suitable, then the charts are best drawn under one another using vertical bars, so that the scales are in alignment.

Time graphs

Simple time charts

In a time graph, the varying values of some measurements are plotted against time, and time is always allotted the horizontal axis.

Simple time graphs consist of a series of points representing the measurements joined by straight lines. If it is desired to emphasise the points used in the construction of the graph a small circle should be drawn surrounding the point, and connecting lines should be stopped at the edge of the circle. If more than one series of measurements are shown on one graph then clearly differentiated lines should be employed. When lines of different colours cannot be used then the type of line must be changed, *i.e.* solid, dotted, pecked. Lines made up of tiny symbols such as crosses, triangles, etc., should not be used, as a graph employing them often takes longer to decipher than it would take to examine the data it is based on. The maximum number of lines is best restricted to three again, to keep the graph simple. A large number of different measurements may be compared by drawing them below one another with sufficient separation to avoid overlapping. A small section of the scale for each measurement is given, but all are referred to the same time scale. Excellent examples of this technique will be found in *Economic Trends*.

Care should be taken in indicating the time scale to avoid ambiguity. When measurements refer to specific times there is no problem and points are placed to correspond to the time. When the measurements are averages over a period, and when the measurements are totals over a period of time the points are placed at the end of the time period.

Band charts

Band charts correspond to component bar charts and show the components of the total line in a time chart. Even more than in

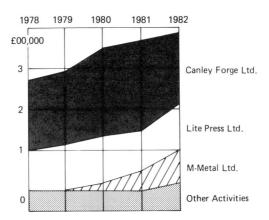

FIG. 10.—*Band chart. Group trading profits*

the component bar charts, the magnitude of the bottom band only is easy to gauge, so this should be reserved for the most important component unless a logical order of components dictates otherwise. The size of the other bands can be very deceptive and care should be taken when using these diagrams.

Percentage band charts

The percentage band chart shows the variation of the relative proportions of the components with time. Here the magnitudes of both the top and bottom bands can be reasonably easily gauged.

Z-charts

A Z-chart is a specialised time graph which can be used to display a series of figures such as sales, production, orders, etc.

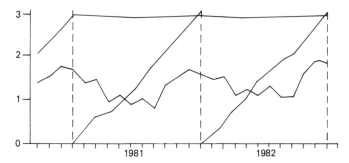

FIG. 11.—*Linked Z-charts showing sales for 1981 and 1982*

The most common Z-chart is one spanning a year and using monthly data, although Z-charts using other time-spans and intervals (see Fig. 11) would be feasible. Three lines are plotted on the chart:

(*a*) monthly totals;
(*b*) cumulative totals;
(*c*) twelve-month moving totals.

In addition a target may be inserted.

To calculate the twelve-month moving total it is necessary to have data for the preceding twelve months; this means that this line cannot be drawn on the first of a series of Z-charts.

The method of calculation of the required totals, and the appearance of the graphs are shown in Table VI and Figs. 11 and 12. Note that the scale for the monthly total has been increased to make variations more obvious.

Table VI—Construction of Z-chart

Month	Mthly. sales	Cum sales	Mthly. sales	Cum sales	month sales	Mthly. sales	Cum sales	month sales
Jan.	162	162	154	154	1632	156	156	1582
Feb.	152	314	156	310	1636	157	313	1583
Mar.	106	420	105	415	1635	104	417	1582
Apr.	131	551	128	543	1632	132	545	1586
May	114	665	103	646	1621	112	661	1595
June	125	790	109	755	1605	124	785	1610
July	89	879	85	840	1601	110	895	1635
Aug.	82	961	81	921	1600	112	1001	1666
Sept.	150	1111	140	1061	1590	164	1171	1690
Oct.	161	1272	162	1223	1591	183	1354	1711
Nov.	186	1458	180	1403	1585	190	1544	1721
Dec.	182	1640	177	1580	1580	187	1731	1731

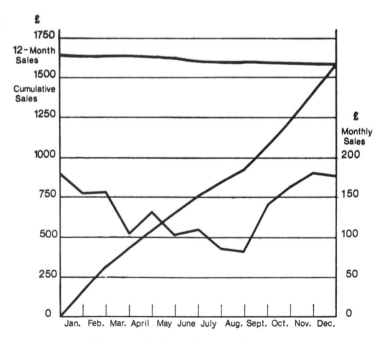

FIG. 12.—Z-chart, showing sales for 1982

Statistical maps

The use of statistical maps

When it is desirable to classify data by their geographical origin, then the data may best be illustrated by statistical maps. As with all statistical diagrams complexity should be avoided if it impairs the clarity of the maps produced. A series of maps illustrating one set of data from different aspects is usually more informative than one map which attempts to include all the data.

As with other statistical diagrams there is much scope for individual initiative in the construction of maps, and only the more common types of map will be indicated. An excellent series of maps, using a variety of techniques, will be found in the *National Atlas*.

Location maps

The simplest maps show the location to which the data refer by placing small bar diagrams or pie charts at appropriate places on the map. Alternatively numerical symbols or simple pictograms may be used.

Density maps

When measurements refer to an area rather than a point on the map, then the density rather than the total of some measurements is often the significant feature. Density may be represented by several methods; the choice is best made by constructing the alternative representations and then deciding which best illustrates the data. The simplest technique is to shade the areas for which the measurements have been obtained so that density of shading corresponds to the density of the measurement. The remarks made earlier regarding shading apply even more strongly here, and care should be taken to obtain clear distinctions between shadings.

If the density figures are available at points on the map, then an *isoline map* may be constructed by drawing in lines of equal density. These are familiar in meteorological maps, where isobars, lines of equal pressure, are a principal feature.

Lastly dots may be placed to represent counted units at the location where the units were counted. The closer the dots the greater the density of units. In constructing a map of this type the size of data and choice of minimum count represented are critical, and several combinations of these should be tried out before deciding on the final form of the map.

Flow maps

Maps are very effective in showing the size of flows between different points, such as flows of commodities or of transport units.

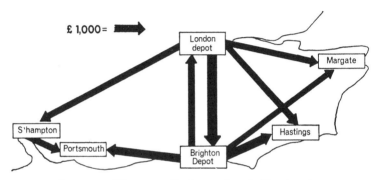

Fig. 13.—*Flow map, Goods transferred, March 1982*

The size of flow may be indicated by varying either the density of the flow lines or their width, and the lines may be combined with other symbols at terminal or interchange points. Flow diagrams can achieve considerable impact, especially when detail is suppressed to allow the principal features of the data to be presented more emphatically.

Questions

1. Discuss the main features to be looked for in a good statistical diagram, indicating the various presentations possible and noting their suitability for different uses.

2. A company markets its products direct in the major towns in the London area, but excluding the Metropolitan area where sales are handled by an agent. By means of sketches show various ways in which the sales levels in different towns could be illustrated on a base map of the area.

3. The quarterly sales for a product over six years are:

	1977	1978	1979	1980	1981	1982
Jan.–March	88	93	102	110	117	130
April–June	80	85	94	100	108	120
July–Sept.	75	81	89	96	103	114
Oct.–Dec.	84	90	100	104	112	128

4. Draw a time graph to illustrate this data.

THE J. B. JOB GROUP, EMPLOYEES 1974		
	Men	*Women*
J. B. Job and Co. Ltd.	2591	1308
Job Motors Ltd.	314	25
E. Land Co. Ltd.	1413	2105
Ridewell Ltd.	491	89

5. Illustrate the following data by constructing a band chart and percentage band chart.

CANLEY SERVICES LTD. PROFITS 1979–82				
Dept.	1979	1980	1981	1982
Industrial	£800	£1000	£1500	£1700
Offices	£40	£400	£800	£1400
Domestic	£0	£100	£506	£600

6. The sales figures in units sold for a company are as follows. Illustrate them by constructing a Z-chart.

	1981	1982
January	54	61
February	50	52
March	56	54
April	59	54
May	65	61
June	73	69
July	85	85
August	85	93
September	70	97
October	60	93
November	65	81
December	80	101

7. A company has three factories and four warehouses. Factory A supplies Warehouse 1 with 90 tons of product and Warehouse 3 with 50 tons of product. Factory B supplies 40 tons to Warehouse 1 and 80 tons to Warehouse 2. Factory C supplies 30 tons each to Warehouse 2 and 3 and 50 tons to Warehouse 4. In addition Warehouse 3 transfers 60 tons to Warehouse 1.

Illustrate the situation by means of a flow diagram.

8. The membership of the Ruritanian Motor Club, and the number of service calls made by members are shown below.

Year	Members	Calls made
1977	101 300	209 000
1978	110 500	234 000
1979	121 600	260 000
1980	128 600	284 000
1981	135 000	304 000
1982	150 000	351 000

Draw suitable diagrams to illustrate this data, showing particularly the ratio of calls per member.

9. Discuss, with examples, some of the ways in which statistical diagrams can be used to give a misleading impression of the data used.

10. A company has four factories. Draw diagrams to show how the contribution of these factories to the overall profits and costs could be illustrated, over a period of three years.

CHAPTER SIX

ANALYTICAL GRAPHS AND DIAGRAMS

THE diagrams described above so far have found their main use as illustrative or descriptive devices. Many diagrams, however, are constructed more to aid in the analysis of data than simply to illustrate it, and the diagrams which are used in this way will now be described. The division between these diagrams and those of the last chapter is an arbitrary one, and certain of the diagrams already described may help in the analysis of data, just as some of the diagrams to be described may also have an illustrative function.

Logarithmic graphs

Use of logarithmic graphs

For many time graphs the main interest is in the rate of growth of the figures shown, rather than in their absolute growth. Rates of growth may best be studied by the use of logarithmic instead of linear scales. On a graph using linear scales lines representing measurements with equal rates of growth will diverge rapidly, and comparisons are difficult.

On a logarithmic graph, a trend showing a constant rate of growth is shown as a straight line. By the use of these graphs the sales production or capital growth of a company or plant may be more easily studied and the rates of growth compared. A line with a decreasing slope indicates a decreasing rate of growth, and with an increasing slope an increasing rate of growth. These would have been difficult to detect on a linear scale graph. Taking logarithms reduces considerably the range of measurements, and series of measurements showing considerable difference in scale may be compared on these graphs. For example the growth of small and large companies or countries may be compared.

Construction of logarithmic graphs

Logarithmic graphs may be plotted on linear scale graph paper by taking the logarithms of the measurements from conventional four-figure tables. As it is difficult to plot points with an accuracy greater than 1%, the logarithms need only be read to the first two figures in the tables. Alternatively, if logarithmic graph paper is available the original data may be plotted on to the logarithmic scale. For time graphs of the type being discussed, the time scale remains linear and the type of paper required is sometimes described as *semi-logarithmic*. The logarithmic scale will be in one to six cycles. Each represents a size range × 10 in magnitude, so that three-cycle graph paper would cover a size range of 1000, *e.g.* measurements: from 1 to 1000, or 100 to 100 000, or 0·01 to 10, etc. Note that there is no zero on a logarithmic scale, and that negative numbers cannot be represented.

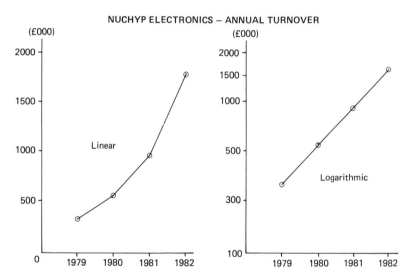

FIG. 14.—*The use of linear and logarithmic scales*

Functional graphs

Variables

We often have sets of data in which two measurements are recorded for each item, and for which it is believed that the size of one measurement for an item affects the size of the other measurements. These may be described mathematically as independent and dependent variables respectively. Their relationship can be shown by representing each item by a point on a graph, located by reference to two scales at right-angles. Conventionally the independent variable is always assigned to the horizontal scale or axis, and the dependent variable to the vertical axis. It will be seen that the time graphs so far discussed obey this rule, as time is always an independent variable.

If the measurements show a regular relationship which can be represented by a mathematical equation, they are said to be functionally related. A common relationship is the linear $Y = a + bX$ where Y is the dependent variable, X the independent variable and a and b constant quantities for the particular circumstances, determining the position and slope of the line on the graph respectively.

Plotting functional relationships

When the functional relationship between two variables is known it may be drawn on a graph. This is done by assuming a series of values for the independent variable and calculating the corresponding values for the dependent variable from the equation linking them. These corresponding values are plotted as points on the graph and connected by a line.

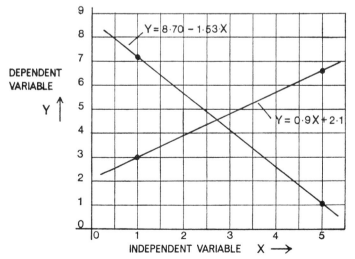

FIG. 15.—*The construction of straight line graphs*

In the case of a linear relationship only two points need be identified, as a straight line is completely fixed by two points. These should be chosen to be near the extremes of the range for the independent variable to give the most accuracy in the position of the line. The position of a point is always given with the independent variable first, *e.g.* (4, 21) implies a point located at 4 in the horizontal axis and 21 on the vertical axis.

Lorenz curves

Purpose of Lorenz curves

The Lorenz curve, or Pareto curve, is used to study the distribution of some property, such as value, among the items possessing it, in particular to compare the degree to which the property is concentrated into a few items. The type of data to which it may be applied includes the distributions

(*a*) of income among individuals,
(*b*) of personnel among companies,
(*c*) of turnover among companies,
(*d*) of trade among retail outlets,
(*e*) of values among stock items.

Construction of Lorenz curves

The required data is the number of items and the amount of the property each possesses. For the first case given above we would require the number of individuals and the income each receives. These will usually be classified; we then require, for each class of income, the number of individuals in the class and the total income received by the individuals in the class. The classes are arranged in descending order of income size, and the cumulative totals and percentage cumulative totals for both numbers of individuals and total incomes are calculated. The curve is obtained by plotting the cumulative percentage of income against the cumulative percentage of individuals. The calculation and the derived curve are shown in Table VII and Fig. 16.

The same calculation would be followed but using the appropriate data for the other applications listed above.

Interpretation of the Lorenz curve

If all individuals receive the same income, then the graph would consist of the straight line between (0%, 0%) and (100%, 100%) shown dotted in the example. The degree to which the curve

Table VII—Calculation for Lorenz Curve

PROFESSIONAL INCOMES—SCHEDULE D

Income range £	Number of incomes thousands	Amount of income £million	Cumulative total of a	Cumulative total of b	% of c	% of d
	a	b	c	d		
Over 4000	69	278	69	278	4	20
3000–	90	190	159	468	10	33
2000–	129	180	288	648	18	46
1500–	90	99	378	747	23	53
1250–	112	105	490	852	30	60
1000–	191	148	681	1000	42	71
800–	208	131	889	1131	55	80
700–	134	73	1023	1204	63	85
600–	144	69	1167	1273	72	90
500–	137	57	1304	1330	80	94
400–	120	39	1424	1369	88	97
300–	102	26	1526	1395	94	99
180–	95	16	1621	1411	100	100

diverges from the straight line is a measure of the inequality of distribution of incomes. Different classes of earners may be contrasted as is done in the example, where the corresponding line for Schedule E wage earners has been inserted. If the data were available, similar comparisons could be made of the distribution of income in different countries. Note that the average level of income is not being studied, only the distribution of the total income available to each class of earner.

An interesting use of this curve occurs in the preliminary investigation of stock levels. If the distribution of value of stock among items stocked is studied it is often obvious from the curve that a large proportion of the stock value is contained in a small proportion of the items. In many cases the ratios are 80% of the value in 20% of the stock or similar figures, and this is sometimes quoted as the 20:80 rule. When this occurs it is good policy to concentrate efforts to control stock levels on the high-value

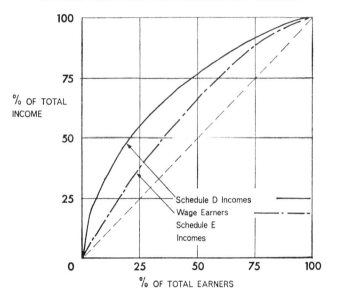

FIG. 16.—*The Lorenz curve*

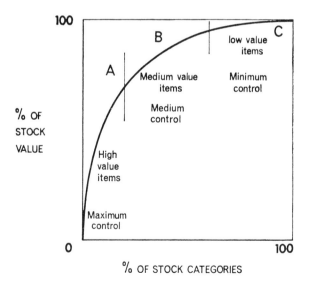

FIG. 17.—*The A–B–C curve*

items, and to use less sophisticated stock control methods on the low-value items.

Representation of frequency distributions

Importance of frequency distributions

A tabulation in which a number of measurements have been classified into classes by numerical size, and the number or frequency in each class is given, is known as a frequency table, or frequency distribution. The analysis and description of such distributions is an important part of statistics, and as a preliminary part of the investigation a diagram of the frequency distribution is drawn. The diagrams used, although mainly illustrative, are more formally defined than those of the last chapter, and their construction follows definite rules. Three types of diagrams can be drawn:

(*a*) histograms;
(*b*) frequency polygons;
(*c*) cumulative frequency curves.

Histograms

The histogram is a development of the simple bar chart, with the following differences:

(*a*) The area of each bar is proportional to the frequency in the class it represents, not its height (except for equal intervals).

(*b*) Each bar is constructed to cover the class it represents, without gaps.

This means that as the vertical scale for a histogram is frequency density, not frequency, the frequency scale must be shown as an area.

As indicated, in the special case where all class intervals are equal, then the heights of the bars are proportional to the frequencies they represent. Even here it is best to indicate the scale by showing what area represents a given frequency.

In the case of discrete data, where only certain values are possible, the bars are drawn to class boundaries which lie midway between permissible values of the measurements:

e.g.   *Class*   *Bar drawn between*
                  4—6   4·5 and 6·5

Construction of histograms

To emphasise the necessity to adjust the heights of bars for differing class intervals, the following method of drawing a histogram is suggested.

(*a*) Decide on classes and class boundaries.

(*b*) For each class calculate the class frequency and class interval.

(*c*) Divide the class frequency by the class interval to give a measure of the frequency density in each class.

(*d*) Construct the histogram with bars drawn between the class boundaries determined in (*a*), and with heights proportional to the densities determined in (*c*).

Table VIII—Calculation for Histogram

Class boundaries	Frequency	Class width	Density
24–27	5	3	1·67
27–30	11	3	3·67
30–33	19	3	6·33
33–36	21	3	7·00
36–42	27	6	4·50
42–48	12	6	2·00
48–60	11	12	0·92

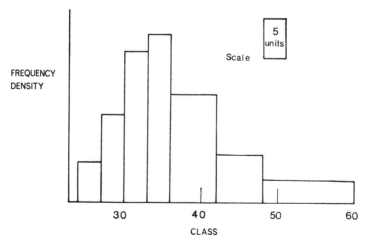

FIG. 18.—*Histogram*

(*e*) Construct a block to give the scale by choosing a suitable class interval and frequency, and determining the height of the block as above.

The routine is illustrated in Table VIII and the resultant histogram shown in Fig. 18.

Frequency polygons

An alternative diagram used to represent the data in a frequency distribution is the frequency polygon. This is constructed by connecting up points plotted at the mid-points of each class and at heights proportional to the frequency density in each class. These heights are determined in the same way as the heights of the bars for a histogram.

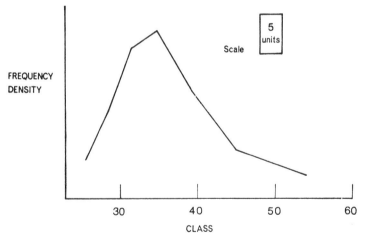

FIG. 19.—*Frequency polygon*

When we wish to compare the shapes of two or more frequency distributions it is often better to use the frequency polygon than the histogram. It is much easier to compare the lines drawn for the frequency polygon, than to use different and overlapping shadings as is necessary if histograms are used. If it is felt that the histograms do give a superior distribution, then they are best compared by constructing several histograms below one another, but with their scales in alignment.

Frequency distribution curves

If a histogram or frequency polygon is constructed from a very large amount of data, then a large number of classes can be used. It is generally found that such diagrams show shapes which tend towards smooth curves. Such curves are called frequency distribution curves, and may be thought of as giving the parent population distribution, of which the sample distribution we have available is an approximation. Many of these curves can be shown to be very similar to mathematically defined curves and the properties of some of these will be described later. The terms used in describing the shape of frequency distribution curves are given at the start of the next chapter.

Probability distribution curves

It was pointed out that the area under a histogram between any given values of the measurement represents the frequency with which the measurement occurs. The same interpretation may be made for a frequency distribution curve. If we divide the total area by the frequency, the area becomes proportional to 1, and we can then regard the area under a curve between given measurements as proportional to the probability that the measurements will be observed in practice. This interpretation and use of the term probability is fully explained in chapters Nine and Ten. A frequency distribution curve which has been rescaled in this way may be described as a probability distribution curve.

Cumulative frequency curves

It is often useful to have information about the proportion of a set of measurements which exceed a given measurement or alternatively what range of measurements contain a given proportion of measurements.

This and similar information is best derived by the construction of a cumulative frequency curve. This is also known as the "ogive" curve, from its resemblance to the curve of this name in architecture, or as the "up to" curve, for reasons which are obvious.

The curve is constructed by plotting the cumulative frequency up to the end of each class, against the upper class boundary. The points are then connected by a line. It is usually possible to draw a smooth curve through the points without difficulty, and so to approximate the parent population curve more easily than can be done when using the histogram. The method of construction is shown by Table IX and Fig. 20.

Table IX—Calculation for Cumulative Frequency Curve

Class boundaries	Upper boundary	Frequency	Cumulative frequency
24–27	27	5	5
27–30	30	11	16
30–33	33	19	35
33–36	36	21	56
36–42	42	27	83
42–48	48	12	95
48–60	60	11	106

If the cumulative frequencies are divided by the total frequency and multiplied by 100 they are converted to percentage cumulative frequencies. This alters the scale of the diagram but not its shape, and may be more useful for reading off proportions as

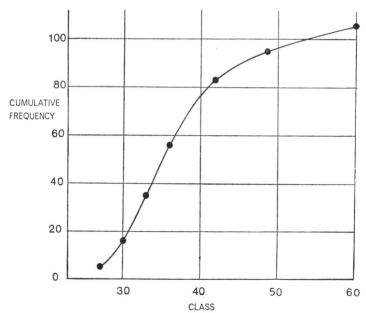

FIG. 20.—*Cumulative frequency curve*

suggested above. The use of the cumulative frequency curve to estimate certain statistical measures will be developed in the next chapter.

Planning diagrams

The use of diagrammatic techniques to aid in the planning of projects and other activities is an important field of study. While the diagrams used may in some cases resemble the statistical diagrams which have been described, and while statistical ideas and methods may be involved in the analysis of planning diagrams, they are not basically a statistical technique. The reader is referred to specialist publications and publications in production planning and operational research for further information concerning these diagrams.

The principal methods involved are the use of Gantt charts, a form of bar chart, for the planning and review of projects, and Network Analysis. This is a recent technique which has now diversified into several interrelated techniques. The two most prominent are Critical Path Method and PERT (Program Review and Evaluation Technique), which were pioneered by Du Pont, Nemours and Co., and by the U.S. Admiralty Polaris Submarine project team respectively.

Questions

1. The following data shows the total number of retail groups and turnover for retail outlets classified by turnover. Draw a Lorenz curve to compare the distribution of retail groups in the trades shown.

BUTCHERS		
Turnover £ p.a.	*Number of groups*	*Total turnover in class £000*
Under 2000	456	588
2001–5000	2196	8479
5001–10 000	6639	50 488
10 001–20 000	8062	114 556
20 001–50 000	4288	126 229
Over 50 000	1134	185 445

GREENGROCERS

Turnover £ p.a.	Number of groups	Total turnover in class £000
Under 2000	4458	4611
2001–5000	8360	29 678
5001–10 000	8884	63 965
10 001–20 000	4791	65 579
20 001–50 000	1507	43 705
Over 50 000	353	49 022

Source: *Based on Census of Distribution*

2. The ages of employees in a department are classified as follows.

Age	Number of employees
17–20	14
21–25	25
26–30	29
31–40	24
41–50	15
51–64	12

Illustrate these figures by constructing a histogram and a frequency polygon.

3. Explain the characteristics which distinguish a histogram from a simple bar chart.

4. Discuss the use of a Lorenz curve. What indication is given by a curve which diverges a large amount from the 45° line?

5. Classify the following fifty measurements of the weight of a component, and illustrate the data by a histogram.

Weight of bolt assembly—ounces				
8·9	9·0	9·3	8·7	9·1
8·5	9·0	8·9	9·3	9·2
8·8	9·1	8·9	9·3	9·1
9·2	8·6	9·1	9·3	9·0
8·9	9·0	9·2	8·8	8·9
9·6	9·0	8·6	9·1	9·5
9·4	8·8	9·3	8·7	9·0
9·2	9·1	9·2	9·5	9·1
9·0	8·8	9·5	9·0	9·2
9·0	9·4	8·9	9·2	9·1

6. Use the data of Question 2 to construct a percentage cumulative frequency curve, and use it to find:

(*a*) what proportion of the employees are below 33 years of age, and

(*b*) what age is exceeded by 50% of the employees.

7. Use the data of Question 6 to construct a cumulative frequency curve. Within what range of weights do the central forty items lie?

8. Plot the following lines over the range:

$$X = 4 \text{ to } X = 14$$
$$(a) \ Y = 5X - 6$$
$$(b) \ Y = 24 + 2 \cdot 2X$$

9. The sales in a newly opened shop are as follows for the first five weeks.

Week	Sales £
1	21
2	47
3	114
4	332
5	419

Show these figures on both linear and logarithmic scale graphs.

10. Demand for a component held in stock in a warehouse varies day to day. The demands recorded over a period are:

Demand per day

10, 14, 9, 15, 6, 10, 11, 12, 13, 9, 14, 18, 10, 9, 11, 14, 11, 12, 13, 7, 14, 8, 12, 12, 16, 10, 9, 11, 10, 15, 7, 11, 5, 12, 13, 9, 10, 10, 8, 12, 8, 9, 10, 10, 11, 7, 13, 13, 14, 11, 6, 11, 9, 10, 17, 8, 7, 9, 8, 9, 16, 9, 6, 12, 10, 12, 11, 10, 5, 15, 11

Draw a histogram to show the pattern of demand, and a percentage cumulative distribution curve. Use this curve to find what percentage of the time the demand is for less than fifteen items.

CHAPTER SEVEN

FREQUENCY DISTRIBUTIONS AND DESCRIPTIVE STATISTICAL MEASURES

Frequency distributions

Population distributions

As stated earlier a set of measurements usually represents a sample from a larger, real or theoretical, population or series of measurements. The shape of a sample distribution may be taken as an indication of the shape of the population distribution from which it is derived, and we will wish to describe the shape so that different populations may be compared.

By using numerical measures to describe the shapes of distribution we can make these comparisons less subjective, and also predict quantities based on the distributions. These studies of the shape and characteristics of distributions are of central interest in statistical work, and the most common types of distributions will now be described.

Normal distribution

Whenever measurements are subject to unbiased variation, then a symmetrical distribution of the type shown in Fig. 21 is most

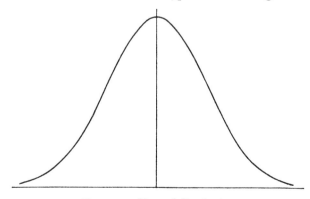

FIG. 21.—*Normal distribution*

commonly found. We may anticipate the theoretical derivation of this shape of curve and call it a normal curve. This and similar shapes to which it is a good approximation are the most common type of distribution curve.

The properties of distributions of this type will be fully discussed later, after the derivation of the theoretical curve has been indicated.

Positive skew distribution

When there is a restriction on the least size of a measurement, such as a minimum value, then a curve similar to the normal curve but with a longer "tail" to the right results.

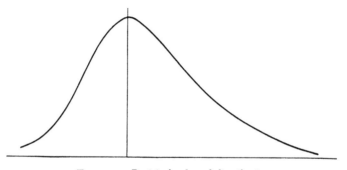

FIG. 22.—*Positively skewed distribution*

This is described as a positively skewed distribution. Such distributions are common in management statistics, *e.g.* distributions of size of salary, size of company, times to complete projects, etc. They also occur when the binomial and Poisson distributions are applicable, as in many sampling situations and in the statistics relating to accidents and other infrequent events. The distribution of ratios or percentages may also be expected to be of this shape. The corresponding negatively skew distribution occurs when there is a restriction on the maximum value of a measurement, but distributions of this shape are not often observed.

J-shaped distribution

An extremely skew distribution may have its maximum frequency at the minimum value; this is then described as a

J-shaped distribution. In addition to its derivation as the limit of a positively skew distribution, a J-shaped distribution may be observed in the study of failure rates for machines or components.

U-shaped distribution

A type of distribution occasionally encountered occurs when the central value of the distribution is the least frequent. This from its shape is described as U-shaped. Fortunately this is rare in business situations, as its treatment by conventional statistical methods is not practicable.

Bi-modal and multi-modal distributions

A distribution having two maximum values is described as bi-modal, and multi-modal distributions may also occur. It will often be found that the occurrence of such a distribution is caused by the mixing of two or more measurements from different

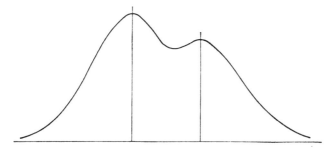

FIG. 23.—*Bi-modal distribution*

populations, and if the sets of measurements can be separated then a better analysis of the data can be made. Such a preliminary examination of data is always valuable and fully justifies time spent on constructing diagrams and graphs before calculating the measures to be described later.

Descriptive measures

Although a diagram may provide a useful visual method of comparing distributions, it is necessary to calculate derived statistics or measures, in order to compare them on an objective basis.

Two measures are sufficient for most instances:

(*a*) a measure of position;
(*b*) a measure of dispersion.

Further measures of shape can be calculated, but are only of interest where the exact mathematical form of a distribution is required to provide highly detailed predictions, as in actuarial work.

Measures of position

Mode

The simplest measure of position is the value of the quantity being studied corresponding to the maximum of its frequency distribution; this is called the mode or modal value.

In the case of discrete data the mode is the most frequent value and is found by inspection of the data.

Table X—Mode by Inspection

Measurement	Frequency
15	25
16	40
Mode → 17	51
18	32
19	12
20	6
21	3

The mode may also be derived from a frequency curve by visual estimation as in Fig. 24.

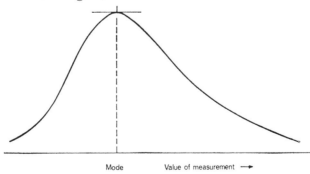

Mode   Value of measurement ➞

FIG. 24.—*The estimation of the mode from a frequency curve*

As a histogram represents a simplification of the original data, we can find only the modal class by direct inspection—that is the class which has the highest frequency density. The position of the mode inside the modal class may be estimated as follows. The modal class, and the two neighbouring classes are drawn as shown in Fig. 25 and the intersection of the diagonals taken as the value of the mode.

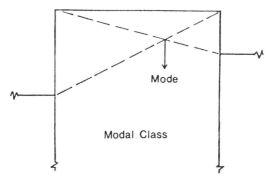

FIG. 25.—*The estimation of the mode from a histogram*

By making this diagram reasonably large, sufficient accuracy for most purposes can be obtained. A diagram with a class width of 2″ on ordinary $\frac{1}{10}$″ graph paper can easily yield an accuracy of 2·5% of the class interval; this is probably as accurate as is justified when using grouped data.

The mode represents a real property of a distribution, *e.g.* there is little point in saying that the average family in the United Kingdom has 2·4 children, but it is very useful to know that the most common family size is of two children. Similarly the modal wage of a group of workmen may give the best indication of their earnings level, as it ignores high and low values which may not be typical of the group as a whole.

The mode is not amenable to easy mathematical handling and is little used in statistical analysis beyond its descriptive function.

Median

The median is the half-way value of a distribution; it is that value which exceeds half the measurements and is exceeded by half the measurements in a frequency distribution.

The median is not affected by alterations in the values of individual measurements away from the centre of the distribution, so long as their relative order does not change. This makes it a good measure of position when extreme values occur in a distribution, and especially when they are very variable in size. It can also be calculated in cases where the exact size of many measurements in a distribution is not known, *e.g.* when "open-ended" classes such as "50 and over" are used. It is particularly useful in the study of distribution of times to complete a given event. If a destructive test is being carried out, then to calculate other measures of position, we require all items being tested to fail before the average time of failure can be calculated. Since the times to failure are automatically derived in order, if all tests start at the same time, the median time to failure is the time when half the items being tested have failed. We then have a measure of the average time to failure, without waiting for the completion of all the tests.

The median is a useful descriptive measure that is widely used in demographic statistics. It is also in use under the name of the "half-life" and provides a good measure of the average time for something to happen, e.g. a failure or a success, when for some items the event to be observed never happens.

Calculation of the median

From ungrouped data the median may best be calculated by first ranking the data. Ranking consists of arranging the individual measurements in order of magnitude, usually ascending, and giving each measurement a number 1, 2, 3, etc., corresponding to its order 1st, 2nd, 3rd, etc., in the array. Such a number is called the rank of the measurement. If we have N measurements, they will have ranks 1 to N and the median rank will be $(N + 1)/2$. For an odd number N this will give a particular measurement which is taken as the median. For an even number N, this gives a fractional figure and the median value is taken as being half-way between the values of the measurements with ranks nearest to this figure.

From grouped data the median cannot be determined exactly; as with the mode, only the class in which it lies can be specified without doubt. To estimate the position of the median within the class we assume that the measurements composing the class are

Table XI—Estimation of the Median

Class	Frequency	Cumulative frequency
Up to 20	52	52
20–30	161	213
Median class → 30–40	254	467
40–50	167	634
50–60	78	712
60–80	64	776
Over 80	52	828

Total frequency $= N = 828$
Median rank $= N/2 = 414$
Median class $= 30\text{–}40$
Median rank is
$(414 - 213)/(467 - 213)$
parts through median class $= 201/254$
∴ median value is $\quad 201/254$ parts through class,
i.e. median value $= 30 + (201/254)(40\text{–}30)$
$= 37\cdot91$

evenly distributed within it. We then take the value of the median to be the same proportion throughout the class as is the rank of the median. If the total frequency is N, then the median is taken as $N/2$.

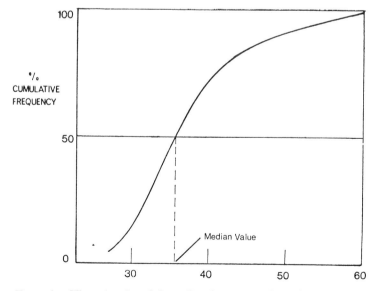

FIG. 26.—*The estimation of the median from a cumulative frequency curve*

Alternatively the median may be estimated from the cumulative frequency graph by reading off the value corresponding to a cumulative frequency of $N/2$ or 50%. As with the mode, sufficient accuracy for most purposes may be obtained in this way.

Mean

The term "mean" without qualification will be taken to refer to the arithmetic mean. It is obtained by summing all measurements and dividing the total obtained by the total frequency, and is usually symbolised by placing a bar over the symbol of the measurement averaged. For example, arithmetic mean of measurements $x_1, x_2, x_3, \ldots x_n$ is $\bar{x} = (x_1 + x_2 + x_3 \ldots + x_n)/n$.

The mean is the most useful measure of position, and is the measure usually referred to when the term "average" is used. It is a good representative of a distribution as it is based on all the measurements composing the distribution, but is susceptible to changes in the extreme measurements. It is easily handled mathematically, and is very widely used in statistical analysis.

Calculation of the mean

In order to calculate the mean of grouped data we assume that the total frequency in each class is concentrated at the mid-point of the class. Then for classes with mid-points $x_1, x_2, x_3, \ldots x_k$ and frequencies $f_1, f_2, f_3, \ldots f_k$,

$$\bar{x} = \frac{f_1 x_1 + f_2 x_2 + f_3 x_3 \ldots f_k x_k}{f_1 + f_2 + f_3 \ldots + f_k}.$$

These formulae may be simplified by the use of the summation sign Σ,

$$\bar{x} = \Sigma f x / n = \Sigma f x / \Sigma f, (\Sigma f = n).$$

It will usually be clear which items are to be summed without employing full mathematical notation.

Coding in calculations

The mean is easily calculated from a small number of measurements by using the method suggested above, but for a large number of measurements it is often useful to lessen the arithmetic labour. The process described is called coding and will be used extensively in more complicated calculations.

If we represent the original data by X_1, X_2, ... X_k and the coded data by x_1, x_2, ... x_k and if the constant quantity subtracted is c then:

$$x = (X - c)$$

This only alters the zero of our measurements and would not make any difference in the shape of the distribution if the histogram were drawn.

If we now calculate $\bar{x} = \Sigma fx/n$ then we can find X from $X = \bar{x} + c$.

Table XII—Calculation of Mean Using Coding

Class	Mid-point	Frequency	X − 45	
	X	f	x	fx
0–20	10	52	−35	−1820
20–30	25	161	−20	−3220
30–40	35	254	−10	−2540
40–50	45	167	0	0
50–60	55	78	10	780
60–80	70	64	25	1600
80–100	90	52	45	2340
		n = 828		+4720
				−7580

$c = 45$ $\Sigma x = -2860$

$\bar{x} = \Sigma fx/n = -2860/828 = -3.45$

$X = \bar{x} + c = -3.45 + 45 = 41.55$

Many electronic calculators now allow the calculation of statistical measures. Typically the calculator is set to "*s.d.*" mode by a switch or suitable key-strokes, and then a sequence of numbers can be entered, usually with a key marked "*x*". When all the data has been entered the number of measurements "*n*", the total "Σx" and the mean "*x*" may be displayed by pressing appropriate keys. Data in a frequency table cannot be easily handled in this way and the table described above should be used. The work is speeded up by the use of a calculator and by the use of a memory function; not all the numbers in the table need be written down, although the general procedure should be followed.

Geometric mean

An alternative method of combining measurements is given by the geometric mean. The geometric mean of n measurements type x:

$$G.M._x = \sqrt[n]{\Pi x},$$
$$\Pi x = x_1 \times x_2 \ldots x_n.$$

This is a more suitable measure of central position for quantities such as ratios, but is not frequently used except in the calculation of some index numbers. The calculation is eased by noting that:

$$log.\ G.M._x = \Sigma\ log.\ x/n.$$

The x values are converted to logarithms, the mean of the logarithms found, and the antilogarithm of the mean logarithm is then the geometric mean.

Table XIII—Calculation of Geometric Mean

x	$\log x$	f	$f. \log x$
5	0·6990	1	0·6990
9	0·9542	1	0·9542
10	1·0000	2	2·0000
11	1·0414	2	2·0828
14	1·1461	2	2·2922
18	1·2553	1	1·2553
26	1·4150	1	1·4150
30	1·4771	1	1·4771
44	1·6435	1	1·6435

$n = 12$ $13·8191 = \Sigma(f. \log x)$

$\log x = \Sigma(f. \log x)/n$
$= 13·8191/12 = 1·1516$
$G.M._x = $ antilog $(1·1516)$
$= 14·18$

Compare $\bar{x} = 16·83$. For a moderately skew distribution, the geometric mean is usually close to the mode.

The three measures compared

A good statistical measure should possess several properties: it should be stable, use all the data available, be easy to understand and easy to handle mathematically. The arithmetic mean satisfies most of these conditions, and can be faulted only in its greater sensitivity to extreme values than the other measures.

The mode and median do not use all the data available and are not easy to handle mathematically, and hence are of less importance than the mean. They find a use, apart from their own value as measures, as estimates of the mean. For symmetrical distributions, which are of very common occurrence, the mean, median and mode are coincident, and the more easily obtained median or mode may be used to estimate the mean.

For moderately skew unimodal distributions, the following relationship is approximately true and may be used to give a quick estimate of the mean:

$$(\text{mean} - \text{mode}) = 3\ (\text{mean} - \text{median}).$$

or
$$\text{mean} = \text{median} + (\text{median} - \text{mode})/2.$$

The danger of averages

While it is necessary to calculate measures of position and shape in order to summarise the information given in a frequency distribution, it should not be forgotten that only the original data gives all the information. The process of summarising necessarily results in a loss of information. Also when the data is sparse then the summary statistics are less reliable, and so the number of measurements on which a calculated statistic is based should be clearly stated. Another source of error is the inclusion of two or more sets of measurements from different sources or from different circumstances in the same calculations. It may not be immediately obvious that this is being done, but it should be watched for. As indicated earlier, a bi-modal distribution may well indicate this state of affairs. In all cases it is wise to have the original data preserved for reference; summary measures can be recalculated from the original data, but the data cannot be reconstructed from summary measures.

Measures of spread

The range

The simplest measure of spread in a set of measurements is known as the range and is the difference between the greatest and least measurements. It is easily calculated, but is very unstable for any number of measurements greater than 12, as it depends only on the extreme measurements and these are the measurements most liable to variation.

For a small set of measurements the range uses a large part of the available information and is almost as useful as the other measures of dispersion. For a given number of measurements, whose distribution is similar to the normal distribution, its relationship to the other measures of dispersion is known, and use is made of the range and this relationship in statistical quality control.

There is no reason why the mean range should not be used more frequently to estimate the standard deviation, the most widely used measure of spread. If we have several independent samples, each of the same size, then if w is the range and $\bar{w}$ the mean range, the standard deviation is given by $s = \bar{w}/d_n$. d_n is found from the following table.

Table XIV—Factors for Use with Mean Range

Sample size n	Factor for standard deviation d_n
2	1·13
3	1·69
4	2·06
5	2·33
6	2·53

The quartile deviation and fractiles

The reason for the instability of the range in large samples is the variability of the extreme values. If we take instead of the range of the whole distribution, the range of a central part of the distribution then we obtain a very much more stable measure. We can divide up a distribution in a manner similar to that used in obtaining the median, by considering the values which exceed a given proportion of the distribution. Such values are known as *fractiles*.

The most commonly used fractiles are the quartiles which divide the distribution into four equal parts. Designating them as Q_1, Q_2, Q_3, then:

Q_1 exceeds one-quarter of the measurements;
Q_2 exceeds one-half of the measurements;
Q_3 exceeds three-quarters of the measurements.

It will be seen that Q_2 is the median.

Similarly we may define deciles, dividing the distribution into 10 equal parts, or percentiles dividing it into 100 equal parts. These are related, *i.e.*

$$5\text{th decile} = 50\% \text{ ile} = Q_2 = \text{median};$$
$$25\% \text{ ile} = Q_1 = \text{1st quartile};$$
$$75\% \text{ ile} = Q_3 = \text{3rd quartile}.$$

We may now define the range of any given part of the distribution by reference to the fractile, *i.e.* the 90% range, or the range of the central 90% of the distribution. This is found as the difference between the 5-percentile and the 95-percentile.

The particular range most used in descriptive statistics is the interquartile range, Q_3–Q_1, or more usually the semi-interquartile range, or quartile deviation.

$$\text{Quartile deviation} = (Q_3\text{–}Q_1)/2.$$

The quartiles may be found by a method similar to the calculation of the median, but are most frequently found by estimation from the cumulative frequency graph. For a distribution of N items, the value of Q_1 corresponds to a cumulative frequency of $N/4$ and of Q_3 to $3N/4$, or in the case of the percentage cumulative frequency graph, to percentages of 25 and 75 respectively.

The quartile deviation is a good measure of dispersion, although it is not fully representative of a set of measurements as it is not based on all the information available. This is sometimes an advantage as it means that the quartile deviation can be calculated even though all the measurements are not known, as with open-ended classes.

It is usually employed with the median as a descriptive measure when further analysis of the data is not undertaken.

The mean deviation

The various ranges do not use all the information available, in that they do not involve all the measurements in their calculation. An attempt to remedy this is given by the mean deviation. This as its name implies measures the mean difference between individual measurements and a measure of central location. If the mean is employed then we must calculate the differences in two stages, as we require the size of the differences only. If we have n measurements x_i with mean value $\bar{x}$, then:

(1) for $x_i > \bar{x}$ sum of differences $= \Sigma(x_i - \bar{x})$,
(2) for $x_i < \bar{x}$ sum of differences $= \Sigma(\bar{x} - x_i)$,

or alternatively, sum of differences $= \Sigma |x_i - \bar{x}|$. Note that we could not find the sum of differences from $(x_i - \bar{x})$ for all values of x_i as it always totals 0, this being a property of $\bar{x}$.

The mean deviation of x is given by

$$(\Sigma |x - \bar{x}|)/n$$

Because we are effectively summing two sets of measurements, the measure is awkward to handle mathematically and is not used in further analysis.

The mean deviation does use all the data available, and is easy to calculate for a small number of measurements, although not so convenient when a large amount of data is available. For a normal distribution the relationship between the mean deviation and the important measure of dispersion the standard deviation is known, and the mean deviation is sometimes used to estimate the standard deviation.

It can be shown that the mean deviation of measurements from a central figure is least when the differences are measured from the median instead of the mean.

The standard deviation and variance

The problem of the sign of $(x - \bar{x})$ may also be resolved by considering instead $(x - \bar{x})^2$ which is always positive. If we now find the mean value of the sum of this quantity we obtain another measure of spread, the mean square deviation from the mean, or variance:

$$\frac{1}{n}\,\Sigma(x - \bar{x})^2$$

This is a most useful measure of dispersion and will be used extensively later. It has the property of being additive; if two normal distributions are combined by adding pairs of measurements, then the variance of the new distribution is the sum of the variances of the separate distributions. The use of this property will be illustrated and developed later.

The variance has the disadvantage that its units are the square of the units of the original data, and to obtain a measure of spread with the same units as the original data we must take the square root of the variance. This measure, the root mean square deviation from the mean, is called the standard deviation:

$$= \sqrt{\frac{1}{n}\Sigma(x - \bar{x})^2}$$

Although the standard deviation is based on all the data available it is not very easy to calculate and its relationship to the original data is not easily visualised. It is, however, of great importance in theoretical statistics and in statistical analysis, and this usefulness completely overrides its drawbacks. The standard deviation and the related measure, the variance, are the most important measures of dispersion.

Some idea of the relationship of the standard deviation to the data it is based on may be obtained by looking at Fig. 27. This

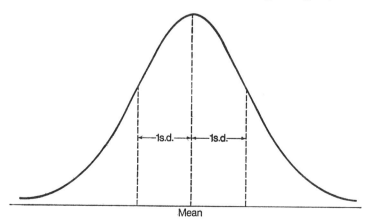

FIG. 27.—*Standard deviation in the normal distribution*

shows a normal distribution, and one standard deviation is the distance from the mean to where the curve changes its direction of curvature (the *point of inflection*).

Calculation of the standard deviation and variance

To calculate the standard deviation or the variance from the formula given on p. 83 would be onerous except when the mean is a whole number, and for purposes of calculation different forms of the formula are preferred. These are:

$$\text{variance of } x = \frac{1}{n}\left[\Sigma x^2 - \frac{(\Sigma x)^2}{n}\right]$$

$$\text{standard deviation of } x = \sqrt{\frac{1}{n}\left[\Sigma x^2 - \frac{(\Sigma x)^2}{n}\right]}$$

Table XV—Calculation of Variance and Standard Deviation

Class	Mid-point	Frequency	$x = X - 45$	fx	fx^2
0–	10	52	−35	−1820	63 700
20–	25	161	−20	−3220	64 400
30–	35	254	−10	−2540	25 400
40–	45	167	0	0	0
50–	55	78	10	780	7800
60–	70	64	25	1600	40 000
80–100	90	52	45	2340	105 300
		$n = 828$		+4720	306 600
				−7580	$= \Sigma fx^2$

$$\Sigma fx = -2860$$

$c = 45$

$\bar{x} = \Sigma fx/n = -3\!\cdot\!45$

$\bar{X} = \bar{x} + c = -3\!\cdot\!45 + 45 = 41\!\cdot\!55$

$$\text{Var. } x = \frac{1}{n}\left[\Sigma fx^2 - \frac{(\Sigma fx)^2}{n}\right] = \frac{1}{828}\left[306600 - \frac{(2860)^2}{828}\right]$$

$$= 358\!\cdot\!36$$

$\text{s.d. } x = \sqrt{\text{Var. } x} = 18\!\cdot\!93$

$\text{s.d. } X = \text{s.d. } x = 18\!\cdot\!93$

Coefficient of variation

When we have measurements which are based on a scale of measurement starting from zero, such as thicknesses, weights or numbers of faults, we may wish to compare the relative variability in the measurements. The measure used to do this is the coefficient of variation, C, and is the standard deviation divided by the mean of the measurements: $C = s/m$.

It may also be given as a percentage: $C = 100s/m$.

C is a ratio, and so dimensionless, making it possible to compare the variability in measurements of differing sizes, but care must be taken to check if the mean is measured from an arbitrary zero, when C is meaningless.

Measures of skewness

Pearson's measure of skewness

As indicated earlier the mean, mode and median will only coincide for symmetrical distributions, and the difference between them may be used as a measure of skewness, or departure from symmetry.

The statistician Pearson suggested the use of (mean — mode) as a suitable measure, standardised for distributions of different dispersions by dividing by the standard deviation, *i.e.* Pearson's measure of skewness:

$$Sk_p = (\text{mean} - \text{mode}) \div \text{standard deviation}.$$

An alternative, which is often easier to apply when the mode is awkward to estimate, is given by:

$$Sk_p = 3 \, (\text{mean} - \text{median}) \div \text{standard deviation}.$$

For moderately skew unimodal distributions, these give the same measure.

Pearson's measure can take values from -3 to $+3$, for a symmetrical curve it is 0, and for positively and negatively skew curves it takes the appropriate sign. For a moderately skew curve the absolute value of Sk_p is less than 1.

Quartile measure of skewness

In a symmetrical distribution the quartiles will be equal distances from the median, for a skew distribution these distances will differ. The difference in distances of the quartiles from the median provides a measure of skewness, and is standardised to allow comparisons between distributions with differing dispersions by division by the quartile deviation. Quartile measure of skewness $= Sk_q$, where:

$$Sk_q = \frac{(Q_3 - \text{median}) - (\text{median} - Q_1)}{\text{quartile deviation}}$$

As with Pearson's measure of skewness, this measure takes the value 0 for a symmetrical distribution and is positive or negative for positively or negatively skew distributions respectively. Its range of values is -1 to $+1$.

This measure is convenient to use with the median and quartile deviation to describe the shape of a distribution.

Population and sample statistics

Symbols

When all the possible measurements which make up a population are known then the measures calculated from these measurements are known as population parameters. The following symbols are used for population parameters:

mean $= \mu$;
standard deviation $= \sigma$;
variance $= \sigma^2$.

The same measures calculated from a sample of measurements taken from a population are known as sample statistics and the following symbols used:

mean $= m$;
standard deviation $= s$;
variance $= s^2 = var$.

Where it is necessary to distinguish the statistics referring to more than one set of measurements the following symbols may be used:

mean of $y = m_y$;
standard deviation of $y = s_y$;
variance of $y = s^2_y = var \cdot y$.

Estimates

If we do not have all the measurements necessary to calculate population parameters we must estimate them from the corresponding statistics for a representative sample. We cannot expect every sample to be representative of the population, but the estimates of population parameters made in this way represent the best estimates with the data available. The mean of a population is estimated by the mean of a sample, and if we could take many samples we would find that the mean of the means of the samples would approach closer and closer to the true population mean. The best estimate of the population mean is symbolised by $\hat{\mu}$ and $\hat{\mu} = m$.

If we calculated the variance of several samples all of size n, we would not find that the mean variance of the samples approached closer and closer to the population variance. Instead we would find that the mean sample variance was lower than the population variance. The sample variance is described as a biased estimator of the population variance. To correct for this bias we must multiply the sample variance by the factor $n/(n-1)$. Symbolising the best estimate of the population variance by $\hat{\sigma}^2$, we now have $\hat{\sigma}^2 = n/(n-1) \cdot s^2$.

For calculation purposes then:

$$\hat{\sigma}_x^2 = \frac{1}{n-1}\left[\Sigma x^2 - \frac{(\Sigma x)^2}{n}\right]$$

or:

$$\hat{\sigma}_x^2 = \frac{1}{n-1}\left[\Sigma f x^2 - \frac{(\Sigma f x)^2}{n}\right].$$

It is necessary to make use of the best estimates whenever we make deductions based on samples, and this includes virtually all the statistical procedures in the following chapters.

If an electronic calculator is used to calculate the standard deviation then a choice of σ_x or $\hat{\sigma}_x$ is usually given, indicated by the symbols σ_n and σ_{n-1} respectively, showing the divisor used. A few calculators calculate $\hat{\sigma}_x$ under the name "s.d." and σ_x in the form "Var. x", read the manual to check which is which.

Questions

1. Describe with diagrams a normal distribution, a positively skew distribution and a bi-modal distribution. Under what circumstances would you expect to find these distributions occurring?

2. Discuss the measures of position used in statistical work and indicate their various faults and virtues.

3. What is meant by skewness? Describe a measure of skewness and explain what is meant by negative and positive skewness.

4. Distinguish between the mean deviation, the quartile deviation and the standard deviation. Indicate the relative usefulness of each of these measures.

5. Find the mode, median and mean of the following distribution.

Class	Frequency
150–	103
158–	98
162–	190
166–	140
168–	116
170–	138
174–	62
178–	24
182–190	22

6. Use the data of Question 5 and estimate the median, quartile deviation and quartile measure of skewness from the cumulative frequency graph.

7. Use the data of Question 5 and calculate the variance and standard deviation of the distribution.

8. The following nine measurements are drawn from a large population: 18·3, 18·1, 19·2, 18·8, 18·5, 19·0, 18·6, 18·7, 18·3. Estimate the population mean and standard deviation.

9. Use the data of Question 8 to calculate the coefficient of variation. A second sample gives estimates of mean = 25·3 and standard deviation = 0·21; compare its variability with the first sample.

10. Calculate the arithmetic and geometric means of the following measurements: 9·3, 9·1, 10·5, 13·2, 12·1, 10·2, 10·5, 9·8, 10·6, 14·0, 10·6, 10·1, 10·1, 9·0, 9·8, 9·7, 16·0, 10·2, 10·0, 9·9.

WEIGHTED AVERAGES AND INDEX NUMBERS

Weighted averages

WHEN information from more than one sample is combined, it is convenient to find average values of the measurements we are interested in from the sample statistics, without having to recalculate them from the original data. In some cases the original data may not be to hand and we have no choice, and must use the sample statistics. Consider two samples:

sample A, size 5, mean = 4;
sample B, size 15, mean = 6.

The mean of the combined sample is not given by $(4 + 6)/2 = 5$ as this does not make allowance for the size of the samples, but by $[(4 \times 5) + (6 \times 15)]/20 = 5 \cdot 5$. An arithmetic mean calculated in this way is described as a weighted mean, and is an example of a weighted average. A similar weighted average can be calculated for the geometric mean.

If we have several means each based on a different number of measurements then we must weight each mean by the number of measurements it is based on to obtain the overall mean. This corresponds exactly to the method of calculating the mean of a set of classified data already described, i.e.

for $\bar{x}_1$ based on w_1 measurements;
$\bar{x}_2$ based on w_2 measurements; and
$\bar{x}_3$ based on w_3 measurements.

The grand mean $= \bar{\bar{x}} = \dfrac{x_1 w_1 + x_2 w_2 + x_3 w_3}{w_1 + w_2 + w_3}$

The calculation of a mean in this way is described as taking a weighted arithmetic mean.

A similar routine is followed when measurements have to be combined which are of varying importance. We may have three estimates of next month's sales figures, and know that the reliability of the sources of the estimates varies, yet feel that a combined figure would be more reliable than any single figure. If the estimates are 100, 80, 120 and the reliabilities of the sources are in the ratios of 4 : 3 : 1 then the best estimate is given by:

$$\frac{(100 \times 4) + (80 \times 3) + 120}{4 + 3 + 1} = 760/8 = 95.$$

The factors 4, 3, 1 are referred to as the weights or weighting factors. The choice of weights is obviously of critical importance when carrying out a calculation of this type, and an important part of the process is to decide on the appropriate weights in a particular situation. In some cases we can use objective reasoning to assign the weights to measurements which are to be combined. In other cases they must be decided on by a mixture of experience and intuition, and the decision is a major management contribution to the correct calculation of the combined statistic.

Index numbers

Relatives

If we have a series of measurements of a similar type, such as the price of a ton of copper over several years, or the gross income per head for a number of countries, we may wish to compare the relative size of the measurements. This may be done by choosing one measurement as a base, assigning to it the value 100, and expressing the others as percentages of it. These percentages are called "relatives," and are the simplest types of index numbers.

Table XVI—Calculation of Price Relatives

Item	Price 1978 per litre	Price 1982 per litre	Relative
	a	b	100b/a
Oil grade 1	18p	25p	139
Oil grade 2	20p	31p	155
Emulsifier	88p	112p	127

Relatives are a very simple device for making comparisons, but can still be misleading. The effect of changing the base may be considerable, and lead to a quite different impression of the relative size of the numbers involved. Where possible a base should be chosen to represent an agreed standard, or normal time or situation, or be based on a significant event or situation. The effect of changing the base year is shown in Table XVII.

Table XVII—Price Relatives—Change of Base

Year	Price	Relative (1972 = 100)	Relative (1978 = 100)
1972	80	100	91
1973	84	105	95
1974	84	105	95
1975	83	104	94
1976	85	106	97
1977	86	108	98
1978	88	110	100
1979	89	111	101
1980	91	114	103
1981	94	118	107
1982	112	140	127

Emulsifier—Price per litre, pence

Composite index numbers

When we wish to compare the change in levels of a number of measurements simultaneously we can construct a composite relative, or "index number." An index number can be completed by taking a weighted average of the relatives for the individual items which are to be combined in the index number. The choice of weights is again of crucial importance, and is the basis of most of the controversy concerning the construction of index numbers. In the case of a price index, the choice commonly made is to use weights proportional to the total sales or purchases of the various components at a given time or place. For an index number which measures the change of some measurement over a period of time, the weights may be chosen to represent the importance of the components at the base time, or at the time of compilation of the index number, or some compromise between these two. If the weights are based on the importance of the components at the base time, then the index is said to be base-weighted. If they are based on the importance of the components at the time of the latest compilation of the index they are said to be current-weighted.

The compilation of an index number for the two extreme cases can be formulated as follows:

let p_0 be the value of a measurement at the base time o;
p_t the value at t units of time later;
w_0 the weights based on the situation at the base time; and
w_t the weights based on the situation at the time t.

If we take the weighted arithmetic mean of the relatives:
index for base-weighting

$$= \frac{\Sigma(Rel. \times Wt.)}{\Sigma Wts.} = \frac{\Sigma\left(\dfrac{100\, p_t}{p_0} \times w_0\right)}{\Sigma w_0}$$

index for current-weighting

$$= \frac{\Sigma(Rel. \times Wt.)}{\Sigma Wts.} = \frac{\Sigma\left(\dfrac{100\, p_t}{p_0} \times w_t\right)}{\Sigma w_t}$$

Table XVIII—Calculation of Index Number from Relatives

INDEX NUMBER FOR RAW MATERIALS

Item	Relative	Weight	Rel. × Wt.
Oil grade 1	139	10	1390
Oil grade 2	155	25	3875
Emulsifier	127	1	127
		36	5392

$$\text{Index} = \frac{\Sigma(\text{Rel.} \times \text{Wt.})}{\Sigma \text{Wts.}} = \frac{5392}{36} = 149 \cdot 8.$$

Base-weighting versus current-weighting

Current-weighting of an index is attractive in that it provides a continuous review of the situation being studied and always represents the current importance of the components in the index. However, the calculation of the weights must be made anew for each calculation of an index value.

If the calculation of the weights requires a considerable expenditure in time and effort, as it often does, then the insistence on current weighting will almost inevitably lead to an increase in expense and possibly to delay in the appearance of an index number. In addition the continuous change in the weights will make comparisons between different parts of an index-number series invalid, and may arouse suspicion in lay users of the index number that it is not reliable.

Base-weighting is attractive in that the weights need only be calculated once, and are then held constant. This has advantages in cost and stability. Base-weights are less desirable in that they progressively become outmoded and over a long series may seriously misrepresent the true situation.

In the case of price index numbers a further consideration arises. If an item rises in price more rapidly than other items, then by the "law of the market place" the demand for this item will decrease and the demand for the other items increase. This means that over a period of time the importance of items showing the greatest increases in price will be lessened. The current-weighted index number will recognise this lessening importance, the base-weighted number will not. Thus a current-weighted index will tend to play down the amount of change in prices compared to a base-weighted index. Which index number is to be preferred may well depend on whether the user's interest lies in emphasising changes or not.

The greater ease and speed with which base-weighted index-numbers can be calculated has tended to make them the more popular. They do have the effect of emphasising changes and in a period in which inflationary increases have been a major preoccupation of government a move towards current-weighted index-numbers which tend to minimise such increases has occurred.

Arithmetic versus geometric weighted mean

So far the relatives have been combined by taking a weighted arithmetic mean of them. This can be criticised on the grounds that ratios, such as price relatives, will follow a distribution whose mean value is better represented by a geometric mean. The method of calculation of a geometric mean is simplified by taking logarithms of the price relatives and an example is shown in Table XIX.

It is found that the geometric mean gives a lower value for an index number than does the arithmetic mean. If the relatives are not far from 100 the difference between the two index numbers will be small and the arithmetic mean is usually preferred for its greater simplicity.

Table XIX—Calculation of Index Number using the Weighted Geometric Mean of Relatives

INDEX FOR RAW MATERIALS

Item	Relative	Weight	Log. Rel.	log. Rel. × Wt.
Oil grade 1	139	10	2·1430	21·430
Oil grade 2	155	25	2·1903	54·7575
Emulsifier	127	1	2·1038	2·1038
		36		78·2913

$$\text{Log. Index} = \frac{\Sigma(\text{log. Rel.} \times \text{Wt.})}{\Sigma \text{Wts.}} = \frac{78 \cdot 2913}{36} = 2 \cdot 1748$$

$$\text{Index} = 149 \cdot 6.$$

Aggregative indices

Index numbers can be calculated without the intermediate step of calculating relatives. If we specify a list of items to be purchased, and choose the quantity of item to represent its importance, then we can compare the cost of purchasing the list of items at different times, or in different places. Since we take a ratio of prices, the actual quantities of items specified are unimportant, so long as the relative quantities are correctly allocated.

Table XX—Calculation of Aggregative Index

INDEX FOR RAW MATERIALS

Item	Quantity	Price 1978	Price 1982	Cost 1978	Cost 1982
	litres	p	p	p	p
Oil grade 1	5	18	25	90	125·00
Oil grade 2	11·25	20	31	225	348·75
Emulsifier	0·10	88	112	8·8	11·2
				323·8	484·95

$$\text{Index} = \frac{\text{Cost 1974}}{\text{Cost 1970}} \times 100 = \frac{484 \cdot 95}{323 \cdot 8} \times 100 = 149 \cdot 8.$$

As with the previous methods of calculating index numbers, we can construct the indices by reference to base-time or current-time conditions. A base-weighted aggregative index is known as a Laspeyre index, and a current-weighted aggregative index as a Paasche index. The names refer to two early workers in this field.

If we use the symbols p_o, p_t as before and let q_o be the quantity of each item specified at time o and q_t be the quantity of each item specified at time t, then:

$$\text{Laspeyre index} = \frac{\Sigma p_t q_o}{\Sigma p_o q_o} \times 100,$$

$$\text{and Paasche index} = \frac{\Sigma p_t q_t}{\Sigma p_o q_t} \times 100.$$

This method of calculating index-numbers is convenient when we are not particularly interested in the relatives or index-numbers of selections of the relatives. Most published index-numbers are partially "aggregative" and partially "weighted relatives" in their construction.

Quantity indices

If we are interested in changes in quantities rather than prices, we can design quantity index numbers in a very similar manner. The weighting is often by price and the type of index number which can be used is shown below.

Base-weighted quantity index

$$= \frac{\Sigma p_o q_t}{\Sigma p_o q_o} \times 100.$$

Current-weighted quantity index

$$= \frac{\Sigma p_t q_t}{\Sigma p_t q_o} \times 100.$$

Value index

If a measure of the change in value of a series of items bought or sold is required then a value index number may be required. In this case only one index number can be constructed and the question of base versus current weighting does not arise.

$$\text{Value index} = \frac{\Sigma p_t q_t}{\Sigma p_o q_o} \times 100.$$

Published index numbers

The use of index numbers

Despite the criticism which has been levelled at the use of index numbers from time to time, they remain one of the most widely used statistical devices. It is true that their uncritical use is dangerous, and the importance of the various components in the construction of an index number, the choice of base, the choice of weights and the choice of type of index, has already been pointed out. Much of the criticism becomes less relevant when the user is well aware of the background of an index number, and any person wishing to use an index number is well advised to seek this information.

Index numbers do represent a way of combining changes in quantities which are not otherwise easily combined together. They are commonly used in several main fields of interest of which:

(*a*) prices and wages,
(*b*) production and trade, and
(*c*) share prices

are the most important.

Price index numbers

One of the most widely quoted index numbers is the Index of Retail Prices, or as it is commonly referred to, the "Cost-of-living Index." The development of this index is of considerable interest as it illustrates a changing approach to the problems of compiling an index number. The forerunner of the present index number was initiated after the First World War. It was a base-weighted index number, the weights being based on a survey on household expenditures of a sample of working-class homes taken just prior to the war. This index number was described as an "Index of the cost of maintaining a standard of living of the same level as in 1914 in working-class households." The weights used were:

food   7·5,
rent/rates   2·0,
clothing   1·5,
fuel/light   1·0,
other   0·5,

and the base was July 1914 = 100.

It should be noted that this index number was mainly concerned with necessities and made little allowance for entertainment or leisure spending. Despite this it remained unchanged until 1947. By the 1930s it was becoming increasingly obvious that the index did not represent any contemporary patterns of spending, and it was claimed that it underestimated the true level of average family expenditure by between 20% and 30%. To remedy this a survey of family expenditure was made involving 10,000 households in 1937–9. Use was not made of this data until 1947 due to the outbreak of war. In 1947 a further short survey was made and the results combined with the pre-war results to establish new weights. This index was titled *The Interim Index of Retail Prices.* It was not intended to represent the expenditure of an average family, but to reflect the general level of expenditure of the majority of families. The weights used were:

(i)	food	348
(ii)	rent and rates	88
(iii)	clothing	97
(iv)	fuel and light	65
(v)	household durable goods	71
(vi)	miscellaneous goods	35
(vii)	services	79
(viii)	drink and tobacco	217

and the index was based on June 1947 = 100. It will be noted that this index was weighted to represent actual expenditure rather than essential expenditure as previously.

Further revisions have been made on the basis of surveys of expenditure and from 1956 the Retail Price Index was established with base 17th January 1956 = 100. The weights at this revision were based on a survey of household expenditure in 1953–4. In this index two classes of households were excluded from the calculation as not being typical. They were those where over 75% of the income was derived from national insurance, national assistance or pensions, and those where the head of the household earned more than £20 per week gross.

From July 1958 a continuing survey of household expenditure has been carried out under the title of the *Family Expenditure Survey.* This is made yearly and is based on information from about 4000 households. The data collected in this survey is now used to revise the weights of the Retail Price Index. The weights are changed annually at the start of the calendar year and are based on the average expenditure pattern in the three years ending the previous June. From January 1975 the revision will be based on the latest annual expenditure pattern figures available. Low-income and high-income families are excluded from the calculation as having non-typical expenditure patterns. The exclusion limit for high-income families has risen steadily to keep in step with changes in income over the years.

The weights used since 1947 are shown in Table XXI. The current values of the index will be found in the *Monthly Digest of Statistics* and in the *Department of Employment Gazette*. The current index is based on 15th January 1974 = 100 and replaces the previous series based on 16th January 1962 = 100. As always when a change is made in the base the new and old series are published together for a year.

Pensioner index numbers

The concern being shown at the effect of inflation on low income and pensioner families has been reflected in the construction of price index numbers based on weighting for pensioner households. These are now published for one-person and for two-person pensioner families and are to be found in the *Department of Employment Gazette*. The series has been extended backwards using the already available data to give figures from 1962. To distinguish it from this series the standard index number is now known as the General Index of Retail Prices.

Use of the retail price index

The index is used popularly as a measure of the value of money and hence of the effect of inflation on wages, and has been much quoted in wage and salary negotiations. But it is not strictly correct to use the index in this way as it is very much an average figure and so not representative for any particular set of workers, or indeed for any particular area of the country. As no good alternative exists it is to be expected that this erroneous view of the index will continue. The index has for many years been used to provide automatic adjustment of earnings as prices rise—cost of living rises are given when the index rises by some agreed amount. The number of employees affected increased dramatically

Table XXI—Retail Price Index Weightings

	1947–55	1956–61	1962	1965	1968	1971	1974	1977	1980
Food	348	350	319	311	263	250	253	247	214
Alcoholic Drink	}217	71	64	65	63	65	70	83	82
Tobacco		80	79	76	66	59	43	48	40
Housing	88	87	102	109	121	119	124	112	124
Fuel and Light	65	55	62	65	62	60	52	58	59
Durable Household Goods	71	66	64	59	59	61	64	63	69
Clothing and Footwear	97	106	98	92	89	87	91	82	84
Miscellaneous Goods	35	59	64	63	60	65	63	71	74
Services	79	58	56	55	56	54	54	54	62
Transport and Vehicles		68	92	105	120	136	135	139	151
Meals bought and consumed out of home					41	44	51	45	41

Note: The last category "Meals out" was assigned half to "Food" and half to all other categories prior to 1968.

in late 1973 when government pay policy deliberately encouraged these adjustments under the name of "threshold agreements," and the monthly publication of the latest value of the index is now of considerable general interest. It might well be asked how many of those who refer to the index in fact know what it is and how it is calculated.

Wholesale price index numbers

Equally important index numbers are calculated and published to measure changes in wholesale prices. These are often regarded as better measures of the change in the value of money than the Retail Price Index, and have a longer history. The simplest of these index numbers take a list of important commodities and measure the general change by averaging the price relatives for each commodity.

Typical is the *Financial Times* Index of Sensitive World Commodity Prices. This includes twelve price relatives which are combined by taking a geometric average. The commodities are selected to represent major items of world trade which are not subject to a large degree of price control, and so are sensitive to world trading conditions.

A large series of index numbers is published by the United Kingdom Government under the title of *Index Numbers of Wholesale Prices*. These are specifically designed to measure the change in wholesale prices generally. The 8000 price relatives which are available are combined for groups of commodities which are of interest to different industries. The composition of these groups and the weightings used to calculate the group index numbers are derived from a variety of sources, including the Census of Production and information from trade associations. Much of the information discovered by the Census of Production is now published in the series of some 163 Business Monitors, each of which includes data relevant to a particular sector of the economy. Revisions to these Monitors are described in the monthly publication *Statistical News*.

To provide similar information for farmers a series of index numbers which measure the changes in prices of materials and services required in different sectors of agricultural production is also published.

Business activity index numbers

Index numbers are often used as a general measure of the level of business activity at a given time. It is probably best in fact to examine several index numbers each of which measures a different aspect of business activity, rather than attempting to design an overall index number.

Index numbers useful in this way include the following:

1. *The Index of Industrial Production.*

This is formed by weighting the relatives for about 880 industries in proportion to their net output in 1975 as shown by the Census of Production taken that year. A corresponding series of index numbers which have been seasonally corrected are also published.

2. *The Indices of Volume of Orders in Engineering, Aircraft Industry and Textile and Clothing Industries.*

These index numbers measure the volume of orders, orders in hand and deliveries in the various engineering industries, the volume of deliveries of aircraft and aero-engines, and the volume of orders and deliveries for textiles and clothing. In the last category index numbers for different subsections of the trade are calculated and combined in proportion to the net output in each subsection.

3. *The Index of Volume of Output of the Construction Industry.*

This measures the output of new work, and a seasonally corrected figure is also published.

4. *The Index Numbers of Retail Sales and Stocks.*

Separate index numbers are calculated for sales in the different categories of shops, and are based on voluntary information from a sample of retail businesses. The weightings used to calculate the index numbers from individual returns are based mainly on the results of the Census of Distribution and Other Services. An overall index number of value of sales for all kinds of business is published, and seasonally corrected index numbers for both value and volume of sales. For stocks, an overall index number only is published.

5. *Index Numbers of Hire Purchase and Instalment Credit.*

With the growing importance of credit trading and its sensitivity to the general availability of money, much interest is now shown in these two index numbers measuring changes in this trade. They measure the new credit given by durable goods shops, and the new credit extended direct to hirers from finance houses in each month.

6. *Index Numbers of Exports and Imports.*

Index numbers are published for exports and imports both by volume and by value. The index numbers by volume are based on the ratio of goods transferred in a given year at base year prices to the value of goods transferred in the base year. It is well to remember that some exports or imports take the form of very large single orders, such as for ships or aircraft. The timing of the delivery of such items may have a substantial effect on individual values of the index numbers.

7. *Index Numbers of Wages and Hours.*

Index numbers of average earnings in various industries are available, classified into employees paid weekly and employees paid monthly, and corresponding overall index numbers are published for all industries and for manufacturing industries. An all-industries index of average earnings of salaried workers is also published.

To remove the effect of overtime or short time, a corresponding series of index numbers is available of weekly and hourly wage rates, and of normal hours of work per week.

8. *Index of Labour Costs.*

An index designed to reflect the changes in total labour costs is now published. This is based on the gross domestic product at current and at constant prices. The series was first published and described in *Economic Trends* (October 1968).

9. *Index Number of House Prices.*

An index number of house prices is published. This shows the change in the prices of houses on which mortgages have been given by the Building Societies.

10. *Index Numbers of Share Prices.*

Apart from the Retail Price Index, perhaps the best known index numbers are those measuring changes in prices on the Stock Market. As with the commodity index numbers a division may be made into sensitive and overall index numbers. Typical of the sensitive index numbers is the *Financial Times* Industrial Ordinary Share Index. The simple geometric mean is taken of price relatives of thirty securities and the index is recalculated three times daily, reflecting its ability to change rapidly with the climate of dealing on the Stock Exchange. The thirty securities included in the index are chosen to be representative of industrial shares generally and the list is subject to revision when this seems appropriate.

By contrast to these sensitive index numbers, the *Financial Times* Actuaries' Share Index Numbers are designed to provide an over-all measure of the changes in price levels of major categories of stocks and shares. Although not based on all prices quoted on the Stock Exchange, they are based on a sample which represents over 90% of the capital value of all shares. The various share price relatives are combined by means of a weighted arithmetic average, the weights being modified when changes in the capital structure of the companies represented take place.

Corresponding index numbers to those described are published in the other countries having active stock markets, and particular mention may be made of the American measures of share prices. Although many index numbers are calculated, probably the best known measures are the Dow Jones Averages. These are not index numbers, and did not have the value of 100 at their base date. However, they are usually referred to in the same way, and as they are based on a small number of securities are the equivalent of the *Financial Times* Industrial Ordinary Share Index.

The tax and prices index number

In 1980 the Chancellor of the Exchequer's Budget contained provision to move some direct taxation, in the form of income tax, to indirect taxation, in the form of value added tax. VAT is included in the price of retail goods and hence increased the Retail Price Index. As this index number is used to measure inflation particularly by trade unions in wage negotiations the Government argued that it would be better to design an index number which took account of changes in direct personal taxation as well as retail prices in order to measure the effect of inflation on a typical family.

This was done and the *Tax and Prices Index* was published and, as its authors hoped, showed a lower rate of increase than the Retail Price Index. There is little evidence that it was regarded as anything other than a "fiddle" by the trade unions—the Retail Price Index with many years behind it being the established measure. At budget time in 1981 the effect of the VAT change was lost and as the Government did not alter tax thresholds in line with inflation direct taxation was also effectively allowed to stay at a higher rate than a year earlier. The total effect was that the Tax and Prices Index now showed a higher rate of increase than the Retail Price Index. Not surprisingly it is not now being commended as the correct basis for pay settlements.

The interpretation of index numbers

Index numbers are statistics which are heavily dependent on the way in which they are calculated. This has been held to discredit them as good statistics, as the subjective element in their calculation is high. Despite this they are widely published and can be of great use. Any liability to draw incorrect conclusions from them, or to be knowingly misled by them should be avoided by making oneself thoroughly familiar with the method of calculation. The basic information required to judge an index number can again be listed as:

(*a*) the base of the index,
(*b*) its constituents,
(*c*) the method of weighting, and
(*d*) the method of calculation.

It is probable that in gaining this information a good familiarity with the index number will also be gained, and the dangers mentioned above will be minimised.

Care must be taken not to confuse absolute and relative changes. It is common to speak of a change in an index number as being of so many "points," meaning units, *e.g.* a change from 113 to 117 is a change of four points. If an index number has diverged far from its base level of 100, then the simple correspondence of "points" to percentages which applies close to the base level will fail, *e.g.* change from

113 to 117 = four points = 4%;
413 to 417 = four points = 1%.

Questions

1. Three men estimate the cost of a job as £75, £120 and £140 respectively. If you rate their knowledge in the ratio of 1:8:4 what is the best estimate of the cost of the job?

2. Distinguish between a base-weighted and a current-weighted index number and discuss their relative merits.

3. What are the principal features of an index number which a prospective user should be familiar with?

4. Discuss the published index numbers suitable for measuring business activity; give the base year and current value of the index numbers you discuss.

5. The prices of three raw materials and amounts used are given below for two years. Calculate a base-weighted index on 1980 = 100, and a current-weighted index on 1982 = 100.

Item	Consumption tons		Price per ton	
	1980	1982	1980	1982
A	1200	1600	£5	£6
B	800	1500	£7	£6
C	2000	800	£5	£9

6. The weights and relatives for three categories in the Index of Retail Prices at 17th November, 1981 were:

Category	Relative	Weight
Housing	345·6	135
Fuel and light	398·5	62
Durable household goods	240·9	65

Source: *Monthly Digest of Statistics*

Calculate an overall index for these three categories.

7. Four share prices move as shown over a year: calculate the arithmetic and geometric weighted index numbers, using the issued shares as weights, and Jan. 1981 = 100.

Share	Shares issued	Price: Jan., 1981	Price: Jan., 1982
		p	p
A	500,000	71	78
B	120,000	53	75
C	1,300,000	45	55
D	400,000	94	85

8. "The Index of Retail Prices has risen 5 points."
"The F.T. Ordinary Share Index has risen 5 points."
Discuss the relative implications of these statements. Discuss any other index numbers of share prices with which you are familiar.

9. Discuss the measurement of price changes by reference to the Index of Retail Prices, and the Indexes of Wholesale Prices.

10. Discuss the ways in which an index number can be designed to give a misleading picture of changes.

CHAPTER NINE

PROBABILITY AND THEORETICAL DISTRIBUTIONS

Probability

The probability problem

THE principal distinction between the use of words in everyday life and in a science is the degree to which we restrict their meaning in a scientific context by defining it more closely. In the case of probability theory this distinction becomes of the greatest importance as many of the words in common use are capable of very wide ranges of interpretation, and yet it is not easy to define them without using equally wide-ranging words. This has led to a large number of definitions of probability, which while they may help to give an intuitive knowledge of its meaning do not define it, or else define its meaning within a very restricted context.

In the study of mathematical probability the problem is resolved either by making an implicit assumption that the meaning of probability is understood, without actually defining it, or else by a definition in terms of quantities and concepts which are not familiar to any but mathematicians.

For the purposes of this book it appears to be best to give a definition of probability which allows the development of statistical methods without confusion, and to use more restricted definitions of probability where required to obtain actual measures of given probability.

Meaning of probability

In everyday life we use words such as chance, likelihood and probability without precise definition, but with a general understanding of what is intended. When we say that the probability of a "head" resulting from one toss of a coin is 50:50, or "evens" we do not expect that out of every two tosses one will result in a head, but after a large number of tosses we would expect equal proportions of heads and tails. In other words, that the proportion of heads after a large number of tosses will tend to half. This idea of the probability of an event as the expected proportion of occurrence of the event in a large number of trials gives us a measure with a numerical value between 0 and 1. We can now identify the event with probability = 0 as an impossibility and the event with probability = 1 as a certainty. Between these limits the more certain we are that an event will happen, *i.e.* that in a large number of trials it would be observed in a majority of instances, the nearer its probability is to 1.

This measure of probability as the ratio of observed events in an infinitely long series of trials is supported by the *Law of Large Numbers*. This states that the observed proportions of events in a series of trials will approach fixed limits as the number of trials increases, assuming that the events are randomly distributed among the trials. By a random event is meant one whose occurrence is independent of the preceding events.

When the occurrences of events are related one to another, then the Law of Large Numbers may not apply, and a different method of calculation of the likely outcomes must be adopted. The assumption of random occurrence of events in a series of trials is basic to most statistical theory, whether it is expected or not, and when it is not valid the usual methods of statistics cannot be expected to hold. Fortunately in the great majority of statistical applications the assumption does hold true, or else appears to be valid as judged by the correctness of the conclusions reached by using it.

The probability of an event happening can be conveniently symbolised by putting a description or symbol representing the event in a bracket following the letter P, *e.g.*

$P(A)$, the probability that (A) will happen,

$P(loss)$, the probability that a loss will occur as the result of a given decision,

$P(z > 3)$, the probability that the variable z, takes a value greater than 3.

Combinations of probabilities

There are two important ways in which probabilities of individual events can be combined to find the probability of a complex event. If two events in the same series of trials are mutually exclusive then the probability that either one or the

other will occur is the sum of their separate probabilities, *i.e.*
$P(either\ (A)\ or\ (B)) = P(A) + P(B)$.

This can be illustrated by the situation facing a stock controller
when considering the demand for a little-used item. The demand
may be for one item, two items, three items and so on in a particular time interval. The stock controller wants to know what the
likelihood is of the demand exceeding his stock level. Obviously
the demand cannot be more than one particular number, and if
we can identify the probability of a particular number of items
being demanded then the required probability is the sum of the
probabilities of any demands greater than the stock level, *e.g.*
if the stock level is k items, and the probability of n items being
demanded is $P(n)$ then,

$$P(\text{stock out}) = \sum_{n=k+1}^{n=\infty} P(n)$$

The use of the Poisson distribution to determine such probabilities is considered later.

If two events are independent, that is the occurrence of one does
not affect the probability of occurrence of the other, then the
probability that they will both occur, either simultaneously or
successively, is given by the product of their separate probabilities,
i.e. $P(both\ (A)\ and\ (B)) = P(A)\ .\ P(B)$.

Imagine a firm which has submitted tenders for two contracts,
both of which will be considered at the same time and which are
for different organisations. The two results are independent, and
so if the probabilities of winning the contracts are P(first contract)
and P(second contract) the probability of winning both contracts
will be P(first contract) $\times$ P(second contract).

In this case the two events described are not mutually exclusive
and the first rule given does not apply. A little thought will show
that if we took P(any contract) $= P$(first) $+ P$(second) we would
be double counting when both contracts were won. This can be
avoided by subtracting the probability of both being won.
e.g. P(any contract) $= P$(first) $+ P$(second) $- P$(both).

If $P(\text{first}) = 0.7,$
and $P(\text{second}) = 0.8,$
then $P(\text{both}) = 0.7 \times 0.8 = 0.56$
and $P(\text{any}) = P(\text{first}) + P(\text{second}) - P(\text{both})$
                $= 1.5 - 0.56$
                $= 0.94.$

Probability values

The question of assigning a value to a given probability has so far been ignored. The definition given cannot be used as it is based on future events which cannot be foreseen, and we must adopt methods which give results which are in agreement with the definition while certain assumptions hold true. These assumptions underlie all statistical work, and may not be explicitly stated in a given problem. Whether stated or not, their validity is basic to the validity of the results obtained, and obviously erroneous results can often be traced to a breakdown of one of these assumptions.

The simplest method of assigning a value to a probability is by intuition or experience, and there is no reason to reject this method if others are not available. In fact it represents the use of the other methods, although not necessarily in a formal or conscious manner.

Theoretical probability

To assign a probability in this case we must know all possible outcomes to our trial. We then examine these outcomes and identify those corresponding to the occurrence of the event we wish to observe. If we know the probability of each outcome then the probability of the desired event is given by the sum of the probabilities of individual outcomes. In general we do not know the probabilities of individual outcomes but may feel justified in saying that they are all equally likely, *e.g.* in a well-shuffled pack of cards, any card is as likely to turn up next as any other when dealing.

In this as in many similar cases we cannot prove that all outcomes are equally likely, but equally we cannot give any reason why they should differ. Ensuring that outcomes are of equal probability is largely a matter of eliminating any reasons for the contrary to be true. In a card game, it is enough to shuffle the pack, at a fête a drum with folded papers may serve to choose raffle winners, but for statistical sampling such techniques are not adequate.

If we have n possible outcomes all of equal probability then we assign to each a probability of $1/n$. This means the probability that one of the possible outcomes will occur is $n \times 1/n = 1$ in agreement with our definition of the probability measure. Then if there are $n(r)$ outcomes corresponding to the occurrence of event (r) we define the probability of (r) as $P(r) = n(r)/n$.

Note that we do not have to make the assumption of equi-probability of outcomes. This is normally a justifiable assumption, but must not necessarily be taken for granted. Care must also be taken in identifying all possible outcomes, *e.g.* if two coins are tossed the outcomes are not three; two heads, head and tail, two tails, but four; two heads, head and tail, tail and head, two tails. In this instance:

$$P(1 \ head) = P(head + tail) + P(tail + head)$$
$$= \tfrac{1}{4} + \tfrac{1}{4} = \tfrac{1}{2}$$

despite the fact that with two similar coins we may be unable to discriminate between the falls, head and tail, and tail and head.

If we do know the probabilities of particular outcomes to a trial, then the probability of an event is given by the sum of the probabilities of the outcome which represents the occurrence of that event.

Historical probability

If we have details of a number of trials we can measure the proportion of the trials which result in the event we wished to observe. If we call this p then:

$$p = \frac{\text{number of times event observed}}{\text{number of trials}}.$$

If we now make the assumption that history will repeat itself, *i.e.* that the same proportion of required events to trials will occur in the future as in the past, then this proportion is the probability that the event will occur.

It may be seen that this assumption will only be reasonable if there is no change in the conditions under which the trials are carried out. We may not be sure of this, and we must treat probabilities derived from a use of the assumption of similar conditions with a measure of reserve, and correct them by the use of later information as it becomes available. Also, by the operation of the Law of Large Numbers, the greater the amount of past information available, the more closely will p approach the true value of the probability. We must always be cautious in using values based on a small amount of past data.

Uses of probabilities

Probability and decisions

The use of probabilities even when they are derived only from intuitive values, and are known to be subject to error, can often lead to an easing of the burden of making decisions. At the simplest we can choose between rival methods of obtaining a desired result by preferring the one with the greatest probability of success. This may seem an obvious method, requiring no knowledge of probability, but it is surprising how often this obvious assessment of probabilities is not made. The statement that a person is taking a calculated risk usually means that the risks or probabilities involved have not been calculated, but that a gamble on unknown odds is being made. The use of any probabilities, even if only "order of size" estimates, can usually clarify a situation, and make clearer the crucial points on which a decision must be taken.

Probability and expectation

In management situations we are usually interested in the financial results of decisions, and the idea of the expectation of a trial can be of use. The expectation is defined as the sum of the products of the probabilities of the possible outcomes, and the financial result associated with each.

To take a simple example, if we bet on a horse at 10 to 1 and the true probability of the horse winning is 0·05 then for a stake of one unit:

Table XXII—Pay-off Table for Horse Bet

Outcome	Value	Probability	Expectation
Horse wins	+10	0·05	+0·50
Horse loses	−1	0·95	−0·95
		Total expectation −0·45	

This does not mean that we would lose money on any given bet, but that in a long series of bets under similar conditions we would lose an average of 0·45 units per bet.

As a further example consider a shopkeeper stocking a perishable commodity. He can order the commodity daily in single units and makes a profit of 10p for each unit sold. Each unit unsold at the end of the day becomes unfit for sale and he incurs a loss of 20p per unit. The shopkeeper wishes to maximise his profit and keeps records of the demand for the commodity. From these results we can estimate the probability of various demands for the commodity.

Table XXIII—Probability of Various Demands

Number demanded	Occasions	Probability
0	2	0·02 = 2/100
1	7	0·07
2	17	0·17
3	27	0·27
4	21	0·21
5	16	0·16
6	7	0·07
7	3	0·03
	100	1·00

We can now estimate the expectation for any number of units the shopkeeper chooses to stock. If he buys 3 units the pay-off table is:

Table XXIV(a)—Pay-off Table for 3 Units Stocked

Event	Profit	Probability	Expectation
0 demanded	−60	0·02	−1·2
1	−30	0·07	−2·1
2	0	0·17	0
3	30	0·27	8·1
4	30	0·21	6·3
5	30	0·16	4·8
6	30	0·07	2·1
7	30	0·03	0·9
		Total expectation = 18·9	

If he buys 4 units the pay-off table is:

Table XXIV (b)—Pay-off Table for 4 Units Stocked

Event	Profit	Probability	Expectation
0 demanded	−80	0·02	−1·6
1	−50	0·07	−3·5
2	−20	0·17	−3·4
3	10	0·27	2·7
4	40	0·21	8·4
5	40	0·16	6·4
6	40	0·07	2·8
7	40	0·03	1·2
		Total expectation = 13·0	

By calculation of the expectation for various numbers of units stocked we can choose the optimum stock strategy. The results are given in Table XXV, and the result is that the maximum profit will be obtained in the long run by stocking 3 units.

Table XXV—Expectation of Profit for Various Strategies

Strategy	Expectation
Stock 0	0
1	9·4
2	16·7
3	18·9
4	13·0
5	0·2

The same ideas can be extended to more complex problems and especially to cases where the probabilities assigned to the various events are derived from a model which is expected to fit the problem being studied.

Decision tree analysis

Expectations may also be calculated for complex events, and the use of decision trees is an example of this. A decision tree shows the various choices open and also the possible outcomes when the future is not certain. Figure 28 shows a simple example. We have to decide whether or not to continue a research project. We can decide to keep expenditure as at present, say £10 000; to increase it to £20 000, or to drop the project. If we discontinue the project our costs will be £5000. If the project is successful within our time limit it will enable us to make profits of £100 000; if it is a failure we will recover nothing.

The probability of success for each of the choices open to us is shown in Fig. 28. Multiplying these by the value of the final outcomes, *i.e.* profit less cost, we arrive at the expectation of net profit for each choice. If this is our only criterion we would choose the branch with the maximum expectation of net profit, and thus increase the expenditure.

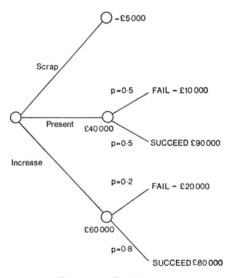

FIG. 28.—*Decision tree*

Theoretical distribution

Derivation of the binomial distribution

Consider the problem "what is the probability of choosing a sample of n items containing r items of a specified type, from a set of N items which contains a proportion p of the specified type?" This can be solved using the information about probabilities that we already have.

To make the situation easier to visualise, imagine a large box containing several thousand apparently identical golf balls. This is our population of N items. A proportion p of the golf balls is faulty. We are asking if it is possible to state the probability that a given sample of n items will contain exactly r faulty balls.

We must first make the assumption that the sample is drawn in a random manner, then the probability of being chosen is the same for all items. Let the items of the specified type be of type (A), then there are Np items of this type in the sample.

The probability we require is the sum of the probabilities of all outcomes to the sampling which satisfy the definition of the required sample. One such outcome would be to choose r items of type (A) and $(n - r)$ items of type $(Not\ A)$. Taking the members of the sample individually:

$P(\textit{first item is an } (A)) \ \ = Np/N = p$
$P(\textit{second item is an } (A)) = (Np - 1)/(N - 1)$
$P(\textit{third item is an } (A)) \ = (Np - 2)/(N - 2)$

If N is large:

$$\frac{(Np - 2)}{(N - 2)} \simeq \frac{(Np - 1)}{(N - 1)} \simeq \frac{Np}{N} = p$$

and this is a reasonable approximation as long as $N > 10n$.

Using this we have for any choice:

$P(\textit{choosing an } (A)) = p$

and by a similar argument:

$P(\textit{choosing a } (Not\ A)) = (1 - p).$

Since we wish to make the choices simultaneously we use the "both . . . and" method of combining probabilities and obtain:

$P(\textit{choosing r items type } (A)) = p^r$
$P(\textit{choosing } (n - r) \textit{ items type } (Not\ A)) = (1 - p)^{n - r}$

and the probability of obtaining a sample of r items type (A) and then $(n - r)$ items type $(Not\ A)$ is $p^r(1 - p)^{n - r}$.

In fact any outcome to the sampling containing r items type (A) and $(n - r)$ items type $(Not\ A)$ has the same probability, and we can combine these probabilities using the "either . . . or" rule, as they are mutually exclusive and in the same series.

We wish then to know how many ways we can arrange a sample of n items containing r of a specified type, as each arrangement represents a different outcome to the sampling. The answer is given by the combination formula $\binom{n}{r}$, and the answer to our problem is, $P(choosing\ specified\ sample) = P(suitable\ outcome) \times (Number\ of\ suitable\ outcomes)$

$$= p^r(1-p)^{n-r} \times \binom{n}{r}$$

Using $P(r)$ to represent the probability of choosing a sample of size n containing r items of a specified type:

$$P(r) = \binom{n}{r} \cdot p^r(1-p)^{n-r}$$

we can interpret p as the probability of choosing an item of the specified type in one choice.

The probability distribution described by this formula is described as the *binomial distribution*.

For a number of samples size n, the number of items type (A) will vary, and this number is said to be "distributed as the binomial with constants n, and p." For such a distribution: mean number of items type (A) per sample $= np$; variance of numbers of items type (A) per sample $= np(1-p)$.

If instead of the number of items type (A) in the sample we are interested in the proportion of items type (A) in the sample these formulae become: mean proportion of items type (A) in a sample $= p$; variance of proportions of items type (A) in a sample $= p(1-p)/n$.

The shape of the binomial distribution for different values of n and p is shown in Fig. 29, where $N > 10n$.

Use of the binomial distribution

The binomial distribution finds its principal use in sampling theory, although it can be used as the basis of certain significance tests. As an example of its use we can derive the operating characteristic curve for a simple sampling plan. A sampling plan specifies that a sample of twenty items must be taken from each batch of items presented for inspection and the batch rejected if there is more than one defective item in the sample. The operating characteristic curve shows the probability that a batch will be rejected when it contains a given proportion of defective items.

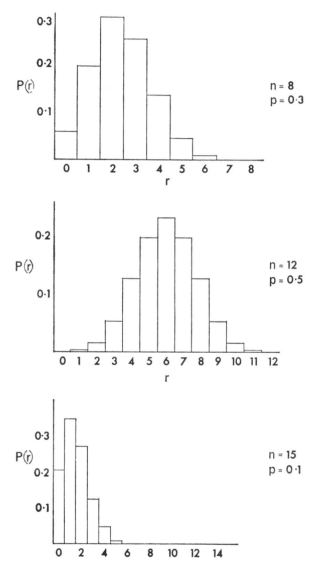

FIG. 29.—*The shape of binomial distributions*

The probability that a batch will be accepted is given by:
P(*no defectives in sample*) + P(1 *defective in sample*).

Table XXVI—Calculation for Operating Characteristic Curve

P	P (0)	P (1)	P (accept)
0	1·000	0·000	1·000
0·02	0·667	0·272	0·939
0·05	0·358	0·377	0·735
0·075	0·210	0·340	0·550
0·10	0·121	0·271	0·392
0·125	0·069	0·198	0·267
0·15	0·039	0·137	0·176
0·20	0·012	0·058	0·070

The operating characteristic curve is shown in Fig. 30.

The operating characteristic curve is used to show the behaviour of a sampling scheme to different inputs, and to enable different schemes to be compared.

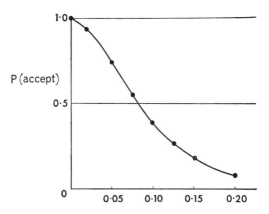

FIG. 30.—*Operating characteristic curve*

Limits to the binomial distributions

The calculation of binomial probabilities is made from published tables, but these are not easily available for $n > 30$ and calculations of this size would be burdensome. The problem is solved by considering limits to the binomial distribution when the sample size becomes large. Two cases may be studied: when the value of p is small and when it is close to 0·5. The first leads to the Poisson distribution and the second to the normal distribution.

The Poisson distribution

Let the size of our sample increase without limit, *i.e.* $n \to \infty$, and let the probability of a specified type of item being chosen tend to zero, *i.e.* $p \to 0$, but let there be a constant number of times when this type of item is chosen, $np = m$. The binomial distribution can then be shown to give the limiting form $P(r) = \dfrac{e^{-m} m^r}{r!}$, this is known as the Poisson distribution. The variable e is a natural constant, being the base of natural logarithms. It should be noted that the size of the sample n, and the probability p, now no longer appear in the formula. The successive values of $P(r)$ only depend on r and the mean number of items observed m.

This distribution predicts the probability of observing a number of items or events, when the number of opportunities of making the observation is high, but the actual number observed is low. Typical situations of this type are the number of phone calls made in a given time, the number of faults in an arbitrary length of paper or cloth, the number of accidents suffered by a person in a given period of time and the number of mistakes made by a clerk in a large number of invoices. The distribution is also of considerable importance in the study of queueing problems.

The mean number of items observed is, as with the binomial distribution, $np = m$ and the variance $np(1 - p)$. Since we have let $p \to 0$, $(1 - p) \to 1$, and $np(1 - p) \to np = m$. We have the result then, that for a Poisson distribution the mean and variance are equal.

The shape of the distribution is shown in Fig. 31 for several values of m. The histograms are drawn as r can only take integral values, as in the binomial distribution.

As can be seen the distribution becomes more symmetrical as m increases and for values of m greater than 5 the distribution may be approximated by the normal distribution with mean and variance both m.

Individual terms of the Poisson distribution may be calculated from a table of values of e^{-m}, but as $m > 5$ is rarely needed it is quite simple to construct a table of values (see Appendix E).

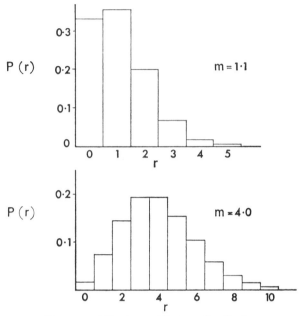

FIG. 31.—*The shape of Poisson distributions*

From this the probability of $P(r)$ can be read off for various values of m and r.

Examples of the use of the Poisson distribution

EXAMPLE I

Consider the following problem: A works maintenance department stocks a certain propeller-shaft which is used on an important piece of machinery. It is essential that a spare be available in the event of a breakage and replacements cannot be obtained in less than one month. If the average requirement is one shaft every two months how many should be stocked so that the chance of none being available is less than:

(*a*) 1 in 1000;
(*b*) 1 in 10,000?

This is a typical situation and $P(r)$ gives the probability that r requests will be made during a month and *Cumulative* $P(r)$ the probability that r or less requests will be made. To satisfy (*a*) *Cum* $P(r)$ must be at least 0·999 and for (*b*) at least 0·9999. From the table we can see that the stock levels must be 4 and 5 respectively. The decision as to which stock level to use would be based on the cost of a machine being idle, the cost of storage and other similar factors, but it can be seen how a statistical model can provide a basis for a decision.

Table XXVII—Use of the Poisson Distribution

$m = 0.5$

r	P (r)	Cum P (r)
0	0·60653	0·60653
1	0·30327	0·90980
2	0·07582	0·98561
3	0·01264	0·99825
4	0·00158	0·99983
5	0·00016	0·99999

EXAMPLE 2

A favourite occupation in Britain is trying to predict the occurrence of drawn football matches so as to win the "Pools." What happens in a football match? There are a large number of occasions on which an attacking player is close enough to the opposing goal to try a shot. Of such occasions very few become goals. In other words we have a large sample with a small probability that any particular member will be of a particular type, *i.e.* a goal. This corresponds to the conditions for a Poisson distribution, and given the mean scoring rate for each team we can predict the probability that it will score no goals, one goal, two goals, etc. A draw means that both teams score the same number of goals and we can use the "both . . . and" rule to combine the probabilities. Table XXVIII shows the calculation for two teams with goal-scoring rates of 2 goals per match and 3 goals per match respectively.

Table XXVIII—Use of the Poisson Distribution

Goals, r	Team A $m = 2.0$ $P(r)_A$	Team B $m = 3.0$ $P(r)_B$	$P(r)_A . P(r)_B$
0	0·135	0·050	0·007
1	0·271	0·149	0·040
2	0·271	0·224	0·061
3	0·180	0·224	0·040
4	0·090	0·168	0·015
5	0·036	0·101	0·004
6	0·012	0·050	0·001
7	0·003	0·022	0·000
		P (draw) = 0·168	

The normal distribution

Consider when the size of the sample increases without limit and let $p = 0.5$. The probability of particular values of r becomes very small and we must consider the probability of a range of values. To mark this change to a continuous distribution let us call the variable x. Then we can derive the probability that x will lie in the range $x_1 - x_2$ from the following formula:

$$P(x_1 < x < x_2) = \int_{x_1}^{x_2} \frac{1}{\sigma\sqrt{2\pi}} e^{-\frac{(x-\mu)^2}{2\sigma^2}} . dx.$$

This is known as the normal distribution. There are two constants in the equation μ and σ and these can be identified as the mean and standard deviation of the distribution respectively. Unlike the binomial distribution the mean and variance are independent for the normal distribution.

The shape of the normal distribution is shown in Fig. 32. It is always symmetrical, and different normal distributions differ only in the position of the central value and the degree of spread

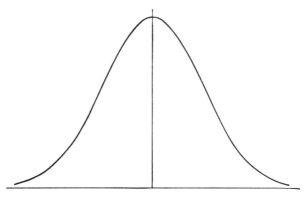

FIG. 32.—*The normal distribution*

around this value. Because of this all normal distributions may be reduced to one standard form with mean = 0, variance = 1, by the transformation $z = (x - \bar{x})/s_x$ where x is the untransformed value of the measurement and z the corresponding standardised value. This is often described as a z score.

The normal distribution occurs very frequently when measurements are centred on a single value and there are no restraints to produce a skew distribution. Many skew distributions may be transformed to a more normal shape by simple non-linear transformations.

Binomial, Poisson or normal?

A decision as to when to use the Poisson or normal limits to the binomial distribution is often required. This must depend on the accuracy required in the particular case, but a general indication can be given as shown below. Note the relationship between the three distributions; when using one to approximate another, the same mean and variance must be used.

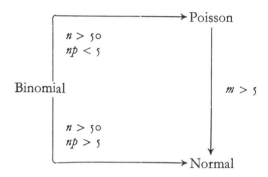

Table XXIX—Constants for Standard Distributions

Distribution	Mean	Variance
Binomial	np	$np(1-p)$
Poisson	m	m
Normal	m	s^2

Questions

1. Discuss the meaning of probability as applied to statistical problems.

2. A shopkeeper buys an item at £2·25 and sells it at £2·90. If it is unsold after a week it is returnable to the supplier and a rebate of £1·95 is allowed. If the shopkeeper knows that sales are distributed like the Poisson distribution, and his average sale is 1·5 items per week, what number of items per week purchased gives him the expectation of highest profit?

3. Discuss the conditions under which you would expect to observe measurements distributed like the Poisson distribution. Indicate typical practical uses of the distribution.

4. A batch of goods has an average of four defectives per hundred items. What is the probability that a sample of twenty items will contain two or less defectives?

5. In a test to distinguish between two brands of coffee a tester correctly identifies eight out of the ten samples given to him. What is the probability of him achieving this result by chance?

How many of the samples must be identified correctly for his ability to distinguish the two brands to be admitted as better than chance? State any assumptions you make in your calculations.

6. In statistical statements it is often necessary to use an estimate of a probability in order to decide if a particular event is likely to occur. Discuss the methods of obtaining such probability estimates, and the choice of probability level at which an event is judged to be not likely.

7. A company can tender for two contracts. The first is worth £100 000 in gross profit, and the company estimates that it has a 0·2 probability of winning the contract. The second contract is worth £140 000 and the chance of winning it is 0·3. Both contracts cannot be accepted, and a tender for each costs £4000 to prepare. Calculate the optimum policy.

8. Two football teams have scoring histories as follows:

Chelford Utd.   (home)   1·8 goals/match
Briggley City   (away)   1·2 goals/match

Calculate the probability that the match Chelford Utd. v. Briggley City will result in:

(a) a home win,
(b) a draw,
(c) an away win.

9. In a competition eight features of a car must be placed in order of merit. The competition can be entered for the cost of a postage stamp (8½p) and the winner receives a car, value £1600. What is the expectation of a completely random entry and hence the best decision on entering?

10. A piece of equipment has four independent control systems. It will stay in operation if at least three are functional. If the probability that any one system fails in a given period is 0·001, what is the probability of total failure?

(Note: at least 6-figure logarithms required.)

CHAPTER TEN

STANDARD DISTRIBUTIONS AND CONFIDENCE INTERVALS

Standard distributions

Summary statistics

THE binomial, Poisson and normal distributions were derived from a consideration of real problems after making a number of simplifying assumptions. They represent the behaviour of variables when the assumptions hold true, but in addition are a good approximation to a large number of other empirical distributions, even though the truth of the underlying assumptions may be unknown or doubtful. In fact since we are often interested only in a comparison of data, or in judging the validity of a statement concerning the data available, rather than in knowing numerical values to a high degree of accuracy, these distributions serve to represent the majority of those met in statistical work.

It is possible to derive a mathematical expression to describe the shape of any curve, but it is only in very specialised fields of work, such as the actuarial forecasting of life expectancies, that such simulations are required. Certain other standard distributions are of use in addition to the three principal distributions described already, and the distributions used in significance testing. In particular the Negative Exponential, Beta and Hypergeometric distributions may sometimes be required.

All standard distributions are completely defined by a knowledge of the constants, or parameters in the equations which describe them. To say that a set of measurements is normally distributed with mean = 5 units and standard deviation = 2 units completely describes the shape of their distribution, and enables us to forecast the behaviour of future measurements belonging to the same set. We can in this way summarise a large amount of data most conveniently.

Confidence intervals

If we know which standard distribution an empirical distribution resembles, and if we know the parameters or constants of the distribution, then we can use this information to make statements about the distribution. This is aided by the availability of tables, giving the probability of observing given values of the quantities being studied. A statement that a variable will lie in a given range of values, with a given probability, is said to define the confidence intervals for the variable.

From the tables of the binomial distribution we can say that for a distribution with $n = 8$, $p = 0 \cdot 1$ the probability of a value of r in the range $r = 0$ to 3 is $0 \cdot 995$. This is the probability that a sample of 8 items taken from a large population with 10% defective items in it will contain between 0 and 3 defectives. To obtain this value, find the part of the table with $n = 8$, $p = 0 \cdot 1$ and add together the probabilities for $r = 0$ to $r = 3$.

An alternative way to state this information is to say that we are $99 \cdot 5\%$ confident that the sample will contain 3 or less defective items. The implication is that we would expect the statement "the sample will contain 3 or less defective items" to be true in $99 \cdot 5\%$ of the instances it is made. As with all statistical statements, we cannot forecast the behaviour of any single sample, but make a statement which we expect to be true in the long run, in the proportion of instances given.

The use of confidence intervals

Confidence intervals are most commonly used in association with the normal distribution, and the intervals are usually either centred on the mean or above or below a given value.

For all normal distributions there is a probability of $0 \cdot 954$ that measurements in such a distribution will lie in the interval, mean ± 2 standard deviations. That is, we are $95 \cdot 4\%$ confident that a measurement will lie in the given interval. For a normally distributed variable x, with mean $= 11 \cdot 2''$ and standard deviation $= 0 \cdot 4''$, $P(x \text{ in range } 11 \cdot 2 \pm 0 \cdot 8) = P(10 \cdot 4 < x < 12 \cdot 0) = 0 \cdot 954$, or $10 \cdot 4 < x < 12 \cdot 0$ ($95 \cdot 4\%$ confidence).

It is conventional to take 95% as a level of good confidence in the occurrence of a specified event, although other confidence levels may be chosen to suit particular circumstances. As noted above a $95 \cdot 4\%$ confidence level is given by the interval mean ± 2 standard deviations, and this range is usually quoted as the expected range of values for a normal distribution. The exact range for a $95 \cdot 0\%$ confidence level is mean $\pm 1 \cdot 96$ standard deviations.

Normal curve tables

The standard normal distribution

The inconvenience of having to refer to a separate table for each combination of values of constants for the binomial and Poisson distributions has been indicated. The situation would be infinitely worse with the normal distribution. Fortunately all normal distributions can be simply reduced to the same shape and we need only construct a table for the standardised form of distribution.

The standard normal distribution is one with mean = 0, and standard deviation = 1. It will be designated in this book as the z distribution. To convert any value of a normally distributed variable x, to the corresponding standardised variable z, the relationship $z = x - mean/standard\ deviation$ is used. The inverse relationship is $x = mean + z\ (standard\ deviation)$.

Normal curve tables

The normal curve or normal distribution tables give the proportion of the area under the curve corresponding to a given range of values of z. This is the probability that a given value of z will be observed. The tables in this book give the probability that a value of z greater than a given value will be observed, that is the proportion of the area under the curve beyond the given value of z. This is illustrated in Fig. 33.

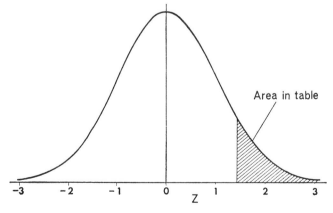

FIG. 33.—*The tabulated area of the normal distribution*

Other tables may give other areas and care should be taken to make sure the exact area tabulated is clearly understood before using unfamiliar tables. Some of the possible variations are shown in Fig. 34, the areas tabulated are shown shaded. There should be no difficulty in using other tables, especially if a diagram is drawn to show the actual areas required.

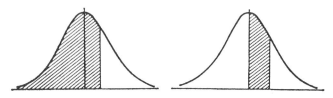

FIG. 34.—*Tabulated areas of the normal distribution*

The use of normal curve tables

The use of the normal curve table is best illustrated by examples. Table A given in Appendix II is used in all the examples.

EXAMPLE I

The heights of men in a certain community are normally distributed with mean = 69·3″ and standard deviation = 1·3″. What proportion of the men in the community would we expect to exceed 6′ 0″ in height, and what proportion would we expect to be less than 5′ 7″ in height?

The proportion of heights greater than 6′ 0″ is represented by the shaded area in Figure 35(*a*). If we let the heights be the variable *x*, then the value $x_1 = 72″$ corresponds to:

$$z_1 = \frac{x_1 - mean}{s.d.} = \frac{72 - 69·3}{1·3} = 2·08.$$

Then referring to the tables this is 0·0188. Hence we expect 0·0188 or 1·9% of the men to exceed 6′ 0″ in height.

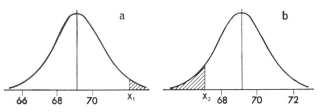

FIG. 35.—*The estimation of proportions using the normal distribution. Example 1*

The proportion of heights less than 5' 7" is represented by the shaded area in Figure 35(b). Here we have $x_2 = 67''$, corresponding to z_2, where:

$$z_2 = \frac{67 - 69 \cdot 3}{1 \cdot 3} = -1 \cdot 77$$

The normal curve is symmetrical, and so $P(z < -1 \cdot 77) = P(z > 1 \cdot 77)$ giving $P(x < 67'') = P(z > 1 \cdot 77) = 0 \cdot 0384$. Hence we expect $0 \cdot 0384$ or $3 \cdot 8\%$ of the men to be less than 5' 7" in height.

EXAMPLE 2

The weights of packets filled on a machine are normally distributed with mean = $32 \cdot 8$ oz and standard deviation = $0 \cdot 5$ oz. What proportion of the packets will weigh more than $32 \cdot 0$ oz?

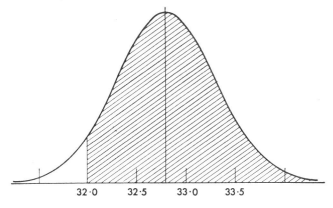

FIG. 36.—*The estimation of proportions using the normal distribution. Example 2*

The required proportion is represented by the shaded area in Fig. 36. This area is not tabulated but the area of the unshaded portion is as shown in the last example. We know that the whole area represents a probability of 1 so we can obtain the required area by difference, *i.e.*

$$P(packet\ over\ 32\ oz) = 1 - P(packet\ under\ 32\ oz)$$

Let the weights be the variable x, then $x_1 = 32$, and corresponds to $z_1 = (32 - 32 \cdot 8)/0 \cdot 5 = -1 \cdot 6$.
Hence $P(packet\ over\ 32\ oz) = 1 - P(x < 32) = 1 - P(z > 1 \cdot 6) = 1 - 0 \cdot 0548 = 0 \cdot 9451$ and we expect $94 \cdot 5\%$ of packets to weigh more than 32 oz.

EXAMPLE 3

A machine produces components whose thicknesses are normally distributed with mean = $0 \cdot 154''$ and standard deviation $0 \cdot 002''$.

Components with thicknesses outside the range 0·150″ to 0·155″ are rejected. What proportion of the production is accepted?

Referring to Fig. 37, the required proportion is that of the shaded area. This is given by $1 - P(less\ than\ 0·150″) - P(more\ than\ 0·155″)$.

Let the thickness be x,

then for $x_1 = 0·150″$, $z_1 = -2·0$
$\qquad x_2 = 0·155″$, $z_2 = 0·5$
and $P(accept) = 1 - P(z > 2·0) - P(z > 0·5)$
$\qquad\qquad\ \ = 1 - 0·0227 - 0·3085$
$\qquad\qquad\ \ = 0·6688.$

Showing that with this setting we can only expect 66·9% acceptable output.

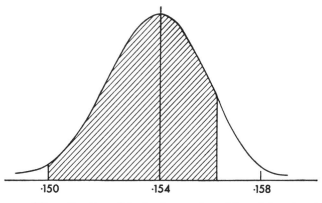

FIG. 37.—*The estimation of proportions and confidence intervals using the normal distribution. Examples 3 and 4*

Consider what would happen if we reset the machine to mean = 0·1525″, with the same variability. We now have:

$P(accept = 1 - P(x < 0·150″) - (x > 0·155″)$
$\qquad\qquad\ = 1 - P(z > 1·25) - P(z > 1·25)$
$\qquad\qquad\ = 1 - 0·1056 - 0·1056$
$\qquad\qquad\ = 0·7888.$

The acceptable output is now expected to be 78·9%, an increase of 12%.

EXAMPLE 4

Using the data of Example 3 find the 90% confidence interval for the thicknesses.

Referring to Fig. 37, this requires finding a range such that the area shaded is 90% of the total area. Assuming we require an interval which is symmetrically placed around the mean we require each of the "tail" areas to be 5% of the whole. Let the range be x_1 to x_2, and the corresponding standardised values be z_1 and z_2.

We want $P(z < z_1) = P(z > z_2) = 0.05$. Reading back from the tables the following values satisfy the conditions,

$z_1 = -1.65, z_2 = 1.65.$

Converting to original units:

$$x = mean + z\ (standard\ deviation)$$

hence

$$x_1 = 0.154 - (1.65) . 0.002 = 0.1507''$$
$$x_2 = 0.154 + (1.65) . 0.002 = 0.1573''$$

or

$$0.1507'' < thickness < 0.1573''\ (90\%\ confidence).$$

EXAMPLE 5

Using the data of Example 2, what must be the mean weight of the packets so that not more than 1% of the packets weigh less than 32 oz?

In this case we require the unshaded area in Fig. 36 to be 0.01 of the total area. Let the bounding value of x be $x_1 = 32$ oz, and the mean weight be m oz. The standardised value corresponding to x_1 is z_1, where:

$$P(x < 32\ oz) = P(z < z_1) = 0.01.$$

From the tables $P(z > 2.33) = 0.01$, and so

$$z_1 = -2.33$$

Using

$$z_1 = \frac{x_1 - mean}{s.d.}$$

$$m = x_1 - z_1\ (s.d.)$$
$$= 32.0 - (-2.33) . 0.5$$
$$= 33.17\ oz.$$

This means that for the given proportion of underweight packets and machine variability, packets must be sold at least 1.17 oz overweight.

Questions

1. Given a normal distribution with mean = 85 kg, standard deviation = 4.5 kg, find 95% confidence limits for the weights. What proportion of weights would you expect to exceed 92 kg?

2. The central 50% of a set of measurements lie in the range 147–159''; assuming they are normally distributed, estimate the mean and variance.

3. Using the data from Question 1, what proportion of weights would you expect to exceed 75 kg, and what are the expected limits for the central 50% of the distribution?

4. The number of people entering a shop per day is normally distributed with mean = 340 and variance = 300. Set 90% confidence

limits for the number of people entering the shop. What proportion of days will between 300 and 400 people enter the shop?

5. Using the data of Question 4 estimate the quartiles Q_1 and Q_3 for the distribution. What proportion of days will more than 320 people enter the shop?

CHAPTER ELEVEN

STATISTICAL SIGNIFICANCE TESTING

Testing an hypothesis

The negative approach to proof

IN scientific research there is a well-tried pattern of inquiry leading to the conclusions and laws which are established. A very similar pattern may be followed in the statistical analysis of a set of measurements.

First the measurements are arranged for examination, and then are examined and a theory or hypothesis suggested which will account for the observed properties of the measurements. Often more than one hypothesis is available to explain the observed data, and if no other information is available, then rival hypotheses can only be judged on emotional or other subjective grounds. As more information becomes available it can be checked against the hypotheses. Agreement between an hypothesis and the further information strengthens our belief in the correctness of the hypothesis, but does not prove it. Disagreement must discredit an hypothesis.

The further information used is usually in the form of predictions made on the basis of the available hypotheses. Disagreement between a prediction and observed fact removes the hypothesis on which it was based from consideration. When a series of hypotheses have been eliminated in this way to leave only one, and this one has proved capable of a large number of correct predictions it is usually dignified with the name of a "Law," although it is still open to disproof by one contrary fact.

In many cases in statistical work we may know that an hypothesis is incorrect, but feel able to use it as it is an adequate explanation of the facts in which we are interested. This would not imply accepting the same hypothesis in a wider context. Such hypotheses or models are extremely useful, and in general the simplest model of a situation which is valid for the inquiry we are engaged in is used.

The null hypothesis

If we wish to decide if a real difference exists between certain figures, let us start by establishing the hypothesis that the difference is due only to chance effects. This is often described as the null hypothesis. On the basis of this hypothesis let us predict the behaviour of a statistic which we can also calculate from the measured data. If the predicted and the calculated figures agree then we can conclude that the hypothesis that the differences observed are due only to chance is tenable. If the figures differ, then we reject the hypothesis and conclude that the observed differences are greater than can be accounted for by chance. Acceptance of an hypothesis does not imply that we believe it to be true, only that the data we have is not such as to lead us to disbelieve it. It is always possible that later data will lead to the rejection of the hypothesis. Rejection of the hypothesis is positive evidence that the difference suspected does exist.

Statistical significance tests

Significance levels

In statistical tests on hypotheses we do not in fact make an absolute acceptance or rejection of an hypothesis. Instead we state our degree of confidence in our decision, as to accept or reject the hypothesis, being correct. The probability of our being in error is called the significance level of the test, and is usually taken at 5%. It should be noted that this corresponds to 95% confidence in our decision being correct, the same confidence level given in the last chapter.

The use of significance levels

The way in which the null hypothesis and the idea of a significance level can be combined to make a significance test is developed in the following example.

EXAMPLE I

"A machine weighs out packets with weights normally distributed with a mean weight of 16·6 oz and a variance of 0·04 oz. A check on a packet gives a weight of 17·2 oz; does this indicate a change in the mean setting of the machine?"

If we set up the null hypothesis that the machine setting is unchanged, then we expect the packet weights to belong to a distribution identical to that described above. This is shown in Fig. 38.

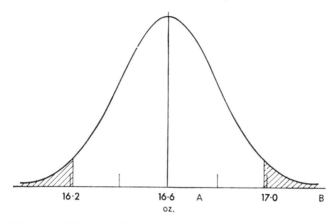

FIG. 38.—*The use of the normal distribution in significance testing*

Let us consider what measurements are consistent with membership of this distribution. If we remember that the area under the curve represents the probability that the corresponding measurements will be observed, we can see that the probability of observing a measurement decreases with its distance from the mean. We would have no doubt in accepting a measurement size (A) as a member of the distribution or rejecting a measurement of size (B). We would take the last decision even though there is a finite probability that (B) does belong to the distribution. The problem is to choose a probability level below which we reject a measurement and above which we accept it. Such levels must be arbitrary and depend to some extent on the problem facing us. As stated above it is conventional to accept a probability of 0·05 as being a reasonable figure.

This means that we will reject the hypothesis that a measurement belongs to the population if the probability that it belongs is less than 0·05. Referring to Fig. 38 these measurements are shown and the area under the curve corresponding to them is shaded. The total area shaded is 0·05 of the total area under the curve, thus there is 0·025 of the total area under each tail of the distribution.

In z scores the values of z corresponding to the boundaries of these areas are 1·96 and −1·96, and we can now test our observed measurement by calculating the z score corresponding to it:

$$i.e.\ z = \frac{observed\ value - expected\ mean}{expected\ standard\ deviation}$$

A value of z greater than 1·96 or less than −1·96 will lead us to reject the hypothesis, but a value of z between −1·96 and 1·96 will lead us to accept it. This range corresponds to the 95% confidence interval for the measurements. In the present case $z = (17 \cdot 2 - 16 \cdot 6)/0 \cdot 2 = 3$.

We reject the hypothesis, and conclude that the weight differs from the mean by an amount greater than we would expect by chance. This may be stated as: "There is a significant difference between the observed weight and the mean value."

One-tailed and two-tailed tests

In the example just given the test was designed to distinguish any difference from the mean value, either higher or lower. This is called a two-tailed test. If we know, before we measure or calculate the statistic we are going to test, that we are only interested in detecting either an increase or decrease, then we can use a one-tailed test. In this case we take the critical value of z, the value which gives an area of $0 \cdot 05$ in one-tail only, *i.e.* $1 \cdot 65$ or $-1 \cdot 65$.

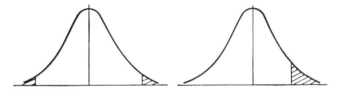

Fig. 39.—*Critical areas for two-tailed and one-tailed tests*

The effect of this is to make it easier to decide that a given deviation from the mean is significant. In fact we may decide that a given deviation is not significant on the basis of a two-tailed test yet is significant when we use a one-tailed test. The explanation is that the more information we put into a test the more powerful it becomes. To avoid using this type of test when we should not we must ask "Is the direction of change we are trying to detect known before we look at the results?" If the answer is "No" then a two-tailed test must be used. If there is any doubt then it is always safest to use a two-tailed test—a significant result on a one-tailed test must be significant on the corresponding two-tailed test.

Reporting significance tests

We can if we wish take other levels of significance at which to test our hypothesis. This is sometimes of use when reporting the results of tests, to indicate how strong the statistical evidence is. The most common levels are 0·05, 0·01 and 0·002 and Table XXX shows the terms usually associated with these, and the critical z values:

Table XXX—Significance Levels

Probability	Description	Critical z-score		Symbol
		1-tail	2-tail	
< 0·05	not significant	1·65	1·96	N.S.
0·01−0·05	significant	1·65	1·96	*
0·002−0·01	highly significant	2·33	2·58	**
< 0·002	very highly significant	2·88	3·09	***

The symbols are of use in reporting results and are used to imply the same significance levels for many tests. On this basis we can restate the conclusions from Example 1.

For the test as given, "There is a highly significant difference between the observed weight and the mean value," or, alternatively, $z = 3·00$**.

If the test had been one-tailed, "There is a very highly significant difference between the observed weight and the mean value," or, alternatively, $z = 3·00$***.

Tests on means
The distribution of sample means

Tests using the z score rely on the assumption that the measurements tested are normally distributed. In many cases this is not a valid assumption. It would, of course, be possible to set up a significance test from an empirical distribution, but an alternative approach is possible and preferable. If we consider a series of samples of the same size from a population, then the means of the samples themselves form a distribution. If the population is normally distributed then the sample means will also be normally distributed. If the population is not normally distributed then the sample means will still be approximately normally distributed. The fit of the distribution of sample means to the normal distribution improves with increasing sample size, but is good even for small samples and quite non-normal populations of measurements. We can assume normality of distribution for sample means, without making any assumptions about the population from which the samples are drawn. If the population has mean $= \mu$, variance $= \sigma$, then the sample will have mean of means $= \mu$. Variance of mean $= \sigma^2/n$. *i.e.* standard deviation of mean $= \sigma/\sqrt{n}$ where n is the size of the sample.

The use of sample means

We can use this property to test if a given sample is likely to have come from a given population.

EXAMPLE 2

Could a sample of sixteen items, mean $= 42$ lb, have come from a population, mean $= 44$ lb, variance $= 10\cdot2$ lb?
Using a two-tailed test, as before receiving the data we do not know if the sample mean will be above or below the population mean, we need $z > 1\cdot96$ for significance.
Take null hypothesis: the sample belongs to the population, then for a sample size 16

$$\text{mean of means} \quad = 44,$$
$$\text{variance of mean} \ = 10\cdot2/16$$

i.e. expected standard deviation of mean $= \sqrt{10\cdot2/16} = 0\cdot8$.

$$z = \frac{observed\ mean\ -\ mean\ of\ means}{standard\ deviation\ of\ means}$$

$$= (42 - 44)/0\cdot8 = -2\cdot5*$$

This exceeds $1\cdot96$ in size, but not $2\cdot58$, therefore we reject the hypothesis at the 5% level and conclude that the sample mean differs significantly from the population mean.

EXAMPLE 3

We want to be 99% certain that the items we are producing are more than 250 g in weight. If we take samples of 5 items, and the standard deviation throughout is known to be 10 g, what must the target mean for the samples be?

$$\sigma_x = 10\ g \quad \therefore \sigma_{\bar{x}} = 10/\sqrt{5} = 4\cdot47\ g.$$
$$\text{For } P(z > z_1) = 0\cdot01,\ z_1 = 2\cdot33$$
$$\textit{i.e. for } P(z < z_1) = 0\cdot01,\ z_1 = -2\cdot33$$
$$\text{Putting } x = 250 \text{ and } \sigma_{\bar{x}} = 4\cdot47$$
$$\text{we have } z = (250 - x)/4\cdot47 = -2\cdot33$$
$$x = 250 + 2\cdot33 \times 4\cdot47$$
$$= 260\cdot4\ g, \text{ which is the required target.}$$

EXAMPLE 4

We have found by experience that our delivery van gives 28 m.p.g. with standard deviation = 2·3 m.p.g. measured over several tanksful of petrol. After tuning, 4 successive tanks of petrol yield an average consumption of 31 m.p.g. Has the tuning improved the performance of the engine significantly?

We are looking for an increase only by tuning, so we have a one-tailed test and take $z > 1·65$ for significance.

Taking the null hypothesis of no increase we expect sample size 4 to have

mean of sample means = 28 m.p.g.
standard deviation of sample means = $2·3/\sqrt{4} = 1·15$ m.p.g.

and to be normally distributed.

$$z = \frac{observed\ mean - expected\ mean}{standard\ deviation\ of\ means}$$

$$= (31 - 28)/1·15 = 2·61**.$$

This value exceeds the critical value and we reject the null hypothesis and conclude that the tuning is effective.

The "t"-distribution

The need for the "t"-distribution

The previous tests have required a knowledge of the population variance. This may not be available and an estimate must be made from the sample, and this introduces an extra element of variability into our test. As a result we must allow for the possibility of error in the variance and require greater differences between the observed and expected sample means for a significant result. The problem of how to do this was solved by the derivation of the "t"-distribution, which replaces the normal distribution in these circumstances. The tests are carried out as before, but instead of stating a value of z which must be exceeded we state a value of "t." As the reliability of the variance estimate increases with sample size, so the value of "t" required for significance decreases, until for very large samples it becomes equal to the corresponding z value. In order to decide on which value of "t" to use we must use a quantity called the "degrees of freedom." This is the sample size less the number of quantities we have fixed in estimating the variance, and is symbolised by v (nu).

The table of values of "t" shows for a series of values of the degrees of freedom, the minimum value of "t" necessary for significance at various probability levels, *e.g.* for a one-tailed test at the 5% significance level and 8 degrees of freedom, "t" must exceed 1·86.

See Table B, Appendix II.

The use of the "t"-distribution

EXAMPLE 5

A process should be set to make items length 4·940″. In a sample of nine items the lengths are 4·946″, 4·944″, 4·939″, 4·947″, 4·949″, 4·940″, 4·948″, 4·942″, 4·950″. Is there any evidence that the process requires resetting? Test at the 5% significance level.

We have to estimate the process variance from the sample, so the "t"-distribution must be used.

We are testing for any difference between the sample mean and the expected value, so we must use a two-tailed test. We must know the mean of the sample in order to calculate the variance, and this removes one degree of freedom leaving $n - 1$, where n is the sample size. In the present problem we have $9 - 1$ giving 8 degrees of freedom. From the tables, for a two-tailed test at the 5% level with 8 degrees of freedom, "t" must exceed $\pm 2·31$ for significance.

To find the value of "t" we need first the estimate of the process or population variance, the calculation may be set out as below.

Table XXXI—Calculation of Population Variance Estimate

X	x	x^2	
4·946	1	1	$c = 4·945$
4·944	−1	1	$h = 0·001$
4·939	−6	36	$n = 9$
4·947	2	4	
4·949	4	16	
4·940	−5	25	
4·948	3	9	
4·942	−3	9	
4·950	5	25	
	0	126	

$x = 0$

$$\text{Estimate of population variance} = \frac{1}{n-1}\left[\Sigma x^2 - \frac{(\Sigma x)^2}{n}\right]$$

$$= \tfrac{1}{8}[126 - 0] = 15·75$$

For simplicity we can use the coded values; this is permissible as "t" is a ratio. Then taking the null hypothesis that the sample does not differ from the required population except by chance, we expect sample size 9 to be distributed as the "t"-distribution with,

mean of means $= -5$ (coded value of required mean)
variance of means $= 15 \cdot 75/9 = 1 \cdot 75$

or standard deviation of means $= 1 \cdot 323$.

$$\text{``}t\text{''} = \frac{observed\ mean - expected\ mean\ of\ means}{standard\ deviation\ of\ means}$$
$$= 0 \quad (\quad 5)/1 \cdot 323 = 3 \cdot 78.$$

This exceeds the critical value of $2 \cdot 31$ at the 5% significance level, and we must reject the hypothesis and conclude that the sample mean differs significantly from $4 \cdot 940''$. The process does require resetting.

Tests for difference of means

For normally distributed variables, the sum or difference of two variables is also distributed normally with mean equal to the sum or difference of their means, and variance equal to the sum of their variances.

A, Normally distributed mean $= m_A$, variance $= s_A^2$.
B, Normally distributed mean $= m_B$, variance $= s_B^2$.
$(A + B)$ is Normally distributed with mean $= m_A + m_B$ and variance $= s_A^2 + s_B^2$, and
$(A - B)$ with mean $= m_A - m_B$, variance $= s_A^2 + s_B^2$.

This property can be used as the basis of a test for a significant difference between the means of two samples, using the hypothesis that they are drawn from the same population. For the difference of means of two sample means m_1, m_2, variance s_1^2 and s_2^2 and sizes n_1, n_2, if the hypothesis is true,

mean of differences $= 0$
variance of differences $= s_1^2/n + s_2^2/n$

s_1^2 and s_2^2 are both estimates of the population variance and must use the divisors $n_1 - 1$ and $n_2 - 1$ in their calculation. The test is made with

$$\text{``}t\text{''} = \frac{observed\ difference\ of\ means\ (m_1 - m_2)}{standard\ deviation\ of\ differences}$$

and is two-tailed, with $n_1 + n_2 - 2$ degrees of freedom. When n_1 and n_2 are both greater than 30, then z may be used instead of

"t." This test is strictly only valid when s_1^2 and s_2^2 are not significantly different but may be used with reasonable confidence even when this is not known. The test is least sensitive to differences in s_1^2 and s_2^2 when $n_1 \simeq n_2$.

EXAMPLE 6

Samples of sales in similar shops in two towns are taken for a new product with the following result.

	Mean sales	Variance	Size of sample
Town 1	57	5·3	5
Town 2	61	4·8	7

Is there any evidence of difference in sales in the two towns? Test at the 10% level.

We do not make any assumptions about the direction of the difference so this is a two-tailed test with $5 + 7 - 2 = 10$ degrees of freedom. From the tables the value of "t" required for significance at the 10% level is greater than 1·81 or less than −1·81. Taking the null hypothesis that the two samples do not differ significantly, we expect the difference of means to be distributed as the "t"-distribution with

mean difference in means = 0
variance of differences in means = $5 \cdot 3/5 + 4 \cdot 8/7 = 1 \cdot 746$
or standard deviation of differences = 1·32.
"t" = $-4/1 \cdot 32 = -3 \cdot 03$.

This is less than the critical value of −1·81 and we must reject the hypothesis and conclude that there is a significant difference in the sales in the two towns.

EXAMPLE 7

We buy four samples of a raw material from each of two potential sources. The moisture contents are as shown below. Do the average values differ significantly?

Source A	Source B
8·4%	8·8%
8·0%	9·1%
8·9%	8·1%
8·5%	8·6%

We calculate estimates of the population variances, the direct method is used as we have a low number of figures to deal with. Source A
$\bar{x} = (8 \cdot 4 + 8 \cdot 0 + 8 \cdot 9 + 8 \cdot 5)/4 = 8 \cdot 45$

x	$x - \bar{x}$	$(x - \bar{x})^2$
8·4	—0·05	0·0025
8·0	—0·45	0·2025
8·9	0·45	0·2025
8·5	0·05	0·0025
		0·4100

$$\delta_x{}^2 = 0.41/3 = 0.137.$$

Source $B\ \bar{x} = (8\cdot8 + 9\cdot1 + 8\cdot1 + 8\cdot6)/4 = 8\cdot65$

x	$x - \bar{x}$	$(x - \bar{x})^2$
8·8	0·15	0·0225
9·1	0·45	0·2025
8·1	—0·55	0·3025
8·6	—0·05	0·0025
		0·5300

$$\delta_x{}^2 = 0.53/3 = 0.177.$$

Neither source can be taken as standard so we cannot specify what difference we anticipate, so we have a two-tailed test. With a 5% significance level and $3 + 3 = 6$ degrees of freedom we find the critical value of "t" = 2·45.

On the null hypothesis of no difference we expect

$$\text{difference of means} = 0$$

$$\text{standard deviation of difference of means} = \sqrt{0\cdot137/3 + 0\cdot177/3}$$
$$= \sqrt{0\cdot1047} = 0\cdot324$$

$$``t" = \frac{observed\ diff. - expected\ diff.}{standard\ deviation\ of\ diff.} = \frac{(8\cdot65 - 8\cdot45) - 0}{0\cdot324}$$
$$= 0\cdot20/0\cdot324 = 0\cdot62 \text{ N.S.}$$

On the evidence we have we cannot say that the two materials differ significantly in moisture content.

The paired comparison test

If we have two sets of measurements in which each measurement in one sample has a corresponding "paired" measurement in the other sample we can carry out a paired comparison test. This uses the distribution of mean differences between paired items, and these may be assumed to be distributed as the "t"-distribution.

Typical examples of the paired comparison test are repeat measurements of the same quantities on the same items, such as before and after measurements to test the effectiveness of a sales campaign, and measurements of the same quantities by different methods, such as two sets of estimates of income for a number of persons.

To carry out the test we calculate d, the difference between the paired measurements, and then the mean $\bar{d}$ and variance s_d^2 of the d values. As we are using the variance of the sample of d values to estimate the variance of a theoretical population of d values we must use the divisor $n - 1$, where n is the number of sets of measurements. On the null hypothesis of no significant difference between the sets of measurements, we expect the mean difference to be distributed as the "t"-distribution with $n - 1$ degrees of freedom, and

mean of mean differences $= 0$

variance of mean differences $= s_d^2/n$.

Then "t" $= \dfrac{observed\ mean\ difference}{standard\ deviation\ of\ mean\ differences}$.

EXAMPLE 8

The sales of an item in six shops before and after a special promotional campaign are:

Shop	1	2	3	4	5	6
Before	53	28	31	48	50	42
After	58	29	30	55	56	45

Can the campaign be judged to be a success? Test at the 5% significance level.

As we are only testing for an increase this is a one-tailed test, and as we use the mean difference to calculate the variance of difference we lose one degree of freedom leaving 5. From the tables the critical value of "t" is 2·02. The calculation may be laid out as follows.

Table XXXII—Paired Comparison Test

x_1	x_2	d	d^2
53	58	5	25
28	29	1	1
31	30	−1	1
48	55	7	49
50	56	6	36
42	45	3	9
		21	121

$\bar{d} = 21/6 = 3\cdot5$

Estimate of population variance of d

$= \dfrac{1}{n-1}\,[\Sigma d^2 - (\Sigma d)^2/n]$

$= \frac{1}{5}[121 - (21)^2/6] = (121 - 73\cdot5)/5$

$= 9\cdot7$

On the basis of the null hypothesis that there is no significant increase in sales we would expect the mean difference to be distributed as the "t"-distribution with

> mean of mean differences $= 0$
> variance of mean differences $= 9 \cdot 7/6 = 1 \cdot 62$
> and standard deviation of mean differences $= 1 \cdot 27$.

Hence "t" $= 3 \cdot 5/1 \cdot 27 = 2 \cdot 76$; this exceeds the critical value, and we must reject the hypothesis and conclude that there has been a significant increase in sales as a result of the campaign.

If desired, the measurements analysed may be coded to simplify the calculations, as before this will not affect the value of "t" found. Both sets of measurements must be subjected to the same coding procedure.

Tests on proportions

The distribution of proportions

As mentioned in the discussion of the binomial distribution, the proportions of a given type of item in a set of samples will be distributed as the binomial distribution, and will have mean $= \pi$, and variance $= \pi(1 - \pi)/n$, where π is the proportion of the given type of items in the population and n the size of the samples.

If we do not know π we can estimate it by p, the observed proportion in the samples, and if $n > 50$ we can approximate the binomial distribution by the normal distribution. Similarly since the variance of the proportions would be estimated from the sample value p, we should use the "t"-distribution in hypothesis testing, but for $n > 50$ the "χ"-distribution may be used instead.

It is very rare for proportions to be based on samples of less than 50 and so we may assume that a proportion p based on a sample size n is normally distributed with mean $= p$, and variance $= p(1 - p)/n$.

Significance tests may be constructed using this property similar to those already described.

EXAMPLE 9

Our market share for a product has been steady at 35%. After a special advertising campaign a survey of 500 housewives shows that 41% now say they will buy our product. Is this increase significant?

$\hat{\pi} = p = 0 \cdot 35$

$$\therefore \text{ standard deviation of proportion} = \hat{\sigma}_p = \sqrt{\frac{p(1 - p)}{n}}$$

$$= \sqrt{\frac{0.35 \times 0.65}{500}} = \sqrt{0.000455}$$

$$= 0.0213.$$

We have a one-tailed z-test, so at 5% significance level the critical value of z is 1.65. On the null hypothesis of no change

expected proportion = 0.35
standard deviation of proportion = 0.0213

$$z = \frac{observed\ propn. - expected\ propn.}{standard\ deviation\ propn.}$$

$$= \frac{(0.41 - 0.35) - 0}{0.0213} = \frac{0.06}{0.0213} = 2.82**$$

We conclude that the campaign has been successful.

Confidence intervals for proportions

Using this information we can set confidence intervals in which we expect the true proportion π to lie, *i.e.*

$$\pi = p \pm 1.96\sqrt{p(1 - p)/n} \text{ (95\% confidence)}.$$

This formula may also be used to estimate the sample size required to estimate a proportion with a given precision. This calculation is much used in work sampling, although usually carried out by the use of a nomograph.

EXAMPLE 10

What size sample is required to estimate a proportion of about 5% to the nearest 1% with 95% confidence?

We require the proportion with a confidence interval of at most ± 0.01, and with 95% confidence the interval is $\pm 1.96\sqrt{p(1 - p)/n}$. This gives the condition:

$$0.01 \geqslant 1.96\sqrt{p(1 - p)/n}$$

Squaring and rearranging we have:

$$n \geqslant \frac{1.96^2 \cdot p(1 - p)}{0.01^2}$$

i.e. $$n \geqslant \frac{1.96^2 \cdot 0.05 \cdot 0.95}{0.01^2}$$

or $$n \geqslant 1825.$$

The calculation is relatively insensitive to the value of p used, and any reasonable estimate of the size of the proportion to be measured may be used in a calculation of this sort. In the example given a sample of about 2000 would probably be used.

Questions

1. A sample of four items gives the values: 0·95, 0·91, 0·93, 0·98. Set 90% confidence limits for the measurement.

2. Another sample of five items has values: 0·93, 0·97, 0·90, 0·88, 0·92. Does it differ significantly in mean value from the sample in Question 1?

3. A sample of ten items has mean = 31 and sample variance = 6. Could the sample have come from a population mean = 35? Test at the 5% significance level.

4. Set 90% confidence limits for a proportion of 0·38 calculated from a sample of 400 items.

5. A consultant claims to be able to increase the efficiency of salesmen. Seven men are subjected to his training and their sales in numbers of items before and after for a period of one week are:

Salesman	1	2	3	4	5	6	7
Before	48	41	52	38	51	44	52
After	53	40	59	40	47	48	54

Is his claim substantiated? Test at the 95% significance level.

6. In a total of 2000 observations a workman is engaged in adjusting the setting of his machine on 300 occasions. Set 95% confidence limits for the proportion of time he spends on this activity. What is the required minimum sample size to estimate a proportion of about 40% within an interval of 2% with 95% confidence?

7. The faults per 1000 articles produced by a number of workmen are recorded both before and after they are subjected to a training routine. Test if the routine has produced a significant decrease in the proportions of faults occurring.

Workmen	Before	After
A	13	11
B	5	5
C	7	5
D	16	12
E	11	10
F	5	4
G	8	7
H	9	7
I	16	14

Justify the choice of significance level you use in your test.

8. A sample of 450 interviews gives Joe Bloggs 52% of the vote in a two-party contest. Has he grounds for confidence in the result?

9. Set 95% confidence limits for the mean of a population given the following four random measurements from it: 104, 121, 110, 115.

10. Does the data in Question 9 contradict a previous statement that the population mean is 108?

CHAPTER TWELVE

STATISTICAL QUALITY CONTROL

The basis of quality control

History

ONE use of the ideas of significance testing which is now of very wide application is that of statistical quality control. The term "quality control" should be understood to include all activities concerned with quality awareness in a production process. Those techniques to be discussed make up a method of providing some of the information necessary for awareness of quality factors.

These techniques were first developed by W. A. Shewhart working for the Bell Telephone Co. in America; the problem he solved was that of checking on the consistency of manufacture of a very large number of components. During the Second World War the methods, which had been slowly finding acceptance, were adopted by the United States Government to help in the mass-production of armaments. After the war the methods spread widely both in the U.S.A. and in other industrial countries, and are now generally accepted. Unfortunately the impression that only mass-production processes are amenable to monitoring by quality control methods has slowed their application in other fields. They can, and have been, of profitable use in very diverse production processes.

Variability in production

Despite the use of the most rigorous care in processing and the use of the best machinery available, it is impossible to manufacture items which are identical in all respects. This is caused by the presence of many individually unimportant and probably unmeasurable variations in the controlling factors in the process. In the majority of cases these will tend to cancel out, but they can combine to produce a measurable effect on the items produced, and hence in the case of processes not stringently controlled, to produce defective items. Variations in manufactured items of this type are implicit in the process, and for a given process can never be entirely removed. One of the aims of statistical quality control is to recognise this variation so that the capabilities of the process being used are known. The lack of defective items from a process does not imply that there is no variation in the items produced, but possibly that the process being used is better than need be for the quality of product required.

The term quality in this context is usually related to some measurement made on the items produced, a good quality item being one which conforms to standards specified for the measurement. Quality does not always imply the highest standards of manufacture, for the standard required is often deliberately below the highest possible. It is almost always consistency of manufacture which represents the most desirable situation rather than the absolute standard which is maintained. A customer buying a product at a cheap rate will not be surprised or disappointed if all his purchase is of an even mediocrity. If some is much better than the rest he may well press for a general improvement—on the grounds that what can sometimes be attained should always be attained.

The distribution of variations

If a large number of items are taken and a quality measurement made on each, then the measurements form a distribution. The shape of this distribution is itself of interest. If the many factors contributing to the variations are unbiased in their effect, then the expected form of the distribution is normal, and the basic methods of statistical quality control are based on the assumption that this is so. However, the methods are robust and are applicable even when considerable deviations from normality exist. As long as the measurements show some central tendency, *i.e.* they are grouped round a central measurement rather than away from it, then the methods will probably be found to be of use.

When the distribution is very markedly non-normal then investigations of the reason will be needed. This may lead to modification in the process or possibly to use of non-standard monitoring methods. The methods of quality control are capable of considerable modification and should always be matched to the process being studied. The application of standard procedures without adequate study of the process is extremely dangerous, and has in the past led to statistical methods being discredited. Statistical methods applied on a production process are a service, and as such must be conditioned by the process to which they are applied.

Process and assignable variations

As has been stated the variations implicit in a process can never entirely be removed. Statistical quality control is a method of recognising these variations and distinguishing them from assignable variations caused by factors which can be removed or altered.

The assignable variations are recognised by their greater magnitude than the process variations, of course small assignable variations do occur, but unless they are of greater size than the process variations they are of no importance.

If we know the mean and standard deviation of the distribution of measurements, then we can calculate the probability that any degree of variation from the mean value will be observed. Variations with a low level of probability of occurrence as process variations are examined as likely to be assignable variations. The levels of probability usually taken are less than 1/40 for a suspicion of non-process variations, and 1/1000 for an almost certainty of non-process variations.

The use of samples

A considerable advantage is gained by considering not single measurements, but a small sample of measurements. The mean of sample will indicate the general level of variation, and the range is available as an estimate of the variability of the variation. As indicated earlier the mean of a sample from a population is much more normally distributed than the individual items in the population; this applies even for distinctly non-normal populations. This means that we can apply the techniques which are based on the assumption of normality, although theoretically they are not completely justified.

For a small sample the range is a good measure of the variability in the sample, and a number of samples may be considered to obtain an estimate of the population variability. To allow this method to be used, the sample size must be below ten, and samples of four or five items have been found most useful.

The Shewhart control charts

The form of control charts

The control charts are the core of statistical quality control. They consist of charts on to which the means and ranges of successive samples are plotted in chronological order. The charts are drawn with lines indicating confidence limits within which the means and ranges would be expected to lie if only process variation is present. The typical appearance of the charts is shown in Fig. 40, the two charts being drawn one above the other so that the two figures calculated for each sample are aligned. Samples are plotted at equal intervals on the graph regardless of the time intervals between them and are not usually connected up as on ordinary time graphs.

The confidence intervals are drawn so that the inner lines would be expected to contain 19/20 of all the points plotted, *i.e.* to be exceeded with a probability of 1/40 for each side. These are often described as Warning Limits. The outer lines are similarly drawn to contain on average 499/500 of all the points, and to be exceeded with a probability of only 1/1000 for each side. These are described as the Action Limits. On the chart for means these lines are symmetrically placed, the expected distribution of the means being normal. However, the expected distribution of the range of the samples is a skew distribution and the lines are placed asymmetrically on the chart for ranges.

The interpretation of control charts

The charts are interpreted as follows: if a pair of points lie within their respective inner limits, then the process is said to be "in control."

If a point lies outside the 1/40 limits, then this is taken as a warning of likely trouble and suggests that a look-out for disturbances or faults in the process should be kept.

If a point lies outside the 1/1000 limits then this is taken as an indication of trouble, and a careful check for its source should be made.

In both cases a further sample is usually taken and the calculated points plotted.

If the second point lies outside the 1/40 limits it may be taken

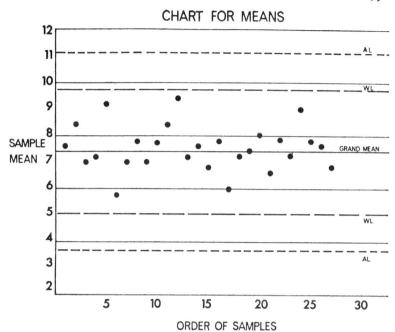

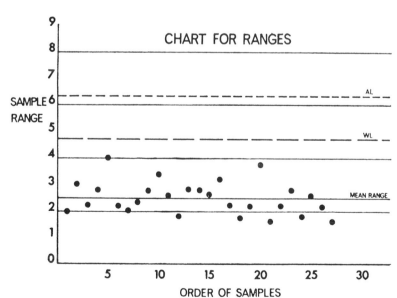

FIG. 40.—*The Shewhart control charts*

as the equivalent of one point outside the 1/1000 limits. If the second point is found outside the 1/1000 limit then it is almost a certainty that there is trouble—and the cause must be found. If the second point lies inside the limits, then it indicates that either the out-of-limits point was just a 1/40 or 1/1000 happening, or else that the disturbance was temporary.

When a set of control charts have been operating for a while then the pattern of points may give useful information. It may be possible to detect a drift, either upwards or downwards on the mean chart, or similar slight increases or decreases on the range chart. Such indications may allow remedial action to be taken before the process goes out of control, or lead to a better knowledge of process capabilities.

The advantages of control chart working

The best control on a process is maintained when there is least delay between the diagnosis and treatment of trouble.

Statistical quality control does give information simply and rapidly, so that the production team can take rapid action. The charts, once set up, can be filled in by plant personnel, and this in itself leads to an awareness of what is happening on the process. A knowledge of the process can be built up, and this may be invaluable in future planning. In particular, estimates of the process capabilities can be made and provide the information necessary for the specification of tolerances on designs, and for the allocation of resources in production planning.

The use of the charts can also lead to more consistent process operation. If a set of dial and lever settings are specified as correct for the operation of the process, then the operative is bound to make adjustments to keep these settings at their specified levels. This can mean much unnecessary adjustment, and may constitute a disturbance in itself. If the operative is told to allow deviations from the specified levels as long as the process remains in control then the amount of interference with the process may be greatly reduced. The operation of the process must, of course, still be kept under scrutiny and the effect of variations of this type noted.

It must be emphasised that the methods of statistical quality control are only an information service. Unless they are used as part of a general quality awareness then they may only lead to a false sense of security. The responsibility for quality and process decisions rests with the manager in charge of the process and not with the statistician. The charts do not reduce the manager's responsibility; simply because they are "in control" does not imply that all is necessarily well with the process.

The installation of control charts

When the mean and standard deviation, μ and σ, of the quality measurements are known from prior work, then the control limits can be set at,

for inner limits $\mu \pm 1\cdot 96\sigma$
for outer limits $\mu \pm 3\cdot 09\sigma$.

Alternatively a sample of measurements may be taken and the mean and standard deviation calculated, and then the same formulae used. However, for small samples the range is a good measure of variability, and for a given sample size is directly related to the standard deviation. It is a simple matter to find the mean range of a series of small samples (say at least ten), and use them to estimate the standard deviation. The routine is further simplified by using tables to go directly from the mean range to the control limits.

Using this approach the calculation of control limits and installation of the control charts proceeds as follows:

(*a*) Decide on a sample size: five is a convenient size and leads to simple arithmetic.

(*b*) Take at least ten samples during a period in which the process is not subject to abnormal conditions.

(*c*) For each sample compute the arithmetic mean $\bar{x}$ and range w and plot $\bar{x}$ and w in chronological order on two graphs on the same sheet of paper with the mean above the range and the same scale for order of sample. A scale width of 2–3″ for each graph is usually adequate.

(*d*) Compute the grand mean $\bar{X}$ and mean range $\bar{w}$. Draw lines representing these levels on the graphs.

(*e*) Compute
$\bar{X} + \bar{w} . A$o·025, and
$\bar{X} + \bar{w} . A$o·001.

Ao·025 and Ao·001 will be found in Table XXXIII. These are the inner and outer limits for the mean and may be drawn in on the graph for the mean.

(f) Compute

$\bar{w} . D$o·975, and

$\bar{w} . D$o·999.

Do·975 and Do·999 will also be found in Table XXXIII. These are the limits for the range and may be drawn on the graph for the range.

These limits should be regarded as temporary, and after at least forty samples have been taken the same routine should be followed to give a better estimate of the limits. If any of the forty samples have given points outside the 1/40 limits these samples should be rejected when calculating the new limits.

The population standard deviation may be estimated when the mean range of a series of small samples is known by using a conversion factor. This depends on the sample size and the standard deviation is found directly, *i.e.*

$$s = \bar{w}/d$$

where d is given in Table XXXIII.

Table XXXIII—Factors for Use with $\bar{w}$ on Control Charts

Sample size	For means		For ranges		For standard deviation
	$A_{0 \cdot 025}$	$A_{0 \cdot 001}$	$D_{0 \cdot 975}$	$D_{0 \cdot 999}$	d
2	1·23	1·94	2·81	4·12	1·13
3	0·67	1·05	2·17	2·99	1·69
4	0·48	0·75	1·93	2·58	2·06
5	0·38	0·59	1·81	2·36	2·33
6	0·32	0·50	1·72	2·22	2·53

Specification limits

Control limits should not be confused with specification limits. Specification limits are set by the designer of the items being produced, and may not have been set with knowledge of the process capabilities. The inner and outer control limits represent limits into which the sample mean and range will fall on average 19/20 and 499/500 times respectively. As such they are a direct result of the behaviour of the process and are specific to a particular process or plant. If it is desired to find how specification limits compare, then the specification limits for the mean of a sample of the size being used may be calculated. If the specification limits are $\pm Y$ units then for a mean of a sample of n they will be $\pm Y/\sqrt{n}$ units. If desired these may be shown on the control charts but care should be taken to make it clear that they are not control limits.

If the specification limits lie between the inner and outer control limits then the process will produce between 0·2% and 5% production out of specification on average. This usually means that the process is adequate for the purpose for which it is being used. If the specification limits lie inside the inner control limits then the process is likely to produce more than 5% production out of specification, and this indicates that the process is not capable of meeting the specification. Either the specification limits must be relaxed or else the process must be improved or replaced. If the specification limits are outside the outer control limits then the process will produce on average less than 0·2% of production out of specification. This means that the process is unnecessarily precise and that possibly a cheaper and less precise process would be adequate in this application.

In this way, the statistical quality control information can give guidance on the correct choice of process and the reasonable settings of specification limits. When the capabilities of different processes are known in this way then the design and costing of new products may be greatly facilitated.

Simplified control charts

The control charts described so far represent the conventional application of statistical quality control. It is desirable that any scheme actually operated should be as simple as is consistent with giving the required information, and considerable modification can take place from the conventional charts.

The control limits can be modified to give a more or less stringent level of control. The usual limits of 1/40 and 1/1000 are arbitrary and are quoted as being of general suitability. It may be desirable to set the outer limits at, say, 1/200 to give earlier warning of trouble, especially where the cost of producing defective items is high.

The inner limits may be omitted. This is standard American practice, the single limits being set at mean ± 3 standard deviations. This gives a probability of greater than 1/1000 of the limits being exceeded, but as the limits are arbitrary the difference is unimportant. In this case judgments as to the need for a greater alertness, which would have been made when a point fell outside the inner limits, are made when points fall near the outer limits.

The lower limits may be omitted on the range chart. We are mainly concerned with excessive variation, and only this need be controlled. If there is a consistent reduction in the range of samples this will be seen in any case, and can be investigated, but does not usually need immediate action. In fact the range chart may be omitted completely, since a situation where the range goes out of control will almost certainly make the mean go out of control as well. The range out of control will be revealed by points on the mean chart going out of control both above and below the control limits, as opposed to a one-way deviation when there is a shift in the mean level of the measurement being controlled.

Other control charts

Control charts for defectives

In many cases a quality judgment is made by comparison with a standard. This produces a very simple test and is applicable when measurements are impossible or very lengthy, *e.g.* colour matching. Similarly a "go," "no-go" gauge may be used to check critical dimensions. This usually takes the form of a gap or aperture into which the item being tested must either fit or not fit depending on whether the set dimension is a maximum or minimum. The result of the tests is expressed as so many defective items and so many effective items.

For a consistent proportion of defective items in a production run, it is possible to predict the probability of a finding, given the number of defective items in a given size sample from the binomial distribution. For a sample size n when the average proportion of defective items is p, the probability of finding r defective items is:

$$P(r) = \binom{n}{r} p^r \cdot (1 - p)^{n - r}$$

For a given situation the cumulative probabilities,

probability of 0 defective items,
probability of up to 1 defective item,
probability of up to 2 defective items, etc.

may be easily calculated or found from tables, and hence the corresponding probabilities,

probability of 1 or more defective items,
probability of 2 or more defective items, etc.

can also be calculated. We can then draw up a control chart with control limits at levels representing a given probability that a number of defective items higher than this level will be found in a given sample.

If we choose our sample size so that the mean expected number of defectives per sample in the set of items we are inspecting is between 1 and 2 we can approximate the binomial distribution by the Poisson distribution. This means that the size of the sample is not needed in determining the control limits, and reference to Poisson distribution tables may be made and the limits set with a knowledge of the mean number of defective items only.

Since we are testing for an excess of defective items in a sample, the limits are set at greater probability levels than in the mean range charts. Levels of 1/20 and 1/200 have been found useful, but are again arbitrary and can be altered if this is felt desirable in a particular application. It should also be noticed that the sample may be large, unlike the samples for mean and range control charts.

Control chart for defects

In many types of production it may not be possible to grade items into defective or effective, or there may be no separate items of production. In this case, the quality is expressed as so many defects per item, or as so many defects per arbitrary units of production, *e.g.* number of faults per TV receiver or number of faults per roll of cloth. If we refer again to the earlier discussion of the Poisson distribution, it will be seen that we expect this distribution to arise in such cases. If we designate a unit of manufacture so that the average number of defects per unit is less than 2 then it will often be found that the number of faults per unit is distributed as the Poisson distribution.

We can then specify control limits for defects per unit in a similar manner to the control limits for defective items per sample above.

It is always wise in both these applications to check that the distribution of defects per unit, or of defective items per sample, is in fact adequately represented by the Poisson distribution. It may be found that defects or defective items are grouped, and that the control charts described are not suitable.

Control limits for defects

The control limits for a given mean number of defects per unit or mean number of defectives per sample may be set by reference to Table XXXIV. The figures shown for the mean values are the limiting figures, *e.g.* if the mean level is 3·88 set the inner limit at 8 and the outer limit at 11. The probabilities used for the inner and outer limits are 1 in 20 and 1 in 200 respectively.

Table XXXIV—Control Limits for Defects

Limit set at	Maximum value for mean	
	Inner	Outer
2	0·36	0·11
3	0·82	0·35
4	1·37	0·68
5	1·97	1·08
6	2·61	1·54
7	3·29	2·04
8	3·98	2·58
9	4·70	3·13
10	5·41	3·72
11		4·32
12		4·94
13		5·59

Note: For cases where the mean exceeds 5, the normal curve may be used to set limits.

Cumulative sum charts

If it is important that the mean setting of a variable does not vary, then the Shewhart charts may not be a very satisfactory control method, as a small change in the mean may not be quickly detected. In this case cumulative sum charts or "Cusum" charts may be used.

On a Cusum chart the value plotted is the sum of the quantities (mean of samples — required mean) and if the process mean is correctly set this sum will vary around 0. If there is a shift in mean it will vary around a line at an angle to the horizontal, and the slope of this line is a measure of the amount of shift. Various methods are available to estimate when a significant change has been observed. These all give much earlier warning of a change than would be expected from the Shewhart charts. It should be noted that it is the slope of the line of points, not their position on the chart, which is critical when using these charts.

Questions

1. Describe the function and form of statistical quality control charts.

2. How does a Cusum chart differ from the conventional control charts? What property of process measurements will a Cusum chart detect?

3. Discuss the installation of control charts for the mean and range. How is the range made use of?

4. A distribution of measurements has mean = 10·50, standard deviation = 0·21. Draw a control chart for the mean of samples of five items. The next ten samples of five items have means: 10·46, 10·48, 10·53, 10·58, 10·35, 10·57, 10·49, 10·50, 10·52, 10·55. Plot these values on your chart and say what conclusions you might draw from this data.

5. Twenty samples of size four taken from a process have mean = 143, mean range = 12. Draw up control charts for the mean and range. The next five samples have the following properties.

| Mean | 142 | 147 | 139 | 155 | 149 |
| Range | 9 | 20 | 15 | 10 | 22 |

Plot these points on your charts and comment on them.

6. A process produces items with a minimum variance in weight of 2·5 grams. The specified limits for the product are 125 grams ± 10 grams. Discuss the suitability of the process for this standard of production. Samples of four successive items taken from the process have the following mean weights.

Sample	Mean weight grams
1	126·4
2	124·8
3	127·2
4	126·8
5	125·5
6	127·0
7	127·3

By plotting a control chart from the information above, discuss the behaviour of the process with regard to its target setting of 125 grams and to the specified limits.

7. It is noted that the number of motor failures per week on a large number of similar drive units is 2·7. Draw up suitable control charts to monitor these failures.

8. A wholesaler keeps records of the number of items returned for replacement under warranty. Suggest suitable charts to keep a check on these returns:

(*a*) when the mean rate is 4 per week,
(*b*) when the mean rate is 24 per week.

9. A process is known to be capable of working so as to produce items with standard deviation = 10 g. It is standard practice to take samples of 4 items for checkweighing. If the items are sold with a specification of ± 8 g draw up a chart for the sample mean showing control and specification limits.

10. Discuss how the ideas of quality control could be used to monitor the performance of a number of copy-typists, and their consumption of type-ribbons, erasers, etc.

CHAPTER THIRTEEN

ACCEPTANCE TESTING

The basis of sampling schemes

Sampling and 100% inspection

IN the normal consumer–producer relationship it is usual for a product to be sold subject to its satisfying certain agreed conditions. This requires inspection of the product and the tests used are described as "acceptance tests." In many cases the inspection instruction is to inspect all items and to reject those found to be faulty. This should give complete protection to the consumer against the purchase of faulty items. However, there is now considerable evidence to show that even in a well-run inspection department 100% inspection is rarely 100% effective. Under these conditions the actual level of faulty items being accepted by the consumer is not known.

In most instances a certain level of faulty items is not a serious bar to the sale of a product, as long as this level is known and the variability in its size is low. If this is so it is possible to specify sampling inspection procedures which give a good indication of the nature of the whole of the items sampled. As samples are not expected to reproduce exactly the population characteristics, there is an element of variability introduced. Despite this a well-designed sampling scheme can often provide a better assurance of quality than 100% inspection.

Sampling schemes

The usual form of a sampling scheme is as follows. A batch or lot of items is presented for inspection, and a random sample taken. If the number of faulty items in the sample is greater than a given number the whole lot is rejected. If the number of faulty items in the sample is equal to or below the given number the whole lot is accepted. This critical number is known as the *acceptance number*. A sampling scheme is defined by the three quantities,

N the lot size,
n the sample size, and
c the acceptance number.

Producer's and consumer's risks

As the sample may be either better or worse than the lot from which it is chosen, an inspection scheme as outlined will inevitably lead to the acceptance of some lots which should have been rejected, and the rejection of some which should have been accepted. These are known as the consumer's and the producer's risks respectively. The level of these risks depends on the actual sampling scheme chosen, and usually forms the basis on which different schemes are assessed and chosen for particular uses.

Operating characteristic curves

A useful way of comparing the characteristics of different sampling schemes is to draw their operating characteristic curves or O-C curves. These show the probability that a lot containing a given percentage of faulty items will be rejected by the sampling scheme. The average percentage of faulty items in the lots presented for inspection is usually called the Lot Percentage Defective or LPD.

The O-C curve for an ideal inspection scheme is shown in Fig. 41. It will be seen that there is a probability of one, *i.e.*

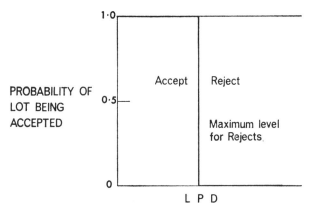

FIG. 41.—*The ideal operating characteristic curve*

certainty, of acceptance of lots with LPD below the critical level, and zero probability, *i.e.* impossibility, of acceptance of lots with LPD greater than the critical level. The nearer an *O–C* curve comes to this ideal shape the better the sampling scheme from which it is derived.

AQL and LTPD

In order to measure the customer's risk we must define maximum percentage of defective items in lots which the consumer wishes to accept. This is called the Lot Tolerance Percentage Defectives or LTPD. Similarly to measure the producer's risk we define a minimum percentage of defective items in a lot below which the lot should be accepted; this is known as the Acceptable Quality Level or AQL. The producer's risk is now defined as the

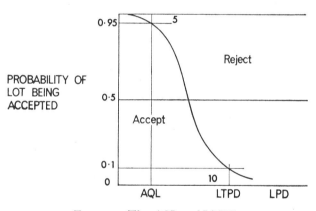

FIG. 42.—*The AQL and LTPD*

probability that a lot having the AQL will be rejected, and the consumer's risk as the probability that a lot having the LTPD will be accepted. These risks are usually taken at 5% and 10% respectively. The actual levels of the AQL and LTPD must be decided by negotiation between the consumer and the producer.

AOQL

In many cases the rejection of a lot leads to its 100% inspection. The inspected lot is then forwarded with the accepted lots. The result of an acceptance/verification scheme of this type is to

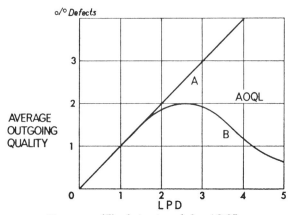

FIG. 43.—*The derivation of the AOQL*

improve the quality of the outgoing lots over the LPD. This can be seen from the two lines on the graph in Fig. 43. Line (A) is based on a sampling scheme in which only accepted lots are forwarded, the Average Outgoing Quality or AOQ cannot be different from the LPD. Line (B) is based on an acceptance/ verification scheme and the AOQ depends on both the LPD and the amount of 100% inspection carried out. As the LPD increases so the amount of 100% inspection increases. Since a large amount of 100% inspection will result in a low AOQ there must be a maximum value which is referred to as the Average Outgoing Quality Limit or AOQL. The existence of such a maximum makes it possible for an assurance to be given that the percentage will not rise above a certain figure when a particular sampling scheme is in operation.

Designing sampling schemes

The construction of O–C curves

To assess the effect of a sampling scheme we must first construct its O–C curve. As we alter the actual proportion of defective items in a lot during the sampling process the binomial distribution is not strictly applicable, as it is based on the assumption of a constant proportion p of defective items in the population being sampled. Under the conditions of changing probability the hypergeometric distribution should be used, but if the ratio n/N, the sampling fraction, is less than 0·1 the binomial distribution is an adequate approximation. Further, for samples of size greater than 50 the Poisson distribution may be used to approximate the binomial distribution. Using this approximation the construction of an O–C curve could proceed as follows.

Construction of an O–C curve for the sampling scheme $N = 1000$, $n = 50, c = 2$.

For each LPD we must calculate the expected number of defective items, $P(0)$, $P(1)$, $P(2)$, and use this to find the probability of finding up to c defective items in the sample. This is the probability of accepting the sample and is plotted against the LPD. The Poisson distribution is used to find the probabilities.

Table XXXV—Calculation for Operating Characteristic Curve

LPD	m	P (0)	P (1)	P (2)	P (accept)
0	0	1·000	0	0	1·000
2	1	0·368	0·368	0·184	0·920
4	2	0·135	0·271	0·271	0·677
6	3	0·050	0·149	0·224	0·423
8	4	0·018	0·073	0·147	0·238
10	5	0·007	0·033	0·084	0·124
12	6	0·002	0·015	0·045	0·062

Note: $m = LPD \times n/100$

The O–C curve is shown in Fig. 44.

An alternative method of calculating an O–C curve using the binomial distribution has already been described as an application of the binomial distribution (see p. 118).

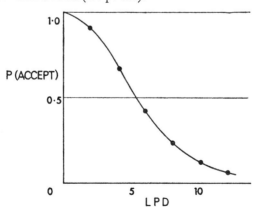

FIG. 44.—*Operating characteristic curve*

The choice of sampling schemes

The principles by which a good sampling scheme is chosen can be illustrated by showing the effect of varying the numbers N, n, c on the O–C curves.

A common misconception is that maintaining a constant percentage of inspection gives a constant level of quality assurance. This is not so, as is shown by the curves in Fig. 45, in which the sampling fraction n/N is kept constant.

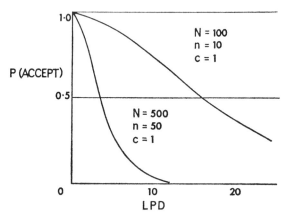

FIG. 45.—*Operating characteristic curves with constant sampling fraction*

It can be seen that the higher the lot size and sample size the more discriminating the sample scheme is.

The effect of changing the lot size but keeping the sample size and acceptance number constant is found to be very small unless n/N is large. From this we can see that the critical quantity is not the lot size or the sampling fraction but the sample size. In Fig. 46 the effect of changing the acceptance number is shown. It will be seen that a greater discrimination, but at a higher LPD, is given by a larger acceptance number. To gain in discrimination at the same LPD the sample size and acceptance number must both be increased.

Using the information from these curves we conclude that a good sampling scheme will have a reasonably large sample size and a non-zero acceptance number. In order to keep the sampling

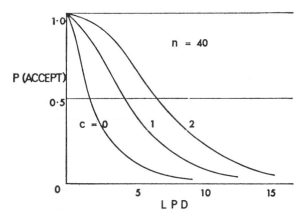

FIG. 46.—*Operating characteristic curves with varying acceptance number*

fractions small this requires large lots. However, too large a lot size can cause trouble as the rejection of a lot becomes a more serious matter with increasing lot size.

If an acceptance/verification plan is in operation, the total inspection required, that is 100% as well as routine, will vary with the sampling scheme chosen and the LPD, and the choice of the scheme used will be influenced by the expected LPD.

Multiple sampling schemes

Double sampling

The schemes discussed so far are described as single sampling schemes, as an accept–reject decision is made on the basis of a single sample. In a double sampling plan the decision to accept or reject is only made for very good or bad samples, and for intermediate cases a further sample is taken. The decision to accept–reject is then made on the basis of the combined sample. The combined sample size in a double sampling plan is larger than the sample size in an equivalent single sampling plan, giving a more discriminating test. The first sample is small, however, and as a reasonable proportion of decisions are made at this stage the average total inspection is less for a double than for a single sampling plan.

The O–C curves for the first stage of a double sampling

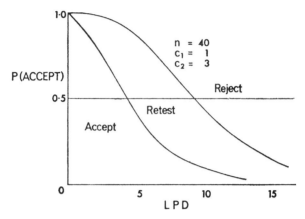

FIG. 47.—*Operating characteristic curves for stages of a double sampling scheme*

scheme are shown in Fig. 47. The probability of acceptance for a double sampling scheme, combined samples, is found as follows:

$P(acceptance) = P(accept\ at\ 1st\ sample) +$
$P(taking\ 2nd\ sample) \times P(accept\ at\ 2nd\ sample)$.

Multiple sampling

There is no reason why a final decision should be taken at the second sample, and three- or four-stage sampling schemes can be designed. There is a further gain in sampling efficiency, and the same O–C curve can be achieved with a lower average sampling effort. The gains made in this direction tend to be offset by the increasing complexity of the scheme, and of administering it. As the greatest gain in efficiency occurs in going from single to double sampling, it is usual not to go beyond double sampling.

Sequential sampling

The most efficient sampling scheme is one in which multiple sampling is carried to its extreme, and each sample consists of only one item. Such a scheme is described as a sequential sampling scheme. The decision to accept or reject is made on the basis of the total defective items found at a stage, and the acceptance or rejection numbers vary with the total number of items sampled. The test may be carried out by use of a graph such as the one in Fig. 48. Single items are sampled and the total number of

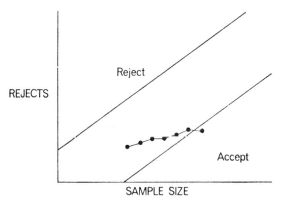

FIG. 48.—*Sequential sampling scheme*

defective items found is plotted against the total number of items sampled. The acceptance and rejection numbers are indicated by the two sloping lines, and the test ends when the plotted line crosses either boundary. It might appear that there is a danger of such a test continuing indefinitely without reaching a decision; this is unlikely, and the average number of items required to reach a decision is lower than the average sample size in any other comparable scheme.

As a sequential sampling scheme does require the least sampling for a given O–C curve, such schemes are used when the cost of taking a sample is high compared to the cost of administering the sampling scheme. This may apply when the testing methods used to detect defective items are expensive to operate, or when a destructive test must be used on high-value items.

Published sampling schemes

The use of published schemes

The labour of calculating O–C curves for a series of possible sampling schemes may be avoided by the use of published sampling schemes. In general a series of suggested schemes are given for various AQL, AOQL or LTPD and for varying expected LPD and lot sizes. The corresponding O–C curves are plotted to enable a choice to be made between alternative schemes. The exact form of the tables of schemes must depend on the philosophy of testing held by the authors and can vary considerably. The study of published schemes, which are usually fully explained and annotated, should make clear the idea on which they are based.

The Dodge and Romig tables

The Dodge-Romig sampling tables are an extensively used collection of sampling schemes. They are based on the assumption that all rejected lots will be 100% by the acceptance/verification system, and are designed to require the minimum total inspection effort. The schemes are indexed in two ways, first by reference to the LTPD with a consumer's risk of 10%. For each value of LTPD from 0·5 to 10% a series of sampling schemes are given, and the scheme giving the minimum sampling effort is found by considering the lot size and the expected LPD. The AOQL which will result from the scheme chosen is given and the O–C curves for the schemes are also shown. In the second instance the plans are indexed by reference to the desired AOQL, and the sampling scheme giving minimum sampling effort under the expected conditions of use is indicated. In this case the LTPD given by the scheme chosen is indicated. As the sampling effort becomes very large with an acceptance/verification scheme the schemes are only given for an LPD less than the AOQL chosen.

The same layout is followed for a second series of sampling schemes, which use double sampling, and again the O–C curves are shown. This makes it possible to choose directly between single and double sampling schemes by comparison of the sampling required and the effectiveness of the schemes.

The Dodge-Romig tables are suitable for situations where re-testing by 100% inspection is simple, as in interdepartmental transfers in a large organisation. If there is no assurance that the 100% inspection will be carried out, then they are no longer directly relevant. This is often true when the transfer of goods is between a customer and producer who are not closely linked.

DEF 131 sampling schemes

A series of sampling schemes to be used in contracts with the Ministry of Defence are published under the reference DEF 131. These are copies of the sampling schemes used in contracts by the United States Government and published as Military Standard 105. They do not assume any 100% inspection of rejected lots, and are designed for cases where the customer wishes to be assured of a quality level, and to encourage the producer to maintain it. The schemes are indexed by reference to the required AQL and expected lot size, and schemes are given for three levels of inspection, reduced inspection, normal inspection and tightened inspection. The producer pays for the inspection.

The provision of three levels of inspection is intended to provide an incentive to the producer to improve his quality, and to protect the consumer against lowered quality standards. If the producer can provide goods at an LPD well below the AQL required and can show a regular production flow at this level, then reduced inspection may be allowed. The reduced inspection plans favour the producer and will only detect large changes from the required quality. Reduced inspection would not normally be agreed to by the customer until a producer has established a good record of quality maintenance, and even then must change to normal inspection as soon as a defective item is found in a sample.

Normal inspection is designed for the situation where there is a steady quality level with the LPD below the AQL, and corresponds to the normal balance between consumer and producer. The decision to move from normal to reduced inspection would require the assurance of reliability as described above, and the observation of a series of defective-free samples. If the LPD is above the AQL, or if the quality level is variable, or production spasmodic, the consumer may require tightened inspection.

Tightened inspection is designed to filter out the reasonable lots from what is expected to be a variable selection. It is expensive to the producer, and represents the consumer's protection against failure to meet quality standards after contracts have been signed. To change from tightened to normal inspection a producer would have to be able to assure the consumer that regularity of production has been established with the LPD below the AQL. The amounts of inspection required at the three levels is in the proportions,

reduced 1,
normal 2, and
tightened 4,

indicating the advantage to a producer in being able to use normal, or reduced inspection.

As with the Dodge-Romig tables, double sampling as well as single sampling schemes are available in the tables.

Continuous sampling plans

The sampling schemes described can be applied to continuous manufacture by inspecting lots of successively produced items. This requires the marking off or alternatively the physical separation of successive times into lots. A continuous system of sampling may be preferred. A typical plan is to set up a scheme as shown. The numbers i, k, l, m are constants chosen to assure a particular AQL with the scheme.

Start

Inspect every item until i perfect items are observed consecutively, then

Inspect every k^{th} item until a faulty item is observed, then

Inspect every l^{th} item, if m perfect items are found then, or else
if another faulty item is found before m items have been checked, then

Safeguards as to homogeneity of production are introduced into the scheme to ensure that the quality produced is not too variable, and that a systematic sampling scheme as proposed is valid.

Acceptance sampling by variables

A variable may be converted to an attribute of the perfect/faulty type by specifying an allowed range for the variable. It is often found that to do so will lead to a cheaper inspection scheme than a scheme in which all items of a sample are measured and a significance test performed on the results. This arises as simpler and cheaper inspection methods may be used, even though the total amount of inspection required may rise. Only when the cost of inspection is high, as for instance with destruction testing, does acceptance testing by attributes normally become preferable.

Questions

1. Explain what is meant by acceptance sampling, explain the difference between double and single sampling and indicate their relative advantages.

2. Discuss the factors relevant to the choice of an acceptance sampling scheme. Explain the meaning of AQL, LTPD and AOQL by the use of suitable diagrams.

3. Describe the construction of an O–C curve, and draw the curve for the sampling scheme $N = 2000$, $n = 45$, $c = 2$.

4. Describe the use of the DEF 131 sampling plans. In what way do they differ from the Dodge-Romig tables.

5. What is meant by sequential sampling? When is it used to best advantage? Illustrate your answer with a diagram.

CHAPTER FOURTEEN

THE CHI-SQUARED TEST

"Goodness of fit" tests

The need for a "Goodness of fit" test

THE results from many statistical investigations take the form of the number of items or members of the sample taken which fall into various classes. We may wish to test if the totals in the classes agree with the totals expected in the classes if a stated hypothesis is true, that is, we wish to test for the goodness of fit between theory and observation. This is made possible by calculating the value of a quantity called chi-squared, χ^2, which is dependent on the deviations between observed and expected class totals. The distribution of this quantity is known and so the probability of observing a given value of χ^2 under a particular set of conditions can be calculated. A low value of this probability may be taken to discredit the hypothesis used to calculate the expected class totals.

As with the "t"-distribution the χ^2 distribution depends on the degrees of freedom in each application, and the same rule for calculation applies, except that the number in the sample is replaced by the number of classes. If n is the number of classes and k the number of restraints used, that is quantities fixed when calculating the expected totals, then the degrees of freedom $= n - k$.

The calculation of χ^2

Let the expected total number of items in a class be E and the corresponding observed total O. Then,

$$\chi^2 = \Sigma \frac{(O - E)^2}{E}.$$

Whether or not this value is greater than the values one would expect by chance is decided by reference to the table of χ^2-distribution with the appropriate degrees of freedom and significance level.

EXAMPLE I

The number of phone calls initiated in two-minute periods on a switchboard are tabulated below. Does the Poisson distribution adequately describe the observed distribution?

Calls per period	0	1	2	3	4	5
No. of occurrences	19	39	42	23	11	6

Using the hypothesis that the observed frequencies are distributed as the Poisson distribution with the same mean and total frequency, the expected frequencies are found as shown in Table XXXVI.

Table XXXVI—Expected Frequencies from Poisson Distribution

$m = 1 \cdot 9$

r	$P(r)$	$P(r) \times 140$
0	0·1496	20·94
1	0·2842	39·79
2	0·2700	37·80
3	0·1710	23·94
4	0·0812	11·37
Over 5	0·0440	6·16

Using these expected frequencies the value of χ^2 is calculated as shown in Table XXXVII.

Table XXXVII—Calculation of χ^2

Calls	O	E	$(O - E)$	$(O - E)^2$	$(O - E)^2/E$
0	19	20·94	−1·94	3·76	0·18
1	39	39·79	−0·79	0·62	0·02
2	42	37·80	4·2	17·64	0·47
3	23	23·94	−0·94	0·88	0·04
4	11	11·37	−0·37	0·14	0·01
5	6	6·16	−0·16	0·03	—
				Total $\chi^2 = 0 \cdot 72$	

We lose one degree of freedom by making the total expected frequencies equal to the total observed frequencies, and another by specifying the mean of the Poisson distribution used. There are six classes, so allowing for the two restraints there are $6 - 2 = 4$ degrees of freedom.

If we test at the 5% significance level we find that with 4 degrees of freedom χ^2 must exceed 9·49 before we reject the hypothesis. The value of χ^2 found is less than 9·49 and we conclude that there is no reason to reject the hypothesis and that the Poisson distribution can be used to describe the observed distribution adequately.

Restrictions on the use of χ^2

The χ^2-distribution is derived by considering what happens when the expected class frequencies increase without limit in the multinomial distribution, a many-variable development of the binomial distribution. The use which can be made of the χ^2-distribution is limited by the validity of the approximations made in its derivation, and care must be taken to observe these restrictions.

Firstly the χ^2-distribution can only be used with integral numbers of items in the classes. It is not valid for proportions, percentages or any other numbers derived from the original data.

Secondly it cannot be used when the expected frequencies in the classes are low. It is best to arrange that no expected class frequency falls below a value of five, although if not more than one in five of the expected frequencies falls below five there is unlikely to be any trouble. Note that this restriction applies only to the expected class frequencies, the observed class frequencies may take any value.

Test of fit for a normal distribution

The use of the χ^2-distribution may be further illustrated by testing if an observed distribution can be adequately described by the normal distribution. This is a very common assumption in statistical work, and it is most useful to have a method of testing the assumption even if it is seldom employed.

In the example given there are nine classes and we lose three degrees of freedom, one by making the expected total frequency equal to the observed total frequency, one by making the mean of the expected distribution equal to the mean of the observed distribution, and one by making the standard deviation of the expected distribution equal to the standard deviation of the observed distribution. Hence we have $9 - 3 = 6$ degrees of freedom.

On the hypothesis that the observed distribution is adequately described by the normal distribution, then the highest value of χ^2 we expect to observe at the 5% significance level is 12·59.

The calculation of the expected frequencies is shown in Table XXXVIII.

EXAMPLE 2

The amounts by which the lengths of 250 components made on a process differ from the target length have been classified as follows.

Deviation	$-0.4 \rightarrow -0.2$	$-0.2-0$	$0-0.2$	$0.2-0.4$			
No. of components	7	11	28	49			
Deviation	$0.4-0.6$	$0.6-0.8$	$0.8-1.0$	$1.0-1.2$	$1.2-1.4$
No. of components	78	41	20	11	5

The mean and standard deviation for this distribution are 0·474 and 0·327; test if the distribution can be adequately described by a normal distribution having the same mean and standard deviation. Test at the 5% significance level.

Table XXXVIII—Expected Frequencies by Use of Normal Distribution

Class boundaries	z_1	$P(z > z_1)$	P (class)	P (class) × 250
$-0.4--0.2$	$\rightarrow -2.06$	·0197	·0197	4·92
$-0.2-\ 0$	$-2.06 \rightarrow -1.45$	·0197--0735	·0538	13·45
$0\ -\ 0.2$	$-1.45 \rightarrow -0.84$	·0735--2005	·1270	31·75
$0.2-\ 0.4$	$-0.84 \rightarrow -0.23$	·2005--4090	·2085	52·13
$0.4-\ 0.6$	$-0.23 \rightarrow\ 0.39$	·4090--3483	·2427	60·67
$0.6-\ 0.8$	$0.39 \rightarrow\ 1.00$	·3483--1587	·1896	47·40
$0.8-\ 1.0$	$1.00 \rightarrow\ 1.61$	·1587--0537	·1050	26·25
$1.0-\ 1.2$	$1.61 \rightarrow\ 2.22$	·0537--0132	·0405	10·13
$1.2-\ 1.4$	$2.22 \rightarrow$	·0132	·0132	3·30

Note that in calculating the entry for P (class) for the class $0.4''-0.6''$ it is necessary to add the two boundary figures from the $P(z > z_1)$ column, and subtract them from 1. If the reason for this is not clear, then the reader should draw a diagram of the z boundaries as discussed in Chapter Ten.

Using these expected frequencies the calculation of χ^2 is as follows.

Table XXXIX—Calculation of χ^2

O	E	$O - E$	$(O - E)^2$	$(O - E)^2/E$
7	4·92	2·08	4·33	0·88
11	13·45	−2·45	6·00	0·45
28	31·75	−3·75	14·06	0·44
49	52·13	−3·13	9·80	0·19
78	60·67	17·33	300·33	4·95
41	47·40	−6·40	40·96	0·86
20	26·25	−6·25	39·06	1·49
11	10·13	0·87	0·76	0·07
5	3·30	1·70	2·89	0·88
250	250·00	0·00	Total $\chi^2 = 10.21$	

The value of χ^2 found is less than the critical value of 12·59, and so we have no reason to reject the hypothesis, and we can conclude that the observed distribution is adequately described by the normal distribution with the same mean and standard deviation.

Note that by examining the contributions to χ^2 in the last column of Table XXXVIII we can identify the classes showing the greatest deviation between observed and expected frequencies. It is obvious that the main deviation in this case is for the class 0·4–0·6″, and if there are no reasons to expect other than a normal distribution, it might well be worth while to investigate why this peak occurs.

Contingency tables

Attributes and contingency

Classifications need not be made only by reference to the numerical characteristics of the items classified. Any characteristic which can be specified unambiguously and which extends over all the items to be classified is suitable. Typical of such classifications by attribute are the classification of a group of persons by sex, or colour of hair, or political opinion, or purchasing preference. We may wish to investigate if possession of one attribute is connected with possession of another; does sex affect consumer tastes in food, or does age-group affect voting characteristics?

Where possession of one attribute is related to the possession of another we describe one as being contingent on the other, and a two-way classification table which might be expected to demonstrate such a relationship is known as a contingency table. Such a table is shown in Table XL, where a random group of purchasers are classified by sex, and by buying preference among four packs of a product.

Table XL—Contingency Table
Product Pack Chosen

	A	B	C	D	
Male	26	48	21	25	120
Female	8	48	7	17	80
	34	96	28	42	200

It appears that packs A and C are more attractive to women than men, but this result could possibly be a chance sampling distribution and one which would not be expected generally in sales of the product. We wish to test if the observed distribution differs significantly from what we would expect if the sex of the purchaser did not affect the choice of pack. If we can predict the expected frequencies in each class, then we can test if the observed frequencies differ significantly by calculating the value of χ^2, and referring to the appropriate critical value.

χ^2-Test for contingency

On the hypothesis that preference for one pack or other is not affected by sex, then we would expect the proportion of packs type (A) chosen by men and women to be in the same proportion as the total number of men and women in the test, *i.e.*

expected proportion of women choosing (A)
= $34 \times 80/200 = 13\cdot6$
expected proportion of men choosing (A)
= $34 - 13\cdot6 = 20\cdot4$

Similarly for (B), (C) and (D) leading to Table XLI.

Table XLI—Expected Frequencies in Contingency Table

Product Pack

	A	B	C	D	
Male	20·4	57·6	16·8	25·2	120
Female	13·6	38·4	11·2	16·8	80
	34	96	28	42	200

We have used a number of restraints on our choice of expected frequencies by making the row and column totals agree in the two tables. Altogether we have used five restraints,

one by making the grand total agree,
one by making the total of women agree,
one by making the total purchases of (A) agree,
one by making the total purchases of (B) agree, and
one by making the total purchases of (C) agree.

The agreement between the totals of men, and purchases of (D) are not counted as they must agree if the five totals listed agree.

There are eight classes altogether and so $8 - 5 = 3$ degrees of freedom are left.

If we test at the 5% significance level then the critical value of χ^2 is $7 \cdot 82$.

The calculation of χ^2 is shown in Table XLII. The only difference from the previous examples is in the method of deriving the expected frequencies, and care should be taken to compare the corresponding frequencies from the two tables.

Table XLII—Calculation of χ^2

O	E	O − E	(O − E)²	(O − E)²/E
26	20·4	5·6	31·36	1·54
8	13·6	−5·6	31·36	2·31
48	57·6	−9·6	92·16	1·60
48	38·4	9·6	92·16	2·40
21	16·8	4·2	17·64	1·05
7	11·2	−4·2	17·64	1·57
25	25·2	−0·2	0·04	0·00
17	16·8	0·2	0·04	0·00
				Total 10·47

The calculated value of χ^2 is greater than the critical value, and so we reject the hypothesis that there is no relationship between the two attributes tested, and conclude that sex and preference for the different pack are related. Note that there is no question of the statistical test investigating a cause and effect relationship; this must rely on knowledge of the data and other information. All that has been shown is that the distribution of frequencies is not one we would expect by chance if there is no relationship between the attributes.

The general case for contingency tables

The use of the χ^2 test for testing contingency tables can be extended to any size of table. If we have a table with r classes of one attribute and c classes of the other attribute, then there are rc classes altogether. If the row totals are $R_1, R_2, R_3 \ldots$ and the column totals $C_1, C_2, C_3 \ldots$ and the grand total S, then for a class corresponding to the second row and fourth column the expected frequencies would be $R_2 . C_4/S$ and similarly for the other classes; *i.e.* fourth row and second class, expected class frequency $= R_4 . C_2/S$.

The degrees of freedom for the general case are found as in the previous example. There are rc classes and we have,

one restraint from the agreement of grand totals, $r - 1$ restraints from the agreement of row totals, and $c - 1$ restraints from the agreement of column totals.

This leaves $rc - (r - 1) - (c - 1) - 1$ degrees of freedom, which simplifies to $(r - 1)(c - 1)$.

In the calculation of χ^2 there will be rc comparisons and the value found is assessed by comparison with the critical value found from the tables as before.

Yates' correction for continuity

The observed frequencies in χ^2 are necessarily whole numbers and must increase in steps of 1 unit. The χ^2-distribution is based on the assumption that the frequencies can increase continuously. The error introduced by this assumption is not large, and is only of importance when the degrees of freedom are 1, as in the case of a 2×2 contingency table, that is one in which the attributes used can only take two forms. The error is compensated for by reducing the absolute value of all deviations between observed and expected frequencies by 0·5. This procedure is usually described as "Yates' correction for continuity." If the deviation is less than 0·5, then the correction is not applied; the contribution to χ^2 will in any case be very small.

EXAMPLE 3

Out of 46 candidates taking an examination, 22 have attended a revision course on the subject being examined. The result of the examination is:

revision course students,   18 pass,   4 fail,
other students,   16 pass,   8 fail.

Is this evidence that the revision course significantly increases a student's likelihood of passing the examination? Test at the 5% significance level.

The tables of observed and expected frequencies are shown in Table XLIII and the calculation of χ^2 in Table XLIV.

In this case there is only one degree of freedom $(c - 1)(r - 1) = 1 \times 1 = 1$, and at 5% level χ^2 is 3·84. Our hypothesis is, of course, that there is no relationship between attending the revision course and passing the examination.

Table XLIII—Observed and Expected Frequencies
2 × 2 Table

	Observed				Expected		
	Pass	Fail			Pass	Fail	
Revised	18	4	22	Revised	16·26	5·74	22
No revision	16	8	24	No revision	17·74	6·26	24
	34	12	46		34	12	46

The value of χ^2 found is 0·7, and so we have no reason to reject the hypothesis, and conclude that there is not enough evidence in the available data to support the theory that the revision course is effective.

Table XLIV—Calculation of χ^2 for 2 × 2 Table with Yates' Correction

O	E	O − E	Yates	$(O − E)^2$	$(O − E)^2/E$
18	16·26	1·74	1·24	1·54	0·09
4	5·74	−1·74	−1·24	1·54	0·27
16	17·74	−1·74	−1·24	1·54	0·09
8	6·26	1·74	1·24	1·54	0·25
				Total χ^2 = 0·70	

The exact test for 2 × 2 tables

By using the binomial distribution it was possible to predict the probability of any arrangement of items in a random sample. Similarly it is possible to predict the probability of observing any given possible distribution of frequencies in a 2 × 2 table by using the multinomial distribution, and assuming that the two attributes used to form the table are not related. From these probabilities the cumulative probability of observing a distribution at least as extreme as a given distribution can be calculated. The calculation of these probabilities is a time-consuming procedure, and is only attempted for a 2 × 2 table in which the frequencies are low and hence χ^2 is not applicable. If possible the situation should be avoided by using a larger sample size and so increasing the frequencies into the range where χ^2 is valid.

Testing proportions by χ^2

It is possible to test whether an observed proportion in a given sample differs significantly from a given proportion, by using the normal distribution as an approximation to the binomial distribution. This is only valid for samples of size greater than 50, and an alternative test based on χ^2 is often useful.

If the hypothesis is that the observed proportion p does not differ significantly from the given proportion of π, then for a sample size n the observed frequencies are np and $n(1 - p)$, and the expected frequencies are $n\pi$ and $n(1 - \pi)$. We use the same total n in both cases which constitutes a restraint on the system; there are two classes and so one degree of freedom is left.

Yates' correction for continuity is necessary but otherwise the calculations and assessment of χ^2 proceeds as in previous applications.

Significance tests with the median

It is possible to use χ^2 to test for significant differences in the position and spread of samples, without any assumptions as to the distribution of the measurements in the samples. If we have two samples A and B, sizes n_1 and n_2, and rank the combined sample in order, then on the hypothesis that the samples have the same central value we would expect $n_1/2$ items from sample A, and $n_2/2$ items from sample B on each side of the median. The observed frequencies can be compared with the expected frequencies by calculating χ^2.

If the result of this test is found to be non-significant, then the spread of the samples can be tested by comparing the observed numbers of items A and B, inside and outside the interquartile range. The expected frequencies on the hypothesis of equal spread are as before.

Questions

1. A survey of accidents in the warehouse of a large factory shows the following pattern of reported accidents during a year.

Accidents	0	1	2	3	4
Employees	169	67	32	20	6

Test whether the Poisson distribution is an adequate fit to the data.

2. Test if the following data would be adequately fitted by a normal distribution.

Class	Frequency
60–	15
120–	20
140–	45
160–	25
180–	15
200–260	.15

3. In a study of attendance records the following pattern of absences is observed for a particular year.

DEPARTMENT

Warehouse		Production	Maintenance
No. absent at			
least once	15	15	10
Total employed	45	110	45

Test if the absentee rate depends significantly on the department in which a person works.

4. An opinion poll is taken in a town to test opinion regarding a proposed redevelopment scheme. The answers to a question are as follows:

OPINION

Age, years	For	Don't know	Against
Under 21	20	10	5
21–29	40	30	40
30–49	40	20	30
50 and over	20	20	25

Test if there is a relationship between the age of a person and his or her opinion on this question.

Explain carefully the hypothesis you adopt in this test, and what the implications of the rejection of this hypothesis are.

5. In a survey 159 out of 290 people stated that they were in favour of a proposed rebuilding scheme. Is this evidence that there is a majority in favour of the scheme in the population as a whole?

6. Forty sufferers from headaches are divided into two groups by a random selection procedure. One group is given a new drug, the other is given an identical neutral tablet.

	Headaches less	Headaches same
Drug	16	4
No drug	12	8

Does this test show the drug to be effective?

7. Two samples are ranked and the numbers of members above and below the common median are counted as shown.

	Sample A	Sample B
Above Median	49	37
Below Median	37	49

Do the samples differ significantly?

8. Five archers in a contest score the following "golds": 10, 12, 15, 8, 16; test if they differ significantly in ability.

9. An observer obtains the following data from a random sample.

	Fat	Normal	Thin
Normal	82	140	78
Neurotic	7	34	19
Psychotic	8	28	4

Is there evidence of any dependence of mental state on physical build?

10. Discuss the implications of a significant result to a χ^2-test when the number of classes tested is large.

CHAPTER FIFTEEN

THE ANALYSIS OF VARIANCE

The variance ratio test

The distribution of variances

THE tests on sample means described in Chapter Eleven were based on the knowledge that sample means are distributed as the normal distribution or closely similar distributions. A similar approach is not possible when designing tests on sample variances, as the distribution of sample variances is a non-normal skew distribution. The distribution of sample variances is closely related to that of χ^2 and the χ^2-distribution can be used to test for significant differences between variances, or to set confidence limits for the size of variances. In most instances, however, it is the relative size of sample variances, rather than their absolute size, which is of interest, and the principal tests relating to sample variances are based on the distribution of the ratio of two sample variances.

The variance ratio

The ratio of two sample variances is given the symbol F, and the distribution of F has been calculated on the assumption that the two variances are based on samples taken from normally distributed parent populations. The F-distribution varies in shape depending on the size of the samples from which the variances have been derived, and there are thus two independent sets of degrees of freedom associated with the distribution. By always taking the greater variance on the top of the ratio, F is always greater than 1 and the tabulation of the F-distribution is made simpler. The values of F which will be exceeded with a given probability on the hypothesis that the two variances involved are both estimates of the same parent population variance have been tabulated. A table with this probability set at 0·05 is given in Table D (Appendix II). The horizontal set of degrees of freedom refers to the degrees of freedom of the sample variance on the top of the ratio, the vertical set of degrees of freedom to the degrees of freedom of the sample variance on the bottom of the ratio.

Confidence limits for variances

The tables of the F-distribution may be used to set up confidence limits for variances as follows. If we use the 0·05 probability level table then we will derive 90% confidence limits. The distribution of sample variances is such that confidence limits for a higher degree of confidence would probably be so wide as to be useless.

Consider a variance s^2 calculated from a sample of n items; this will have $n - 1$ degrees of freedom and let the 90% confidence limits be σ_1^2 and σ_2^2. The two limiting values σ_1^2 and σ_2^2 are the extreme values that a population variance can take consistent with the sample coming from the population, and so have an infinite number of degrees of freedom.

We can find the two variance ratios $F_1 = s^2/\sigma_1^2$ and $F_2 = \sigma_2^2/s^2$, and from the tables find the highest value they are likely to take with 95% confidence (0·05 probability that this value is exceeded). With F_1, F_2 and s^2 known, σ_1^2 and σ_2^2 can now be calculated.

EXAMPLE I

Find 90% confidence limits for a population variance given that a sample of ten items from the population had variance $= 8$. Let the limits be σ_1^2 and σ_2^2 and let the variance ratios be $F_1 = 8/\sigma_2^2$ and $F_2 = \sigma_1^2/8$. The variance estimate from the sample has $10 - 1 = 9$ degrees of freedom, and so F_1 has 9 and ∞ degrees of freedom, and F_2 has ∞ and 9 degrees of freedom. Reading from the 0·05 probability level table:

$F_2 \leqslant 1·88$ (95% confidence)

The value for F_1 is obtained by interpolation between the values of F with 8 and ∞, and 10 and ∞, degrees of freedom.

$F_1 \leqslant 2·71$ (95% confidence)

This gives $\sigma_1^2/8 \leqslant 2·71$

or $\sigma_2^2 \leqslant 21·68$ (95% confidence)

and $8/\sigma_2^2 \leqslant 1·88$

or $\sigma_2^2 \geqslant 4·26$ (95% confidence)

Combining these $4·26 \leqslant \sigma^2 \leqslant 21·68$ (90% confidence) where σ^2 is the population variance.

The analysis of variance

Tests on many means

When we have a group of observations of a variable for each of a series of different values of what may be a controlling factor, we may wish to test if the mean values of the groups differ significantly from one another. We would carry out a test for difference of means between all possible pairs of groups of observations, but this would require a very considerable amount of calculation. Also the interpretation of the results obtained would not be easy. An alternative approach is to test for homogeneity of means by a single test, and this is the purpose of the analysis of variance.

Contributions to variability

Let us arrange the measurements in columns, each column being those measurements forming the group of measurements for one value of the factor to be tested. If the factor does not influence the measurements then the variability between measurements will be constant through all the measurements. If the factor does affect the measurements then the means of the columns will differ, and there will be more variability between measurements in different columns than between those in the same column. We can estimate the variance of measurements within columns, and this will represent the underlying variability of the measurements. Similarly we can estimate a variance between columns, and this will represent the underlying variability plus any variability due to a difference in column means. If the variance ratio found from

$$F = \frac{between\ columns\ variance\ estimate}{within\ columns\ variance\ estimate}$$

is found to be significantly greater than 1, then we conclude that the column means differ significantly. Note that the test does not identify any particular column as the source of variation. A value of F significantly less than 1 would be meaningless, and probably indicate measurements are not distributed normally within the columns. The assumption of this normality of distribution is always made, even if the actual distribution of the measurements is unknown. The test becomes invalid when there are gross deviations from normality, and a transformation of the original data may be necessary.

The analysis of variance

The test outlined above has been formalised as the *analysis of variance*, and relies on being able to partition the variability present in a set of measurements between the various sources. This variability is measured by the sum of squares of deviations of measurements from the mean of the measurements. This is the corrected sum of squares we have used before with the symbol C. In the present case we can regard this as partly derived from variability within the columns, and partly from variability between the columns.

The variance estimates to be tested are obtained by dividing each contribution to the variability by an appropriate number of degrees of freedom. The whole calculation after the preliminary calculations is conveniently presented in an analysis of variance table, or Anovar table. The typical form of this is shown in Table XLV.

Table XLV—Anovar Table

Source of vari- ability	Sum of squares	Degrees of freedom	Variance estimate	F
Between Cols	C_{COL}	$c-1$	$S^2_{COL} = C_{COL}/_{c-1}$	$S^2_{COL}/_{s^2}$
Within Cols	$C_{TOT} - C_{COL}$	$n-c$	$s^2 = C_{TOT} - C_{COL}/_{n-c}$	
Total	C_{TOT}	$n-1$		

Note that the table is for C columns with a total of n measurements. C_{TOT} is the total corrected sum of squares and C_{COL} the corrected sum of squares for between columns variability.

The value of F is tested at say the 5% significance level with the degrees of freedom indicated in the table.

Calculation for one-factor Anovar

Before calculating an Anovar it should be noted that the final quantity tested is a ratio, and so dimensionless. This means that the original measurements can be coded to simplify calculations without the need for any subsequent adjustment of the results.

EXAMPLE 2

Three nominally identical chemical plants are used to manufacture a substance. The percentage purity of the product is noted for five successive batches on each plant; the results found are:

Plant A   74   78   72   77   75
Plant B   75   71   76   69   70
Plant C   77   79   82   72   81

A more flexible notation for the measurements and their sums is helpful in Anovar calculations and is a development of the use of suffixes. If we let the measurements be represented by X, then X_{13} is the first measurement in the third group. The first suffix refers to the number of the measurement, the second to the group it is in. The general term is X_{ij} and sums are indicated as follows:

$$\sum_i X_{ij} = X_{ij} + X_{2j} + \ldots \text{ for all the measurements in the } i\text{th group,}$$

and

$$\sum_j X_{ij} = X_{i1} + X_{i2} + \ldots \text{ for the } i\text{th measurements in all the groups.}$$

The grand sum of all measurements is shown by $\sum_i \sum_j X_{ij}$ but this will be shown by $\sum\sum X_{ij}$ where there is no chance of ambiguity. The total number of measurements can be symbolised by n the number of groups by c and the number of measurements in each group by r. Returning to the Anovar, let the 15 measurements be coded to 15 values of x_{ij}. The total variability in the measurements is

$$\sum\sum x_{ij}^2 - (\sum\sum x_{ij})^2/n,$$

the second term is the correction for the mean and will be abbreviated to $C.F.$ The variability between groups is given by, $\sum_j (\sum_i x_{ij})^2/r - C.F.$, and the variability within groups can be found by difference.

The layout of the calculation is shown in Table XLVI.

Table XLVI—Calculation for One-way Anovar

$x_{ij} = X_{ij} - 75$				x_{ij}^2		
A	B	C		A	B	C
−1	0	2		1	0	4
3	−4	4		9	16	16
−3	1	7		9	1	49
2	−6	−3		4	36	9
0	−5	6		0	25	36

$\sum_j x_{ij}$ 1   −14   16 $= 3 = \sum\sum x_{ij}$ 23   78   114 $= 215$

$\sum_i x_{ij}^2$ 1   196   256 $= 453 = \sum_j (\sum_j x_{ij}^2)$ $= \sum\sum (x_{ij})^2$

$C.F.$ $= 3^2/15 = 0.6$
C_{TOT} $= 215 - 0.6 = 214.4$
C_{COL} $= 453/5 - 0.6 = 90$
$C_{TOT} - C_{COL} = 214.4 - 90 = 124.4$

There are 15 measurements altogether and we use the mean in calculating the overall variability, leaving a total of 14 degrees of freedom. For the between-groups variability we have 3 groups and use the mean to leave 2 degrees of freedom. For the within-groups variability we lose one degree of freedom by using the mean of each group leaving $15 - 3 = 12$ degrees of freedom. Note that the total of within-groups and between-groups degrees of freedom equals the total degrees of freedom.

The source of variability, variability as measured by the sums of squares and the degrees of freedom are shown in the Anovar table in Table XLVII. The variance estimates are found by dividing the sums of squares by the appropriate degrees of freedom, and F is the ratio of the between- and within-groups variance estimates.

Table XLVII—Anovar Table—One-way

Source	S.S.	d.f.	Var. est.	F
Between	90	2	45	4·33
Within	124·4	12	10·4	
Total	214·4	14		

$F = 4·33$ (2, 12) significant

As indicated in the Anovar table, the value of F found is greater than the critical value, at the 5% significance level, with 2 and 12 degrees of freedom, of $3·9$. From this we conclude that the mean percentage purity does differ significantly between the plants. This might well justify further research to identify the source and cause of the variability.

One-way Anovar with unequal groups

If the number of measurements in each of the groups is not constant the formulae quoted must be modified. If we let there be w_j measurements in the jth group then the various quantities required are,

total variability $= \Sigma\Sigma x^2_{ij} - C.F.$

between-groups variability $= \underset{i}{\Sigma}[(\Sigma x_{ij})^2/w_j] - C.F.$

The degrees of freedom are found as before. The only change in computation is that the quantities $(\Sigma x_{ij})^2/w_j$ must be calculated separately before they are summed.

Interpretation of variance estimates

The exact nature of the extra contribution to the variability which may be found "between groups" depends on the model taken for the situation. It is possible to regard the series of values taken for the factor as either a selected set of values in which we are interested, or as a sample from the population of all possible values of the factor. These are described as Model I and Model II, or fixed effect and random effect models respectively. The distinction between these is important only at the interpretation stage of the Anovar and does not influence the calculations. If the random effect model applies, then it is possible to estimate the variance which is caused by the effect of different values of the factor independent of the background variability. If σ^2 is the background variance, and $\sigma_F{}^2$ the variance due to the factor, then within-groups variance estimate $= \sigma^2$, between-groups variance estimate $= \sigma^2 + r\sigma_F{}^2$. In the fixed effects model the extra component in the variance depends on the values of the factor chosen, and has no general interpretation.

Assuming the data of Example 2, which is a random effects model:

$$\hat{\sigma}^2 = 10 \cdot 4$$
$$\hat{\sigma}^2 + r\hat{\sigma}_F{}^2 = 45$$
$$\therefore \hat{\sigma}_F{}^2 = (45 - 10 \cdot 4)/5$$
$$= 6 \cdot 92.$$

Note that a significant effect may be of little practical importance. As in all tests, if we have large samples small effects are found to be significant. This is seen clearly by the effect of r above.

Two-factor analysis of variance

Contributions to variability

It is possible to extend the analysis of variance to a study of the effect of more than one factor at a time. Consider the measurements in Table XLVIII; each column represents a series of measurements for a single value of Factor A, and each row represents a series of measurements for a different value of Factor B. Each measurement in the table represents an observation made with a different combination of Factors A and B. We can as before make an estimate of the underlying variance plus a contribution caused by Factor A, and may also make a similar estimate from the rows which estimates the underlying variance plus a contribution caused by Factor B. If we assume that Factors A and B act independently then we can also derive an estimate of the underlying variance by itself, and can compare the between-rows and between-columns estimates with the underlying or residual estimate. This will let us decide whether either Factor B or Factor A or both have a significant effect on the measurements.

Table XLVIII—Data for Two-way Anovar

	Factor A		
Factor B	20·4 20·2 20·8 20·5	20·5 19·9 20·4 20·0	19·7 19·5 20·0 19·8

Two-way Anovar table

The calculation of the variance quantities required is an extension of the previous calculations and is shown in Table XLIX. Using the same notation, the cr measurements of x_{ij} represent

Table XLIX—Calculation for Two-way Anovar

$x_{ij} = (X_{ij} - 20 \cdot 0) . x10$			$\sum_{j} x_{ij}$	$(\sum_{j} x_{ij})^2$
4	5	−3	6	36
2	−1	−5	−4	16
8	4	0	12	144
5	0	−2	3	9
$\sum_{i} x_{ij}$ 19	8	−10	17	205
$(\sum_{j} x_{ij})^2$ 361	64	100	525	

	x_{ij}^2	
16	25	9
4	1	25
64	16	0
25	0	4
109	42	38 = 189

$$
\begin{aligned}
C.F. &= 17^2/12 = 24 \cdot 08 \\
C_{TOT} &= 189 - 24 \cdot 08 = 164 \cdot 92 \\
C_{COL} &= 525/4 - 24 \cdot 08 = 107 \cdot 17 \\
C_{ROW} &= 205/3 - 24 \cdot 08 = 44 \cdot 25 \\
C_{RESID} &= C_{TOT} - C_{COL} - C_{ROW} \\
&= 164 \cdot 92 - 107 \cdot 17 - 44 \cdot 25 = 13 \cdot 50
\end{aligned}
$$

c measurements at each of the r values of Factor A and r measurements at each of the c values of Factor B. The variability contributions or sums of squares are,

total sums of squares $= \Sigma\Sigma x_{ij} - C.F.$
sum of squares between columns $= \underset{j}{\Sigma}(\Sigma x_{ij})^2/r - C.F.$
and sum of squares between rows $= \underset{i}{\Sigma}(\underset{j}{\Sigma}x_{ij})^2/c - C.F.$

There are a total of 12 degrees of freedom and,

between-rows degrees of freedom $= 4 - 1 = 3$
between-columns degrees of freedom $= 3 - 1 = 2$

The Anovar table is shown in Table L.

Table L—Anovar Table—Two-way

Source	C	d.f.	Var. est.	F
Between cols	107·17	2	53·58	23·8
Between rows	44·25	3	14·75	6·6
Residual	13·50	6	2·25	
Total	164·92	11		

$F_A = 23\cdot8$ (2, 6) significant
$F_B = 6\cdot6$ (3, 6) significant

We now test two values of F, F_A with two and six degrees of freedom, and F_B with three and six degrees of freedom. As shown we conclude that the variance contribution from Factor A is significant, and that the variance contribution from Factor B is significant.

Interactions between factors

When, as is often the case, two factors affecting a variable are not independent, that is, the effect of them acting together differs from the sum of their separate effects, we may wish to check if the effect of their interaction is significant. In a similar way to that in which we tested for the significance of a single factor, we may test for the significance of an interaction. The term described as the residual in the previous example does in fact estimate the underlying variation plus variability due to an interaction. If we use this estimate then we no longer have a residual term from which to make an estimate of the underlying variance, and the size of the study must be increased to provide such an estimate, against which the other estimates can be tested. The simplest way to arrange this is to repeat the measurements for all combinations of the two factors; this is termed a replication. The Anovar table will now take the form shown in Table LI. This is for one repeat of a Random Effects model.

Table LI—Anovar with Replication

Source	S. of Sq.	d. of f.	M.S.	Var. est. F.
Main A	C_A	$c-1$	$C_A/c-1$	$\sigma^2 + 2\,\sigma_{AB}{}^2 + 2r\,\sigma_A{}^2$
Main B	C_B	$r-1$	$C_B/r-1$	$\sigma^2 + 2\,\sigma_{AB}{}^2 + 2c\,\sigma_B{}^2$
Inter AB	C_I	$(c-1)(r-1)$	$C_I/(c-1)(r-1)$	$\sigma^2 + 2\,\sigma_{AB}{}^2$
Residual	C_R	cr	C_R/cr	σ^2
Total	C_{TOT}	$n=2cr$		

We test Interaction against Residual and Main Effects against Interaction.

Irregular variances

The models for the analysis of variance assume that the underlying variation is constant throughout all the measurements, and independent of the means of the various groups of measurements tested. When the variance of the measurements being studied is related to the mean, then this is no longer true, and the results of the analysis may be unreliable. The measurements can be successfully analysed if the variance is first made independent of the mean for the measurements, and simple transformations of the data can be used to effect this.

For measurements which are distributed as the Poisson distribution, which may give trouble in this way, the appropriate transformation is:

$$X'_{ij} = \sqrt{X_{ij}},$$

where X'_{ij} is the transformed measurement.

This may be useful when the measurements analysed are counts of items in the various classes.

If the measurements are ratios such as proportions or percentages, then the transformation is:

$$X'_{ij} = arc\ sin\ .\ \sqrt{X_{ij}}$$

This means find the size in radians of the angle whose sine is $\sqrt{X_{ij}}$. For situations where the factors act relatively instead of additively, as in some economic measurements, the following transformation may be used:

$$X'_{ij} = log. X_{ij}.$$

The analysis of variance proceeds normally after the appropriate transformation has been used.

Factorial designs

Confounding

When more than two factors are tested at the same time the number of interactions increases rapidly, and includes the interactions of factors three at a time, etc., as well as two at a time. In order to test the significance of all interactions, the size of the study must be very large. The object of factorial designs is to allow the testing of factors and interactions in which we are interested with the minimum amount of measurement. In a confounded design the measurements are made on combinations of factors chosen so that the variance estimates derived are of the type,

underlying variance + variance due to the main effect of a factor
    + variance due to interaction effects.

If such a variance estimate is found to differ significantly from the underlying variance it is not possible to decide whether the main effect of the factor or the interaction effect is significant. The main effect of the factor and the interaction effect are said to be confounded.

As the main intention in the analysis of variance is to estimate the significance of the main effects of factors, the design should be planned so that it is safe to assume that the interaction effects are not significant. It is usual to assume this for most interaction effects involving three or more factors.

Latin squares

If we wish to test the main effects of three factors and can assume that all interaction effects are negligible, then a most economic experimental design is possible. It is necessary that each factor takes the same number of values n and we select n^2 out of the possible n^3 combinations of factor values. These are chosen so that no value of one factor occurs more than once in combination with a given value of either of the other factors. This is displayed diagrammatically in Table LII.

Table LII—Latin Square

a	b	c	d	e
e	a	b	c	d
d	e	a	b	c
c	d	e	a	b
b	c	d	e	a

The columns represent different values of Factor A, the rows different values of Factor B, and the five values of Factor C are shown by the letters a, b, c, d, e. A design of this type is described as a latin square.

A latin square design may well be useful when we wish to remove from an analysis of data the effect of a factor which we are not interested in, but which is known to be significant. If we are not careful to arrange our experiments so that the effect of the factor is separable from the other effects, we may find that we have confounded that effect with an effect in which we are interested.

Consider an investigation into the performance of a series of men on a series of machines. If we can only make a limited number of measurements per day, it may be necessary to spread the investigation over several days. If one machine was used each day then the effect of day-of-measurement would be confounded with the machine effect. This might not cause any trouble, but by arranging to make the investigation in the form of a men × machine × days latin square, the three effects can be unambiguously measured.

Questions

1. Analyse the following measurements to see if the three levels of the factor differ significantly.

Level factor	Items counted				
A	5	7	4	9	6
B	8	5	12	7	7
C	3	5	4	9	5

2. Two factors affecting a measurement are tested at five levels each. The measurements made are:

Factor A

		1	2	3	4	5
	1	157	159	164	188	161
	2	167	157	164	179	157
Factor B	3	149	147	153	160	147
	4	185	163	182	191	187
	5	169	173	159	185	171

Test whether there is any significant difference between measurements at the different levels of the factors.

3. Explain what is tested in the analysis of variance, and what assumptions are made about the measurements analysed.

4. What is meant by:

factorial designs,
confounding,
replication, and
latin squares?

5. Explain what is meant by interaction in a two-way analysis of variance. In what way can the number of experiments needed to estimate the effect of different factors on a measurement be reduced?

6. In an investigation into a testing routine the same mixture is supplied to four testers and each uses three different testing procedures to find the percentage of a component present. Assuming all testers are equally proficient in all procedures, test for significant variations between testers and procedures.

Percentages found:

	TESTER			
Procedure	A	B	C	D
1	18·4	18·1	18·2	18·2
2	18·2	18·0	18·2	18·0
3	18·6	18·3	18·5	18·3

7. Explain how the analysis of a Two-way Random Effects model can be extended to study the variances of the three sources of variability present.

8. Explain how increasing the number of observations makes it easier to obtain significant results in the analysis of variance. Discuss how the number of measurements can be decreased without losing the ability to test several factors simultaneously.

9. (*a*) What is the purpose of replication? Invent an example to illustrate your answer.

(*b*) Similarly explain confounding.

10. A test of four levels of one Factor (*A*) against three levels of another Factor (*B*), both random effects, is replicated once and the following results obtained.

$$C_{TOT} \quad = 249\cdot14$$
$$C_{RES} \quad = 22\cdot18$$
$$C_{MAIN\ A} = 39\cdot41$$
$$C_{MAIN\ B} = 108\cdot23$$

Draw up the Anovar table and test all effects for significance.

CHAPTER SIXTEEN

CORRELATION AND LINEAR REGRESSION

Correlation

Related measurements

W HEN two series of measurements are made at the same time, or on the same object, then we may wish to investigate possible relationships between corresponding pairs of measurements. A relationship between two such sets of measurements such that the value of one is affected by the value of the other is described as a correlation.

If the measurements in one series increase as the measurements in the other series increase, then they are said to be positively correlated; and if the measurements in one series decrease as the measurements in the other series increase, then they are said to be negatively correlated. A measure to assess the degree of correlation between two sets of measurements can be developed by first constructing a diagram of the data.

Scatter diagrams

If there are n measurements of type X and a corresponding set of n measurements of type Y then they can be shown on a graph whose axes have scales for X and Y and whose points are the n pairs of measurements (X, Y). Such a diagram may be described as a scatter diagram and an example is shown in Fig. 49.

If we calculate the two means $\bar{X}$ and $\bar{Y}$ and draw lines parallel to the axes through the point $(\bar{X}, \bar{Y})$ we will divide the scatter diagram into four quadrants, as shown in Fig. 50. The extent to which the points are concentrated in diagonally opposite quadrants represents a measure of the correlation between X and Y. Referring to Fig. 50 the signs of the quantities $(X - \bar{X})$ and $(Y - \bar{Y})$ are shown and the signs of the product term $(X - \bar{X})(Y - \bar{Y})$. As the term $(X - \bar{X})(Y - \bar{Y})$ takes the same sign in opposite quadrants, the size of the sum $\Sigma(X - \bar{X})(Y - \bar{Y})$ will be a measure of the correlation between X and Y.

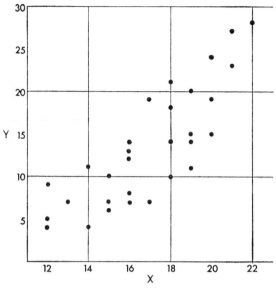

FIG. 49.—*Scatter diagram*

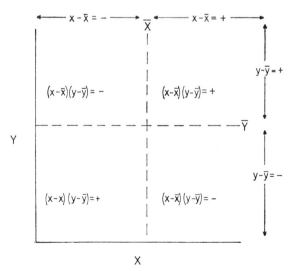

FIG. 50.—*The signs of the quadrants in the scatter diagram*

When the measurements are positively correlated this sum will be large and positive and when the measurements are negatively correlated it will be large and negative. When there is little correlation the points will be evenly scattered around the diagrams and the terms will tend to cancel out leaving a small sum.

The correlation coefficient

While the sum $\Sigma(X - \bar{X})(Y - \bar{Y})$ is a measure of correlation, it is not suitable for comparisons with other sets of figures, as it depends on the number of terms summed and on the variabilities of X and Y. A satisfactory measure is derived by dividing the sum by the number of terms summed, and by the standard deviations of X and Y. The measure so obtained is called the product moment correlation coefficient, and is symbolised by the letter r.

$$r = \frac{\Sigma(X - \bar{X})(Y - \bar{Y})}{n \cdot s_X \cdot s_Y}.$$

The letter ρ can be used to symbolise the population value of the correlation coefficient, and if the sets of measurements are a random sample from the possible population of values of X and Y, then r is an estimate of ρ. The formula given for r can then be rewritten as

$$r = \frac{\frac{1}{n}\left[\Sigma XY - \frac{\Sigma X \cdot \Sigma Y}{n}\right]}{s_X \cdot s_Y}.$$

The top line of this equation represents a quantity known as the co-variance of X and Y; its similarity to the variance of X or Y should be noted. If we are estimating a population value from a sample, then the variances of X and Y and the co-variance must be calculated with the divisor $n - 1$ to avoid bias. Writing out the formulae in full we find that this divisor cancels out and the formula for r is simplified.

$$r = \frac{\Sigma XY - \frac{\Sigma XY}{n}}{\sqrt{\Sigma X^2 - \frac{(\Sigma X)^2}{n}} \cdot \sqrt{\Sigma Y^2 - \frac{(\Sigma Y)^2}{n}}}.$$

It is convenient to use symbols for the sums of squares and products, as in the last chapter, *i.e.*,

$$C_{XX} = \Sigma X^2 - (\Sigma X)^2/n$$
$$C_{YY} = \Sigma Y^2 - (\Sigma Y)^2/n$$
$$C_{XY} = \Sigma XY - \Sigma X \cdot \Sigma Y/n,$$

and this notation will be used in the calculation of r.

In this form $r = C_{XY}/\sqrt{C_{XX} \cdot C_{YY}}$.

The terms C_{XX}, C_{YY}, C_{XY} are corrected for the means of X and Y and r is a dimensionless number, as units of X and Y occur equally on the top and bottom of the fraction. This means that any coding applied to X or Y will not affect the value of r, and in calculating r we may choose a coding from X and Y to x and y which most eases calculation, and then use $r = C_{xy}/\sqrt{C_{xx}} \cdot \sqrt{C_{yy}}$.

The calculation of the correlation coefficient

EXAMPLE I

The sales figures per day of lemonade, and the maximum temperature during each day are recorded by a store manager. Calculate the correlation coefficient as a measure of the dependence of the sales on the temperature.

Temperature °C	12	12	13	15	16	18
Sales, bottles	5	9	7	7	14	18

Temperature	18	16	19	20	21	18
Sales	14	13	20	19	27	10

Temperature	17	14	12	11	15	17
Sales	7	4	4	5	10	19

Temperature	19	20	20	19	16	15
Sales	15	15	24	11	8	6

Temperature	16	16	18	21	22	19
Sales	7	12	21	23	28	14

Note that only thirty readings are given in this example; it is preferable to have as large a sample as possible but the calculation is best illustrated by a limited amount of data.

We can reduce the arithmetic by coding, and we then require the quantities n, Σx, Σy, Σx^2, Σy^2 and Σxy. The layout of the calculation is shown in Table LIII.

LIII—Calculation of Correlation Coefficient

X	Y	X − 17	Y − 15	x^2	y^2	xy
		x	y			
12	5	−5	−10	25	100	50
12	9	−5	−6	25	36	30
13	7	−4	−8	16	64	32
15	7	−2	−8	4	64	16
16	14	−1	−1	1	1	1
18	18	1	3	1	9	3
18	14	1	−1	1	1	−1
16	13	−1	−2	1	4	2
19	20	2	5	4	25	10
20	19	3	4	9	16	12
21	27	4	12	16	144	48
18	10	1	−5	1	25	−5
17	7	0	−8	0	64	0
14	4	−3	−11	9	121	33
12	4	−5	−11	25	121	55
14	11	−3	−4	9	16	12
15	10	−2	−5	4	25	10
17	19	0	4	0	16	0
19	15	2	0	4	0	0
20	15	3	0	9	0	0
20	24	3	9	9	81	27
19	11	2	−4	4	16	−8
16	8	−1	−7	1	49	7
15	6	−2	−9	4	81	18
16	7	−1	−8	1	64	8
16	12	−1	−3	1	9	3
18	21	1	6	1	36	6
21	23	4	8	4	8	32
22	28	5	13	25	169	65
19	14	2	−1	4	1	−2
		+34	+64	218	1366	+480
		−36	−112			−16
		−2	−48			464

n = 30, Σx = −2, Σy = −48
Σx^2 = 218, Σy^2 = 1366, Σxy = 464
C_{xx} = 218 − (−2)²/30 = 218 − 0·13 = 217·87
C_{yy} = 1366 − (−48)²/30 = 1366 − 76·6 = 1289·4
C_{yx} = 464 − (−2) (−48) 30 = 464 − 3·2 = 461·8
$\sqrt{C_{xx}}$ = 14·76
$\sqrt{C_{yy}}$ = 35·91
r = 461·8/(14·76) (35·91) = 461·8/530·0
= 0·87

The significance of the correlation coefficient

The correlation coefficient can take values between -1 and $+1$ and has the following significance:

$r = 1$,   measurements show perfect positive correlation,
$r < 1$,   measurements positively correlated,
$r = 0$,   measurements uncorrelated,
$r < 0$,   measurements negatively correlated, and
$r = -1$, measurements show perfect negative correlation.

The appearance of the scatter diagrams for these cases is shown in Fig. 51.

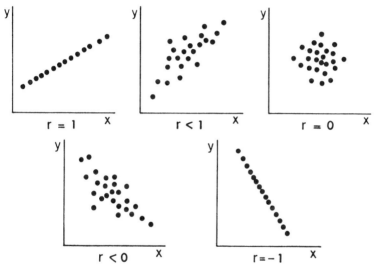

FIG. 51.—*Scatter diagrams for various values of* r

To test if the value of r found is greater than would be expected by chance when the measurements are not correlated, we must test the value of r against the hypothesis that $r = 0$. The distribution of r is known, and on the assumption that the measurements are from normally distributed populations, the hypothesis may be tested by calculating $t = r \cdot \sqrt{n-2}/\sqrt{1-r^2}$ and referring to the "t" table with $n - 2$ degrees of freedom.

An approximate test is given by calculating the quantity $2/\sqrt{n}$, then if $|r| > 2/\sqrt{n}$ the hypothesis is rejected at the 5% significance level and the correlation accepted as real.

The interpretation of correlation

When a value of r is found to be significantly different from o, we say that the measurements are correlated. This means only that the measurements we have examined show a straight line relationship. This may be the result of a cause and effect relationship between the measurements, but this can only be established by other information, and not from the statistical results alone. On the other hand, the absence of a significantly large value of r does not indicate that the measurements are totally unrelated. If the form of the relationship is not linear, then the highest value r can take is limited. Figure 52 shows a case in which measurements are perfectly related, but the value of r is o!

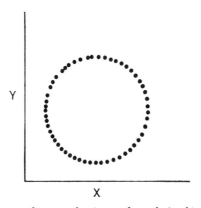

FIG. 52.—*Scatter diagram showing perfect relationship with $r = $ o*

A common situation in which a high value of r is found, in the absence of a true relationship between sets of measurements, occurs when the measurements examined are related to a third set of measurements. Any two series of measurements showing a steady change with time will be found to be correlated. This does not give us any information about them unless we allow for their dependence on time. This can be done by the use of partial correlation coefficients (see p. 224).

Rank correlation

Other correlation coefficients can be designed which are not tied to the linear model as is r. A useful coefficient is Spearman's rank correlation coefficient, which will be symbolised by r_{sp}. To calculate this coefficient each of the series of measurements must be ranked from 1 to n. The ranks of each pair of measurements are compared and the difference in ranks d noted. Then, $r_{sp} = 1 - 6\Sigma d^2/n(n^2 - 1)$. The measure was derived by considering the maximum disarrangement of one series of ranks relative to the other which was possible. It measures the degree to

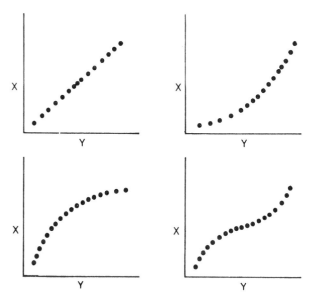

FIG. 53.—*Scatter diagrams with* $r_{sp} = 1$

which the two series of measurements are related to any continuously increasing or decreasing relationship. This is illustrated in Fig. 53 where all the relationships have $r_{sp} = 1$ although only the linear relationship would have $r = 1$.

When calculating r_{sp} it may be found that there is more than one of a given value in the measurements. Each of the measurements is assigned the average of the ranks which span the measurements, *e.g.*

Measurement	0·1	0·5	0·6	0·6	0·7	1·3
Rank	1	2	3·5	3·5	5	6

The value of r_{sp} found may be tested against hypothesis that it represents a chance deviation from the value o in exactly the same way as r, and the same problems of interpretation also apply.

EXAMPLE 2

The average output of sixteen men is measured and compared with the length of time they have been employed. Is there evidence of increasing output with time?

Time employed, weeks			4	6	6	$6\frac{1}{2}$	8	10	12
Output, units			164	170	175	170	180	192	196
Time	16	18	18	20	20	24	24	26	28
Output	193	192	200	196	198	196	203	195	201

The calculation is shown in Table LIV.

Table LIV—Calculation of Rank Correlation Coefficient

X	Y	Rank X	Rank Y	d	d²
4	164	1	1	0	0
6	170	2·5	2·5	0	0
6	175	2·5	4	1·5	2·25
6·5	170	4	2·5	1·5	2·25
8	180	5	5	0	0
10	192	6	6·5	0·5	0·25
12	196	7	11	4	16
16	193	8	8	0	0
18	192	9·5	6·5	3	9
18	200	9·5	14	4·5	20·25
20	196	11·5	11	0·5	0·25
20	198	11·5	13	1·5	2·25
24	196	13·5	11	1·5	2·25
24	203	13·5	16	2·5	6·25
26	195	15	9	6	36
28	201	16	15	1	1

$$98$$

$$r_{sp} = 1 - 6 \times 98/16^3 - 16$$
$$= 1 - 0·14 = 0·86$$

The value of r_{sp} found is significant at the 5% significance level, and we conclude that there is a relationship between the time on the job and output. For comparison, the value of r for these measurements is 0·87.

The rank correlation coefficient is useful when the measurements are known to be derived from grossly non-normal distributions and the product moment correlation coefficient is not reliable. It is, of course, also useful when the data is in the form of ranks and is not available as numerical measurements. This often occurs when comparison judgments are possible, but measurement difficult.

Linear regression

Linear relationships

When a correlation exists between two sets of measurements we may wish to use one measurement to predict the other. In the example given earlier, the store manager might wish to use the forecast temperature for the next day to decide on his stock level. We can do this by deriving an equation which represents the relationship between the measurements, and the simplest and most commonly used equation is based on the assumption of a linear relationship. The equation which represents this relationship is $\hat{Y} = a + bX$, where $\hat{Y}$ is the estimate of Y given by the equation. a and b are the constants which define the position of the line. b defines the slope of the line and is called the regression coefficient, and the equation is described as the line of regression of Y on X.

If we wish to predict the value of X from values of Y we require the line of regression $\hat{X} = a_1 + b_1 Y$.

The least squares criterion

By taking different values for a and b we can draw many lines through the points, and we require some criterion by which to decide which line gives the best estimate $\hat{Y}$. The one employed is that the sum of the squares of the deviations between actual and predicted values of Y is a minimum. If $\hat{Y}_i$ is the predicted value of Y corresponding to $X = X_i$ and Y_i is an observed value of Y corresponding to X_i, we require that $\Sigma(Y_i - \hat{Y}_i)^2$ be a minimum. Substituting the equation $\hat{Y}_i = a + bX_i$ for $\hat{Y}_i$ we require $\Sigma[Y_i - (a + bX_i)]^2$ to be a minimum, and by expanding this expression and using differential calculus to satisfy the condition of minimum value, we obtain two equations which between them give the required values of a and b. These may be solved to give,

$$b = C_{XY}/C_{XX} \text{ and } a = \bar{Y} - b\bar{X}.$$

The regression line of X on Y can be treated in an exactly similar way, to give,

$$b_1 = C_{XY}/C_{YY} \text{ and } a_1 = \bar{X} - b_1\bar{Y}.$$

The two regression lines do not coincide unless X and Y show a perfect linear relationship; this arises as the least squares criterion used differs for each equation. The regression line of X on Y minimises deviations in the Y direction, the regression line of Y on X deviations in the X direction.

The calculation of a regression line

The quantities required to calculate a and b have already been calculated when finding the correlation coefficient. However, a and b are not independent of the units of X and Y, and if coding is used the coding must be reversed before the equations given are used to find a and b. If the coding is

$$x = (X - c_X)/b_X \text{ and } y = (Y - c_Y)/b_Y$$

then we must note that

$$\bar{X} = \bar{x} \cdot b_X + c_X \qquad\qquad b = b_x \cdot b_Y/b_X$$
$$\bar{Y} = \bar{y} \cdot b_Y + c_Y \qquad\qquad b_1 = b_y \cdot b_X/b_Y$$

where $b_x = C_{xy}/C_{xx}$ $b_y = C_{xy}/C_{yy}$.

EXAMPLE 3

Using the data from Table LIII.

$$c_X = 17, c_Y = 15, b_X = b_Y = 1, n = 30, \Sigma x = -2, \Sigma y = -48,$$
$$C_{xx} = 217\cdot87, C_{xy} = 461\cdot8.$$
$$\bar{X} = -0\cdot07 + 17 = 16\cdot93$$
$$\bar{Y} = -1\cdot6 + 15 = 13\cdot4$$
$$b = 461\cdot8/217\cdot87 = 2\cdot12$$
$$a = 13\cdot4 - 2\cdot12 \cdot 16\cdot93 = -22\cdot49$$
$$\therefore \hat{Y} = 2\cdot12 X - 22\cdot49.$$

The measurements and the regression line are shown in Fig. 54.

Anovar for a regression line

We can regard the total variability shown by Y as derived from two sources, the variability which would exist in Y if X were constant, and the variability caused in Y by changes in X. This is usually described as:

variability in Y = variability about regression line
+ variability due to regression line.

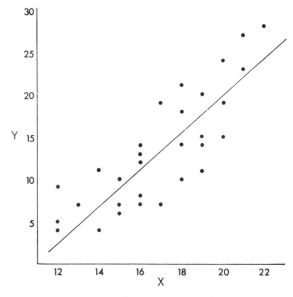

Fig. 54.—*Linear regression line*

The variability in Y is C_{YY}, and that due to the regression line is given by bC_{XY}; the variability about the regression may be found by difference. The total variability has $n - 1$ degrees of freedom, and the variability due to the regression line 1 degree of freedom, leaving $n - 2$ degrees of freedom for the variability about the regression.

These may be combined in the Anovar table shown in Table LV.

Table LV—Anovar for Regression Equation

Source	S.S.	d.f.	Var. est.	F
Regression	bC_{XY}	1	$s_R^2 = bC_{XY}$	s_R^2/s^2
About regression	$C_{YY} - bC_{XY}$	$n - 2$	$s^2 = C_{YY} - bC_{XY}/$ $n - 2$	
Total	C_{YY}	$n - 1$		

The significance of the regression may be tested by comparing the variance due to the regression and the variance about the regression, using the F-test.

Proportion of variability explained

The amount of the total variability explained by the regression is bC_{XY}, and so the proportion explained is bC_{XY}/C_{YY}. This can be rearranged to give,

$$b \cdot C_{XY}/C_{YY} = (C_{XY}/C_{XX}) \cdot C_{XY}/C_{YY} = r^2.$$

This gives a useful way of estimating the efficiency of a regression when models other than the linear regression model are used. The higher r^2, the better the regression model.

Estimates from regression line

The purpose of regression analysis is to show where there are relationships between sets of measurements, and then to use the relationship found to predict one measurement from the other. In addition, we require some measure of the confidence we can place in the estimates.

The estimate of Y is easily found by substituting the relevant value of $\bar{X}$ in the equation of the regression line. There are three sources of error in this estimate, the variability about the regression line, the variability in the mean $\bar{Y}$ and the variability in the regression coefficient, and these must all be taken into account when setting confidence limits for an estimate of Y. We have already found the variance about the regression $= s_Y^2$. The variance of the mean $\bar{Y}$ is given by s_Y^2/n and the variance of b_Y by s_Y^2/C_{XX}. The effect of the variance of b_Y on the variance of an estimate of $\bar{Y}$ will depend on the distance from the mean $(X - \bar{X})$ as errors in the slope will be most noticeable at the ends of the line. The contribution to the variance of an estimate of $\bar{Y}$ from this source is

$$s_Y^2 \cdot (X - \bar{X})^2/C_{XX}.$$

These contributions may now be combined to give the total variance of an estimate of

$$Y = s_Y^2 + s_Y^2/n + s_Y^2(X - \bar{X})^2/C_{XX}$$

or

$$s_Y^2[1 + 1/n + (X - \bar{X})^2/C_{XX}]$$

For small samples this estimate will be distributed as the "t"-distribution with $n - 2$ degrees of freedom, and the 95% confidence limits for Y are

$$Y = \hat{Y} \pm t_{0.025} \cdot s_Y \sqrt{1 + 1/n + (X - \bar{X})^2/C_{XX}}$$

$t_{0.025}$ is the value of "t" at the 0.025, probability level with $n - 2$ degrees of freedom. For large samples, $n > 30$ the normal distribution is a good approximation and the limits become

$$Y = \hat{Y} \pm 1.96 s_Y \sqrt{1 + 1/n + (X - \bar{X})^2/C_{XX}}.$$

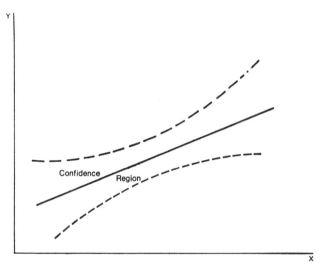

FIG. 55.—*Confidence limits for regression*

Transformations

If we have sets of measurements which are related by a non-linear relationship, it may be possible to set up a linear regression between them by use of a transformation. A common example of this is where the measurements we wish to predict are related to time by a growth or decay relationship. The typical form of the relationships is,

either $Y = Ae^{+Bt}$, growth,

or $Y = Ae^{-Bt}$, decay.

If we take logarithms these become,

log. $Y = log.\ A + Bt$, and
log. $Y = log.\ A - Bt$.

Log. A and B are constants as in the simple linear regression, and the regression of Y on t can be found and used to predict Y for future values of t.

Questions

1. Sales of ice-cream appear to be dependent on the maximum temperature reached during a day. The following information has been collected:

Max. Temp. °C	10	12	15	18	20	17		
Sales kg	1100	1050	1250	1500	1550	1600		
Max. Temp. °C	21	22	21	18	17	15		
Sales kg	1650	1800	1850	1700	1600	1200		
Max. Temp. °C	18	20	20	22	17	14	13	9
Sales kg	1800	1850	1750	1950	1800	1500	1300	1000

Plot the data on a scatter diagram.

Calculate the product moment correlation coefficient between these two quantities and hence estimate how much of the variability in ice-cream sales is dependent on temperature.

Obtain the regression line of ice-cream sales on temperature and plot this on your scatter diagram.

Calculate the 90% confidence interval for the estimate of ice-cream sales when the temperature is 21°C.

2. The product moment correlation coefficient measured between fifty pairs of measurements is found to be $r = 0.24$. Comment on the significance of this result. The Spearman's rank correlation coefficient for the same data is $r_{sp} = 0.82$. Comment on the significance of this result and the possible reasons for its wide divergence from the value of r.

If it is necessary to use one of the measurements to predict the other, what kind of adjustments may be necessary to the data?

3. Two judges in a beauty contest rank the twenty contestants in the following ways.

Contestant	First Judge	Second Judge
A	6	5
B	12	11
C	2	6
D	5	1
E	11	16
F	1	3
G	10	14
H	16	7
I	18	12
J	14	18
K	3	2
L	17	8
M	9	13
N	20	15
O	4	10
P	19	20
Q	13	17
R	7	9
S	15	19
T	8	4

Is there any significant difference in the judging methods used by the two judges?

State clearly and justify your choice of significance level at which to carry out the test.

4. A sales manager proposes to predict sales for the next year by extrapolating the line of best fit to the last four years' figures. Discuss the dangers in this procedure.

5. The correlation between two quantities is 0·83, the two quantities show correlations of 0·91 and 0·75 with time respectively. If 26 sets of measurements have been used, comment on the results.

CHAPTER SEVENTEEN

MULTIVARIABLE METHODS

The multivariable problem

Uncontrolled factors

MOST of the methods of investigating the interrelations between measurements described so far have been limited to very simple situations. In scientific investigations situations of this type may be created by the careful control of the experimental environment, so that the effect on a system of a change in one factor at a time can be examined. In most industrial and commercial investigations this is no longer possible. The factors effective in a given situation may be uncontrollable, as in much market research, or their adjustment may be limited practically, as in investigations on operating industrial processes. Faced with this situation, there are two courses open to the investigator. Either the situation is simplified by assuming that only the major factors are important, and that the other influences are part of the general variability of the situation, or the analysis must be capable of handling many factors or variables. The first alternative may be useful in investigating the gross characteristics of a situation, but limits very largely the scope of the investigator. The second inevitably leads to a very large amount of calculation, which is in general beyond the capabilities of hand computation.

The use of computers

The methods suitable for the investigation of multivariable situations were suggested long before they were practical. The tool which made the needed large-scale computations feasible is the electronic digital computer. A computer is very well suited to the carrying out of a large number of repetitive calculations, and this is precisely the requirement in statistical calculations. This means that it is now possible to consider the analysis of almost any size of multivariable problem, the main restriction being the time and effort needed to collect the basic data, and arrange it in a form suitable for computer processing.

The development of computer programming languages such as Fortran and Algol has made it possible for investigators to program their own material and so keep a close control on the analysis. There are also a number of programs which will perform the more frequently required statistical calculations and which have lead to a vast increase in the ease with which a computer can be used by a non-specialist, and so of the statistical work which is carried out by computer.

The convenience of using already written and tested programs does present a slight danger in that it may encourage a stereotyped approach to problems. The standard programs are best used for parts of problems or for when they exactly suit the situation being investigated.

Factorial investigations

The interpretation of factorial investigations

The extension of the analysis of variance to the study of the effects of many factors has already been indicated. The number of experiments required to estimate the effects in a factorial investigation increases rapidly with the number of factors considered, and the size of the investigation is usually limited by the use of factorial designs. For many factor investigations it is usual to allow each factor two values only, and even then to estimate all main effects and interactions would require 2^{n+1} observations for n factors. The size of the investigation is reduced by confounding, so that the higher interactions are confounded with the main effects and lower interactions.

The interpretation of these many-factor investigations does raise one new point: if an interaction is found to be significant, then the corresponding main effects, even if significant, may not be meaningful. If we are studying fixed effect factors then the presence of an interaction implies that the main effect of one interacting factor is different for the different values of the other interacting factor. If a factor and its interactions are not found to be significant, it does mean that the factor can be omitted from future investigations in the same range of values of the factor.

Multiple regression

The multiple regression model

The methods used to find the equation showing the dependence of one measurement on another by linear regression can be extended to the case of dependence of a measurement on many others. Again the model usually adopted is to assume that all the relationships are linear as this allows a straightforward solution. If the measurement we are studying is Y and the measurements on which it may depend are $X_1, X_2, X_3 \ldots$, then the equation used is

$$\hat{Y} = b_o + b_1 X_1 + b_2 X_2 + b_3 X_3 \ldots$$

where b_1, b_2, b_3 are regression coefficients, and b_o a numerical constant ($= a$ in the simple linear model). The values of b_1, b_2, b_3 ... are as before found by using the least squares criterion, but it is not possible to give a direct visualisation of the model, as the equation now describes a hyperplane in a multidimensional space.

Application of the least squares criterion leads to a set of equations relating b_o, b_1, b_2 . . . and the sums of squares and products

$$C_{Y1}, C_{Y2}, C_{11}, C_{12} \ldots$$

where $\quad C_{Y1} = \Sigma Y X_1 - (\Sigma Y . \Sigma X_1)/n$

and $\quad C_{12} = \Sigma X_1 X_2 - (\Sigma X_1 . \Sigma X_2)/n$

These equations are called the normal equations and for the equation $\hat{Y} = b_o + b_1 X_1 + b_2 X_2 + b_3 X_3$ would be,

$$C_{11} b_1 + C_{12} b_2 + C_{13} b_3 = C_{Y1}$$
$$C_{12} b_1 + C_{22} b_2 + C_{23} b_3 = C_{Y2}$$
$$C_{13} b_1 + C_{32} b_2 + C_{33} b_3 = C_{Y3}$$

and $\quad b_o = \bar{Y} - (b_1 \bar{X}_1 + b_2 \bar{X}_2 + b_3 \bar{X}_3)$

The simultaneous equations can be solved by conventional algebraic methods but, especially as the number of equations increases, may more conveniently be solved by the use of the methods of matrix algebra. As indicated earlier, the routine of calculations necessary, first to find the sum of products and squares, and then to solve the equations, increases extremely rapidly with the increasing size of the model, and these calculations are best carried out by a digital computer.

Tests on regression equations

The methods of testing for the significance of a linear regression equation can be extended to the multiple regression equation, and the analysis of variance is particularly useful. The total variability in Y is as before and the variability due to the regression is given by $b_1 C_{Y1} + b_2 C_{Y2} \ldots b_k C_{Yk}$ with k degrees of freedom, and the variability about the regression is found by difference. The variance due to the regression can now be tested against the variance about the regression by testing

$$F = \frac{variance\ due\ to\ regression}{variance\ about\ regression},$$

with k and $n - k - 1$ degrees of freedom.

When there are many possible measurements which could be included in the analysis, we may wish to test if the addition of further quantities $X_{k+1} \ldots X_{k+q}$ will lead to significant increase in the amount of the variability of Y explained. We can do this by calculating the regression on the k, X measurements, and then on the $k + q$, X measurements. The amount of variability accounted for in each case is found and the difference is ascribed to the additional q, X measurements included. The Anovar table is shown in Table LVI, and the significance of the extra measurements tested by

$$F = \frac{variance\ due\ to\ extra\ measurements}{variance\ about\ regression}$$

with q and $n - (k + q + 1)$ degrees of freedom.

Table LVI—Test of Significance of Extra Factors

Source	Sums of Squares	d.f.	Var. Est.	F
$k + q$ factors	C_{k+q}	$k + q$		
k factors	C_k	k		
q factors	$C_q = C_{k+q} - C_k$	q	$s_q^2 = C_q/q$	s_q^2/s^2
Residual	$C_{RES} = C_{TOT} - C_{k+q}$	$n - (k + q + 1)$	$s^2 = C_{RES}/(n - k + q + 1)$	
Total	C_{TOT}	$n - 1$		

Test: $F_q = s_q^2/s^2$ with q and $(n - (k + q + 1))$ degrees of freedom.

The use of multiple regression equations

One advantage of the multiple regression model is that the addition of further quantities as suggested above cannot lead to a reduction of the variability in Y being explained. This can lead to the temptation to add into the equation every available measurement and this is possible, but should be followed by a routine aimed at rejecting the quantities whose contribution to the variability explained is not significant.

In the model there is no restriction on the nature of the quantities X and these may well be closely interrelated. When this is so, then the major effect of these quantities will usually be ascribed to one of them by the equation, and the quantity which appears to be most important in this way may vary considerably as other quantities are added to or deleted from the equation. These apparently large changes in the equation do mean that all the regression coefficients must be recalculated when a change is made, but do not indicate any change in the validity of the equations. It is not possible simply to delete a non-significant measurement and its corresponding regression coefficient from the equation, without altering the other regression coefficients.

This variation in emphasis does mean that the size of regression coefficients should not be used as a measure of the relative importance of the corresponding measurements, when the measurements are closely interrelated.

When a multiple regression equation is used as an aid in forecasting it may be desirable to give confidence limits for the estimate obtained. These are derived as before from the variance about the regression and contributions for the variance about the mean of the forecast quantity, and for the variance due to each of the regression coefficients.

Proportion of variability explained

The amount of the total variability explained by the regression is

$$b_1 C_{Y1} + b_2 C_{Y2} + b_3 C_{Y3} \ldots$$

and so the proportion explained is

$$(b_1 C_{Y1} + b_2 C_{Y2} + b_3 C_{Y3} \ldots)/C_{YY}.$$

By analogy with the simple linear regression, this is given the symbol R^2. The value R is termed the coefficient of multiple correlation, and may be interpreted in a similar manner to r.

Curvilinear regression

The analysis of a curvilinear regression line by transforming the measurements so that it can be treated as a linear regression line has been mentioned. An alternative approach which is of general application is to regard curvilinear regression as a special case of linear regression. A curve may be approximated by a suitable polynomial equation, and the corresponding regression model would be,

$$\hat{Y} = a + b, X + b_2X^2 + b_3X^2 \ldots$$

If we regard the successive powers of X as separate quantities X_1, X_2, then this becomes, $\hat{Y} = a + b_1X_1 + b_2X_2 + b_3X_3 \ldots$ and the analysis proceeds as above.

The improvement in fit obtained by changing to a higher order polynomial is tested by the Anovar table, the extra term being treated as an extra quantity in the equation as before.

Regression on independent measurements

Although the use of a computer eases the labour, the necessity to recalculate all the regression coefficients when changing the number of measurements used in a regression equation is burdensome. If a measurement is independent, that is, uncorrelated with any other measurements in the regression equation, then its regression coefficient will stay unchanged, and the measurement can be added to or deleted from the equation without affecting any other regression coefficients. There is obviously a considerable advantage in using such independent measurements, and they are described as being *orthogonal* to one another and to the other measurements.

A series of measurements can be transformed into a new series of quantities which are orthogonal to each other, and this is a part of the field of correlation analysis. A special case occurs in curvilinear regression, where, by suitable choice of combinations of the powers of X involved, the effect of changing to a higher order polynomial can be studied without altering the regression coefficient used for the lower order polynomial. The combinations of powers of X used are known as orthogonal polynomials.

Multiple correlation

Partial correlation coefficients

We have been discussing the situation where several series of measurements are closely related, and it may be of interest to examine the correlation between pairs of such measurements when the effect of the others is allowed for. Consider three sets of measurements X_1, X_2, X_3 and let the correlation coefficients between them, calculated by taking in pairs and using the standard calculation, be r_{12}, r_{13}, r_{23}. We are interested in the correlation between X_1 and X_2 and find r_{12} is large, but we know that X_1 and X_2 are both strongly correlated to X_3 as shown by r_{13} and r_{23}. The correlation between X_1 and X_2 which is not caused by their relationship to X_3 is given by $r_{12 \cdot 3}$, and this is found from the formula

$$r_{12 \cdot 3} = \frac{r_{12} - r_{13} \cdot r_{23}}{\sqrt{(1 - r_{13}^2)(1 - r_{23}^2)}}$$

EXAMPLE

Given $r_{1 \cdot 2} = 0.79$, $r_{13} = 0.91$, $r_{23} = 0.85$ what is the value of r_{123}?

$$r_{12 \cdot 3} = \frac{0.79 - 0.91 \times 0.85}{\sqrt{(1 - 0.91^2)(1 - 0.85^2)}} = 0.076.$$

If there are fifty measurements of X_1, X_2, X_3, r_{12} would be significant at the 5% significance level but $r_{12 \cdot 3}$ would not.

This illustrates the ease with which spurious correlations can arise, especially when the existence of measurements such as X_3 is not realised.

The method can be extended to more than three measurements, but the arithmetic involved increases rapidly, and the interpretation of the results may not be as easy as in the example given. Even when the relationship between two measurements, as measured by the partial correlation coefficient, is known, it may be impossible to observe the measurements independently of other factors, and the relationship may be of no practical interest.

The correlation matrix

When a large number of sets of measurements have to be compared the investigation of their interrelation can be started by the calculation of the correlation matrix. This is the array of all possible correlation coefficients between the sets of measurements. For measurements X_1, X_2, X_3, X_4, X_5 the matrix is,

$$
\begin{array}{ccccc}
| & r_{12} & r_{13} & r_{14} & r_{15} \\
r_{21} & | & r_{23} & r_{24} & r_{25} \\
r_{31} & r_{32} & | & r_{34} & r_{35} \\
r_{41} & r_{42} & r_{43} & | & r_{45} \\
r_{51} & r_{52} & r_{53} & r_{54} & | \\
\end{array}
$$

The array is symmetrical as any correlation coefficient r_{12} is symmetrical with respect to the measurements X_1 and X_2 and so $r_{12} = r_{21}$. The diagonal consists of the correlations of the measurements with themselves, which are necessarily perfect and so all have the value one.

The array is calculated by first finding the array of sums and products,

$$
\begin{array}{ccccc}
C_{11} & C_{12} & C_{13} & C_{14} & C_{15} \\
C_{21} & C_{22} & C_{23} & C_{24} & C_{25} \\
C_{31} & C_{32} & C_{33} & C_{34} & C_{35} \\
C_{41} & C_{42} & C_{43} & C_{44} & C_{45} \\
C_{51} & C_{52} & C_{53} & C_{54} & C_{55} \\
\end{array}
$$

and then dividing the rows by $\sqrt{C_{11}}$, $\sqrt{C_{22}}$, etc., and the columns also by $\sqrt{C_{11}}$, $\sqrt{C_{22}}$, etc. This means that any sum, say C_{34}, is divided by two square root terms, and $C_{34}/\sqrt{C_{33}} \cdot \sqrt{C_{44}} = r_{34}$. A visual examination of the matrix will reveal which of the sets of measurements show strong correlations, and by interchanging rows or columns, strongly related measurements can be grouped together. The clusters of interrelations apparent in this way can then be isolated for further investigation. Alternatively the whole of the matrix may be analysed to try to identify the components of variability in it.

Component analysis

If we have a series of sets of measurements $X_1, X_2, X_3 \ldots$ then we can combine these to form a new series of quantities $T_1, T_2, T_3 \ldots$. The new quantities can be linear functions of the originals of the type, $T_1 = k_{11}X_1 + k_{12}X_2 \ldots$ where $k_{11}, k_{12} \ldots$ are numerical constants, and can be chosen so that the total variability in the T quantities is the same as in the X quantities.

There are an infinite number of ways in which this can be done, but the choice can be restricted to find useful combinations only.

In particular we can choose the first combination T_1 to have the maximum possible variability, the second to have the maximum variability of what is left and to be orthogonal to T_1, and so on. This will give us a series of combinations which account for decreasing amounts of the variability present and which are mutually orthogonal. If we start from the correlation matrix, these are described as the principal components of the matrix. The exact combinations of the original quantities which they represent will depend on the data available and will change as other quantities or data are available. They can, however, indicate which combinations of the original quantities represent the largest sources of variability in the overall system and may indicate future lines of inquiry.

It is usual to find that the first few combinations account for the majority of the variability present, and that we can replace quantities of type X by, say, three of type T. Where the combinations appear to have some real meaning they can be used in a multiple regression equation, and are easy to handle, being orthogonal to one another. This means that it may be possible to replace a regression on n interdependent quantities by one on, say, three orthogonal quantities, a great increase in simplicity.

The principal components are extracted from the matrix by iterative methods, and these by definition require a large amount of repetitive calculation which is best carried out by the use of a computer. Standard programmes are available to ease this part of an investigation and to make such investigations feasible.

Factor analysis

The principal components may not represent combinations of the original quantities with any apparent real meaning, and yet it may be obvious that there is a series of common factors, of sources of variation, in the original data. The principal components are not the only orthogonal combinations of the original quantities possible, and combinations may be chosen which are more easily interpreted, although still mutually orthogonal. Such combinations are described as factors and the methods of finding them factor analysis. The methods have been developed considerably, originally for the analysis of psychological data, but recently in the analysis of large-scale market research investigations, particularly for identifying purchaser characteristics.

The interpretation of components and factors

To give any meaning to a principal component of a matrix, or to a factor, requires a considerable knowledge of the data involved. This identification of mathematical quantities with real effects and relationships is not strictly a part of the statistical analysis of the data, and should not be attempted except with expert knowledge of the data. This is especially true of factor analysis as the factors, unlike principal components, are based on a computational process which includes a large subjective element. Despite this the methods do give a way of attempting to simplify the large amounts of data which are often available for analysis, and certainly are capable of creating new ideas for the arrangement and analysis of such data.

CHAPTER EIGHTEEN

TIME SERIES AND FORECASTING

Time series

Time-based measurements

MUCH data obtained in the course of regular business activity is in the form of a series of figures or values, taken at regular intervals of time. Sales figures, share prices, absentee figures, commodity prices and many other sets of figures are of this type, and are described as time series. Such figures are usually recorded at regular intervals of time, and as the analysis of a time series is based on this regularity, this should be regarded as a characteristic of a time series.

The preliminary examination of a time series is made by graphing the data to form a time-graph, but too much should not

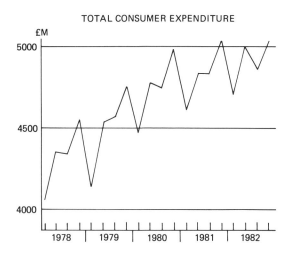

TOTAL CONSUMER EXPENDITURE

FIG. 56.—*Time series*

be read into the variability observed at this stage. The time graph may suggest what patterns of variability are present, but should not be regarded as good evidence to promote or refute any theories.

Components of variability

The variability in the measurements in a time series may be studied by assuming that the variability is compounded of several separate contributions. These may be described as:

(*a*) regular variations or trends,
(*b*) rhythmic variations; either cyclical variations or seasonal variations,
(*c*) catastrophic variations, and
(*d*) random or background variations.

The distinction between cyclical and seasonal variations, which are both cyclical, is that seasonal variations have a period of variation related to the calendar year. The term catastrophic variations refers to sudden changes in a time series which are unlikely to be repeated, and the reasons for which can usually be identified. Examples are changes in the method of measurement, or in the data collected, and in the case of business data, major events in the history of the organisation being studied. Fires, strikes, take-overs or major changes in processes could all be such events.

The term trend refers to regular changes in the measurement being studied. A trend may represent a section of a long-term cyclical variation especially when the data is not extensive enough for the cycle to be detected. The extrapolation of trends is always suspect whenever this situation is possible.

The object of time-series analysis is to identify the direction and magnitude of any trend present in the data, to estimate the effect of seasonal variations, and to estimate the size of the random variations.

Examination for trends

Line fitting

In order to reveal the trend present in data it is necessary to remove the effect of seasonal variations and random variations. This may be accomplished by fitting by eye a trend line to the data available, but this will obviously give variable results. Alternatively a line may be fitted by the least squares method, but this requires assumptions as to the nature of the trend in order to choose whether a linear, exponential or other relationship should be fitted. The methods of fitting lines have been described, and the tests given may be used to decide between competing theories as to the shape of the trend line. If the nature of the trend is unknown or variable then the method of moving averages is often employed to smooth out the variation in the time series.

Moving averages

The technique of using moving averages is to replace a particular measurement by the arithmetic mean of a series of measurements of which it is the centre. Any number of measure-

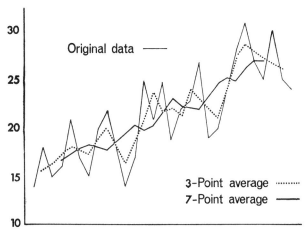

FIG. 57.—*The effect of a 3-point and 7-point moving average on a time series*

ments may be chosen, but an odd number is preferable as the moving average is then centred as an observed measurement. Where an even number of measurements is chosen, the moving average is centred between two observed measurements, and must be recentred before comparisons can be made between the average and the measurement.

The effect of seasonal variations can be removed by taking a moving average over a time span equal to the cycle of the seasonal variation. Annual variations are removed by taking a 4-point average of quarterly data, or a 12-point average of monthly data. In the last case a 13-point average of four-weekly data can also be used and has the advantages of not requiring recentring, and of being based on exactly equally spaced measurements.

The smoothing effect of a moving average increases with the number of measurements taken in the average, but there is a loss of data with the larger size averages, as we cannot calculate moving averages to correspond to the measurements at either end of the series. The effect of different size averages is shown in Fig. 57.

The calculation of moving averages

The calculation of a moving average is best carried out by the following routine, which is illustrated for a 5-point average in Table LVII.

(a) Add the first 5 measurements together to form the total, 80.

(b) Tick the next measurement, 16, and tick off the first, 15.

(c) Add the difference $16 - 15 = 1$ to the 5-point total to give the next total 81.

(d) Repeat to obtain all the totals, then divide each by 5 for the required averages.

When a long series is being studied it is advisable to check an occasional total, and always to check the last total.

Table LVII—Calculation of Moving Averages

Measurement	5-pt. total	5-pt. average
√15		
√17		
√13	80	16·0
√16	81	16·2
√19	84	16·8
√16√	92	18·4
√20√	93	18·6
21√	93	18·6
17√	99	19·8
19√	103	20·6
22√		
24√		
20		

Examination for seasonal effects

Seasonal deviations and factors

Where a consistent seasonal effect exists we may estimate the seasonal effect for each quarter or month. If there is little or no

Table LVIII—Calculation of Seasonal Effects

		Sales	4-pt. total	8-pt. total	8-pt. av.	Devn.	Ratio
1979	1st Qtr.	140					
	2	196					
			758				
	3	219		1537	192·1	26·9	1·14
			779				
	4	203		1600	200·0	3	1·01
			821				
1980	1	161		1680	210·0	−49	0·77
			859				
	2	238		1729	216·1	21·9	1·10
			870				
	3	257		1735	216·9	40·1	1·18
			865				
	4	214		1705	213·1	0·9	1·00
			840				
1981	1	156		1648	206·0	−50	0·76
			808				
	2	213		1609	201·1	11·9	1·06
			801				
	3	225		1598	199·8	25·2	1·13
			797				
	4	207		1586	198·3	8·7	1·04
			789				
1982	1	152		1586	198·3	−46·3	0·77
			797				
	2	205		1596	199·5	5·5	1·03
			799				
	3	233					
	4	209					

Average Seasonal Effects

	Deviation	Factor
Quarter 1	−48·4	0·77
Quarter 2	13·1	1·06
Quarter 3	30·7	1·15
Quarter 4	4·2	1·02

trend, then the absolute size of the effect will stay constant and seasonal deviations may be calculated. The seasonal deviation for a particular month or quarter is the mean difference between the observed figures and the trend figures as given by a moving average or a regression line estimate.

The seasonal factor is similarly the mean ratio of the observed figures and the trend figures. Strictly, the geometric mean should be used for ratios, but the arithmetic mean will produce no great error unless the individual ratios differ considerably. Seasonal factors are more appropriate when a trend is present, and we may expect the seasonal effects to have the same relative effect each year.

The calculation of both quantities is illustrated in Table LVIII.

Removing seasonal effects

When it is required to compare successive values in a time series without confusing seasonal variation, the measurements may be deseasonalised by the use of seasonal deviation or factors.

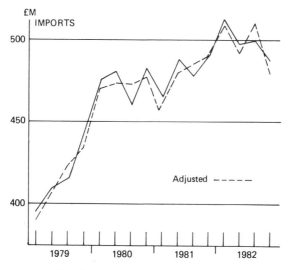

FIG. 58.—*The effect of removing seasonal effects from a time series*

Deseasonalised   measurement = observed   measurement
— seasonal deviation,

$$\text{or deseasonalised measurement} = \frac{\text{observed measurement}}{\text{seasonal factor}}.$$

The effect of these operations is to leave the trend, cyclical and random components of the series for examination—an example is shown in Fig. 58. The use of seasonal factors in this way is common in many of the statistical series published by government offices. In particular, monthly data for unemployment, finance, imports and exports are published both in their original and seasonally adjusted forms.

Adding seasonal effects

If an extrapolation of a trend line is made, then it is desirable to "correct" the estimate for seasonality when this is present. The relationships required are, seasonalised estimate = trend estimate + seasonal deviation, or seasonalised estimate = trend estimate × seasonal factor.

Examination for cyclical effects
The use of correlation coefficients

When a long series of measurements is available then an examination for significant cycles may be made. This may be done by inspection or by the use of serial correlations. Symbolising the measurements by t_1, t_2, t_3, t_4, ... t_n for a series of n measurements, then the correlation coefficient r is calculated for pairs of values t_1 and t_2, and t_2 and t_3, etc. Similar values of the coefficient are calculated for pairs two apart, t_1 and t_3, t_2 and t_4, etc., and so on for increasing separations of pairs. A graph of the value of r against the difference between pairs is plotted. Significant cycles will be shown by peaks on the graph, repeating at the periods of the cycles. It should be emphasised that examination for cycles is unlikely to be fruitful unless a long series of measurements, unaffected by catastrophic movements, is available.

Also a spasmodic variation with an irregular period may appear as a cycle to the visual examination of a time series, but would not be clearly identified by the method described. Such a variation would be of little use in predicting future movements of the series, and its presence is probably a warning not to attempt any other than short-term forecasts.

Forecasting

Forecasting from trend lines

When a trend line has been identified in a time series, then it is possible to extrapolate the line to obtain a forecast of the future behaviour of the series. There are dangers in this, although it is often a necessary course of action. As shown in the discussion of linear regression, the error in an estimate from a regression line increases with distance from the centre of the line. This is true for all trend lines, and the further a line is extrapolated, the less reliable forecasts based on it will become.

In addition the data available may not indicate that the trend line fitted is only an approximation to a trend of an entirely different shape. A small section of any curve is approximated by a straight line, but any extension of the section immediately makes the straight line approximation invalid. There is little that can be done statistically to resolve this problem, and where extrapolations are made, particularly of straight line trends, every effort should be made to obtain other information to help in the forecast.

Forecasting from multiple regression

Where the investigation of a quantity in which we are interested has led to the identification of the factors which influence it, of which time may be one, a multiple regression equation may be used to forecast its behaviour. This requires the knowledge of the future values of the controlling factors and also relies on all the major controlling factors being included in the regression analysis. As with a simple linear regression, extrapolation beyond the values of the factors used in establishing the regression equation is dangerous and should be avoided if possible.

Lead-lag forecasting

A particular forecasting method which has been used is applicable to several business and economic situations. We often have series of measurements which are affected by the same factors, but which react with different speeds. Any change in the more sensitive series will anticipate the corresponding change in the other series, and can be used as a forecasting indicator. This is usually referred to as a "lead–lag" relationship and has been especially used in the investigation of the movements in share prices.

The presence and size of the relationship can be established by calculating the correlation coefficient r between the series, first between corresponding measurements, and then between pairs taken at different times. Let the series be x_1, x_2, x_3 . . . and y_1, y_2, y_3 . . . where the suffixes refer to the time at which the measurement was taken, and let x "lead" y. We first calculate r between all the pairs (x_1, y_1), (x_2, y_2), etc., then between (x_2, y_1), (x_3, y_2), etc. The maximum value of r will identify the lead period and r^2 will measure the variability in y which is accounted for by variability in x. If the maximum r is between values k units of time apart, then we set up the regression equation $y_t = a + bx_{t-k}$, the suffixes again referring to the time scale.

Exponential forecasting

Discounted averages

Consider a series of measurements which is showing no regular trend, but varying if at all, only slowly, apart from random fluctuations. We could make an estimate of the most likely value for the next measurement by averaging a part of the available series. If there is a change in the mean level of the measurements, then there will be a lag before this is reflected in the estimates. This can be lessened by weighting the measurements, so that the most importance is given to the most recent measurements. Changes will now be more quickly allowed for.

It might be expected that the use of a weighted rather than a simple average would lead to more, not less, calculation. However, if the weights form a negative exponential distribution the calculation can be carried out very simply by use of the formula:

$$Estimate = a \ (last \ measurements) + (1 - a) \ (last \ estimate).$$

The term "last estimate" refers to the previous estimate made in the same way and a is called the smoothing factor. At the start of the series any reasonable value can be chosen for the "last estimate" term; it is quickly discounted by the method and any effects due to an error in the initial value quickly disappear. This system using a discounted average is referred to as *exponential smoothing* or *adaptive smoothing*. The calculation is illustrated in Table LIX and Fig. 59.

The equation is more conveniently written as

$$S_t = S_{t-1} + a(x_t - S_{t-1})$$

where S_t is the new smoothed figure (*estimate*)
    x_t is the last measurement
    S_{t-1} is the old smoothed figure (*last estimate*).

Table LIX—Exponential Smoothing of Time Series

Date		S_{t-1}	x_t	$(x_t - S_{t-1})$	$x\alpha(0\cdot3)$	S_t
1973	Jan.	42·0	40	−2·0	−0·6	41·4
	Feb.	41·4	34	−7·4	−2·2	39·2
	Mar.	39·2	47	7·8	2·3	41·5
	Apr.	41·5	40	−1·5	−0·4	41·1
	May	41·1	46	4·9	1·4	42·5
	June	42·5	33	−9·5	−2·9	39·6
	July	39·6	39	−0·6	−0·2	39·4
	Aug.	39·4	42	2·6	0·8	40·2
	Sept.	40·2	46	5·8	1·7	41·9
	Oct.	41·9	34	−7·9	−2·3	39·6
	Nov.	39·6	51	11·4	3·4	43·0
	Dec.	43·0	45	2·0	0·6	43·6
1974	Jan.	43·6	51	7·4	2·2	45·8
	Feb.	45·8	40	−5·8	−1·7	44·1
	Mar.	44·1	55	10·9	3·3	47·4
	Apr.	47·4	45	−2·4	−0·7	46·7
	May	46·7	43	−3·7	−1·1	45·6

Choice of smoothing factor

A low value of the smoothing factor corresponds to taking an average over a large number of measurements. This is the best policy when the mean level of the measurements is constant, and minimises the effect of random fluctuations. If the mean level is changing, a higher value of the smoothing factor is more suitable in order to avoid too long a lag in the estimate following the change. A regular value of 0·1, with a value of 0·3 when change is expected, are typical values to choose. It should be noted that the smoothing factor can be changed at will in the same series, and can be altered ready to accommodate change before the change occurs, where prior information is available.

An alternative procedure which gives an automatic choice of

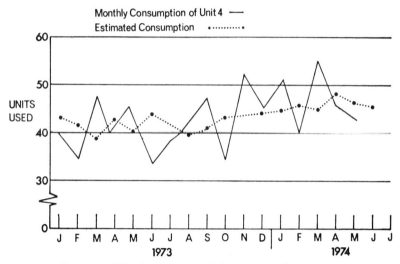

Monthly Consumption of Unit 4 ——
Estimated Consumption •••••••••••

Fig. 59.—*The simple exponential smoothing of a time series*

smoothing constant has been described. For this it is necessary to smooth the deviation $(x_t - S_{t-1})$ and the absolute deviation $|(x_t - S_{t-1})|$. This gives us the smoothed mean deviation—SMD and the smoothed mean absolute deviation—$SMAD$. For both these simple smoothing with a constant of about 0·2 is adequate. The smoothing constant is now given by $\alpha = SMD/SMAD$. The principle is that if the deviations from our smoothed figures are equally distributed above and below the smoothed figures, then our smoothing is unbiassed and so successful. This will give a small value for α, as SMD will be close to zero and $SMAD$ will be larger. If there is a change in the series which our smoothed figure does not follow, then successive deviations will have the same sign and SMD will increase. This automatically increases α and allows our smoothed figures to catch up with the series. α is always taken as positive.

EXAMPLE

Suppose the current values are:

$SMD = 1\cdot06$ $SMAD = 6\cdot34$ $S_{t-1} = 64\cdot8$ (last value of α was $1\cdot06/6\cdot34 = 0\cdot17$).
The next result is $x_t = 70$, this gives $x_t - S_{t-1} = 5\cdot2$
new SMD = old $SMD + 0\cdot2(5\cdot2 - \text{old } SMD)$
$= 1\cdot06 + 0\cdot2(5\cdot2 - 1\cdot06) = 1\cdot06 + 0\cdot83 = 1\cdot89,$

similarly new $SMAD$ = old $SMAD$ + 0·2(5·2 − old $SMAD$)
$$= 6·34 + 0·2(5·2 − 6·34) = 6·34 − 0·23 = 6·11$$
new a = 1·89/6·11 = 0·31
and lastly $S_t = S_{t-1} + 0·31(x_t − S_{t-1})$
$$= 64·8 + 0·31(80 − 64·8) = 64·8 + 1·61$$
$$= 66·4.$$

The values SMD = 1·89, $SMAD$ = 6·11 and S_t = 66·4 are stored until the next result is obtained, S_t being used as our forecast of the average level of the results.

Smoothing series with trend

If a steady trend is present in a time series, then the simple smoothing models described will always lag behind the true values. By adding a trend factor to the model the rate of increase can be tracked as well as the average value, and so forecasts which give a linear extrapolation of the trend can be obtained. The simplest system is to smooth the trend as measured by $(S_t − S_{t-1})$. A small value of a is suitable for this. The average figure given by S_t will still lag and a catch-up factor of $(1 − a)/a$ is used. If the smoothed trend is given by T_t, then

$$T_t = T_{t-1} + a'((S_t − S_{t-1}) − T_{t-1}),$$

and the forecast for k time periods ahead is

$$F_{t+k} = S_t = (1 − a)/a . T_t + kT_t.$$

The alternative is to use "double smoothing," that is to smooth the smoothed figures S_t. The forecast is then obtained as a function of the single and the double smoothed figures.

By the use of triple smoothing, an attempt may be made to track non-linear trends, and such models using the automatic choice of smoothing constant described earlier have been used.

Advantages of exponential smoothing

In order to make a forecast using exponential smoothing, it is only necessary to know the last value in the series and the previous estimate. This represents a considerable saving over any other method involving conventional averages or regression lines, especially when a large number of estimates have to be made. This might be the case in controlling the inventory levels of a large number of items by reference to expected demand. The methods are specially useful when using computers, and make only small demands on memory capacity.

Exponential smoothing and seasonal variation

Exponential smoothing of the simple type described is not suitable for forecasting the behaviour of measurements exhibiting cyclic variation. The forecasts will also be cyclical, but out of phase with the true cycle, that is, with the peak forecast lagging behind the peak observed values. In order to make a forecast including a seasonal effect, further terms would have to be included in the forecasting equation. Alternatively, where the seasonal effect is known and constant, it could be allowed for before and after applying exponential smoothing to a time series.

Questions

1. Discuss the characteristics of a time series and indicate briefly how you could estimate the trend of the series.

2. Explain what is meant by seasonal variation and indicate how seasonal factors can be used to deseasonalise data.

3. Discuss the methods available for forecasting the future behaviour of a time series.

4. What is meant by exponential smoothing? Explain with formulae how it can be used for short-term forecasting.

5. Use a 5-point moving average to identify the trend in the following measurements. Plot the original and average measurements on a time graph: 37, 36, 38, 34, 35, 40, 37, 34, 32, 31, 33, 29, 26, 32, 33, 25, 29, 27, 28, 25, 24, 21, 28, 25, 22, 21, 18, 25, 24, 21, 19, 22, 18, 17, 20, 19, 16, 18.

6. The quarterly sales for a product over six years are:

	1969	1970	1971	1972	1973	1974
Jan.–March	88	93	102	110	117	130
April–June	80	85	94	100	108	120
July–Sept.	75	81	89	96	103	114
Oct.–Dec.	84	90	100	104	112	128

Predict the total and quarterly sales for 1975. Explain carefully any assumptions you make.

7. Describe the use and effect of moving averages in the analysis of a time-series, indicating their use in removing random and seasonal variations.

Under, what circumstances might a weighted moving average be preferred?

8. Using a starting value of 38 and a smoothing constant of 0·2, smooth the series given in Question 5 and plot the original and smoothed figures on the same graph.

9. Discuss the problems of analysing a time series which has a strong seasonal variation.

10. Plot the following sales figures on a time graph and estimate next week's sales. Explain your method.

Week:	1	2	3	4	5	6	7	8	9	10
Sales:	5	8	2	4	9	3	5	5	10	4

APPENDIX I

Selected Books for Further Reading

In each case, only the most up-to-date edition should be used.

Statistical Mapping and the Presentation of Statistics, G. C. Dickinson. Edward Arnold (Publishers) Ltd.

Statistical Methods in Management, T. Cass. Cassell.

Statistical Methods in Management 2, T. Cass. Cassell.

Sampling Methods for Censuses and Surveys, F. Yates. Charles Griffin & Co., Ltd.

Survey Methods in Social Investigations, C. A. Moser & G. Kalton. Heinemann Educational Books.

Statistical Methods in Research & Production, O. L. Davies & P. L. Goldsmith (Eds). Oliver & Boyd.

Control Charts, J. Murdoch. Macmillan.

Statistical Tables, J. Murdoch & J. A. Barnes. Macmillan.

APPENDIX II

Table A: Area under the normal curve
Table B: "t"-distribution
Table C: χ^2-distribution
Table D: F-distribution
Table E: Poisson probabilities
Table F: Random sampling numbers

Table A—Area Under the Normal Curve

The quantity given is the probability that Z would be exceeded for a measurement drawn from a standardised normal distribution

Z	0	1	2	3	4	5	6	7	8	9
					Second Decimal Place of Z					
0·0	·5000	·4960	·4920	·4880	·4840	·4801	·4761	·4721	·4681	·4641
0·1	·4602	·4562	·4522	·4483	·4443	·4404	·4364	·4325	·4286	·4247
0·2	·4207	·4168	·4129	·4090	·4052	·4013	·3974	·3936	·3897	·3859
0·3	·3821	·3783	·3745	·3707	·3669	·3632	·3594	·3557	·3520	·3483
0·4	·3446	·3409	·3372	·3336	·3300	·3264	·3228	·3192	·3156	·3121
0·5	·3085	·3050	·3015	·2981	·2946	·2912	·2877	·2843	·2810	·2776
0·6	·2743	·2709	·2676	·2643	·2611	·2578	·2546	·2514	·2483	·2451
0·7	·2420	·2389	·2358	·2327	·2297	·2266	·2236	·2206	·2177	·2148
0·8	·2119	·2090	·2061	·2033	·2005	·1977	·1949	·1922	·1894	·1867
0·9	·1841	·1814	·1788	·1762	·1736	·1711	·1685	·1660	·1635	·1611
1·0	·1587	·1562	·1539	·1515	·1492	·1469	·1446	·1423	·1401	·1379
1·1	·1357	·1335	·1314	·1292	·1271	·1251	·1230	·1210	·1190	·1170
1·2	·1151	·1131	·1112	·1093	·1075	·1056	·1038	·1020	·1003	·0985
1·3	·0968	·0951	·0934	·0918	·0901	·0885	·0869	·0853	·0838	·0823
1·4	·0809	·0793	·0778	·0764	·0749	·0735	·0722	·0708	·0694	·0681
1·5	·0668	·0655	·0643	·0630	·0618	·0606	·0594	·0582	·0571	·0559
1·6	·0548	·0537	·0526	·0516	·0505	·0495	·0485	·0475	·0465	·0455
1·7	·0446	·0436	·0427	·0418	·0409	·0401	·0392	·0384	·0375	·0367
1·8	·0359	·0352	·0344	·0336	·0329	·0322	·0314	·0307	·0301	·0294
1·9	·0287	·0281	·0274	·0268	·0262	·0256	·0250	·0244	·0238	·0233
2·0	·0227	·0222	·0217	·0212	·0207	·0202	·0197	·0192	·0188	·0183
2·1	·0179	·0174	·0170	·0166	·0162	·0158	·0154	·0150	·0146	·0143
2·2	·0139	·0136	·0132	·0129	·0126	·0122	·0119	·0116	·0113	·0110
2·3	·0107	·0104	·0102	·00990	·00964	·00939	·00914	·00889	·00866	·00842
2·4	·00820	·00798	·00776	·00755	·00734	·00714	·00695	·00676	·00657	·00639
2·5	·00621	·00604	·00587	·00570	·00554	·00539	·00523	·00508	·00494	·00480
2·6	·00466	·00453	·00440	·00427	·00415	·00403	·00391	·00379	·00368	·00357
2·7	·00347	·00336	·00326	·00317	·00307	·00298	·00289	·00280	·00272	·00264
2·8	·00256	·00248	·00240	·00233	·00226	·00219	·00212	·00205	·00199	·00193
2·9	·00187	·00181	·00175	·00169	·00164	·00159	·00154	·00149	·00144	·00140
3·0	·00135	·00131	·00126	·00122	·00118	·00114	·00111	·00107	·00104	·00100
3·1	·00097	·00094	·00090	·00087	·00084	·00082	·00079	·00076	·00074	·00071
3·2	·00069	·00066	·00064	·00062	·00060	·00058	·00056	·00054	·00052	·00050
3·3	·00048	·00047	·00045	·00043	·00042	·00040	·00039	·00038	·00036	·00035
3·4	·00034	·00032	·00031	·00030	·00029	·00028	·00027	·00026	·00025	·00024
3·5	·00023	·00022	·00022	·00021	·00020	·00019	·00019	·00018	·00017	·00017

Table B—"t"-distribution

The quantity tabulated is the value of "t" which must be exceeded for significance at the level given

d.f.	Two-tailed Test		One-tailed Test	
	P = 0.05	0.01	P = 0.05	0.01
1	12.71	63.66	6.31	31.82
2	4.30	9.92	2.92	6.97
3	3.18	5.84	2.35	4.54
4	2.78	4.60	2.13	3.75
5	2.57	4.03	2.02	3.37
6	2.45	3.71	1.94	3.14
7	2.37	3.50	1.90	3.00
8	2.31	3.36	1.86	2.90
9	2.26	3.25	1.83	2.82
10	2.23	3.17	1.81	2.76
11	2.20	3.11	1.80	2.72
12	2.18	3.06	1.78	2.68
13	2.16	3.01	1.77	2.65
14	2.14	2.98	1.76	2.62
15	2.13	2.95	1.75	2.60
16	2.12	2.92	1.75	2.58
17	2.11	2.90	1.74	2.57
18	2.10	2.88	1.73	2.55
19	2.09	2.86	1.73	2.54
20	2.09	2.84	1.72	2.53
22	2.07	2.82	1.72	2.51
24	2.06	2.80	1.71	2.49
26	2.06	2.78	1.71	2.48
28	2.05	2.76	1.70	2.47
30	2.04	2.75	1.70	2.46
∞	1.96	2.58	1.65	2.33

Table C—χ²-distribution

The quantity tabulated is the value of χ^2 which must be exceeded for significance at the level given

d.f.	P = 0.05	0.01
1	3.84	6.63
2	5.99	9.21
3	7.81	11.3
4	9.49	13.3
5	11.1	15.1
6	12.6	16.8
7	14.1	18.5
8	15.5	20.1
9	16.9	21.7
10	18.3	23.2
11	19.7	24.7
12	21.0	26.2
13	22.4	27.7
14	23.7	29.1
15	25.0	30.6
16	26.3	32.0
17	27.6	33.4
18	28.9	34.8
19	30.1	36.2
20	31.4	37.6
22	33.9	40.3
24	36.4	43.0
26	38.9	45.6
28	41.3	48.3
30	43.8	50.9

For degrees of freedom greater than 30 $\sqrt{2\chi^2}$ is distributed as normal with mean $= \sqrt{2\chi^2 + 1}$ and variance $= 1$

Table D—F-distribution

The quantity tabulated is the value of F which must be exceeded for significance at the 5% level

d.f.2	d.f.1 = 1	2	3	4	5	6	7	8	12	16	24	40	100	∞
1	161	200	216	225	230	234	237	239	244	246	249	251	253	254
2	18·5	19·0	19·2	19·3	19·3	19·3	19·4	19·4	19·4	19·4	19·5	19·5	19·5	19·5
3	10·13	9·55	9·28	9·12	9·01	8·94	8·88	8·84	8·74	8·69	8·64	8·60	8·56	8·53
4	7·71	6·94	6·59	6·39	6·26	6·16	6·09	6·04	5·91	5·84	5·77	5·71	5·66	5·63
5	6·61	5·79	5·41	5·19	5·05	4·95	4·88	4·82	4·68	4·60	4·53	4·46	4·40	4·36
6	5·99	5·14	4·76	4·53	4·39	4·28	4·21	4·15	4·00	3·92	3·84	3·77	3·71	3·67
7	5·59	4·74	4·35	4·12	3·97	3·87	3·79	3·73	3·57	3·49	3·41	3·34	3·28	3·23
8	5·32	4·46	4·07	3·84	3·69	3·58	3·50	3·44	3·28	3·22	3·12	3·04	2·98	2·93
9	5·12	4·26	3·86	3·63	3·48	3·37	3·29	3·23	3·07	2·98	2·90	2·82	2·76	2·71
10	4·96	4·10	3·71	3·48	3·33	3·22	3·14	3·07	2·91	2·82	2·74	2·67	2·59	2·54
12	4·75	3·88	3·49	3·26	3·11	3·00	2·92	2·85	2·69	2·60	2·50	2·42	2·35	2·30
14	4·60	3·74	3·34	3·11	2·96	2·85	2·77	2·70	2·53	2·44	2·35	2·27	2·19	2·13
16	4·49	3·63	3·24	3·01	2·85	2·74	2·66	2·59	2·42	2·33	2·24	2·16	2·07	2·01
18	4·41	3·55	3·16	2·93	2·77	2·66	2·58	2·51	2·34	2·25	2·15	2·07	1·98	1·92
20	4·35	3·49	3·10	2·87	2·71	2·60	2·52	2·45	2·28	2·18	2·08	1·99	1·90	1·84
25	4·24	3·38	2·99	2·76	2·60	2·49	2·41	2·34	2·16	2·06	1·96	1·87	1·77	1·71
30	4·17	3·32	2·92	2·69	2·53	2·42	2·34	2·27	2·09	1·99	1·89	1·79	1·69	1·62
40	4·08	3·23	2·84	2·61	2·45	2·34	2·25	2·18	2·00	1·90	1·79	1·69	1·59	1·51
60	4·00	3·15	2·76	2·52	2·37	2·25	2·17	2·10	1·92	1·81	1·70	1·59	1·48	1·39
125	3·92	3·07	2·68	2·44	2·29	2·17	2·08	2·01	1·83	1·72	1·60	1·49	1·36	1·25
∞	3·84	2·99	2·60	2·37	2·21	2·09	2·01	1·94	1·75	1·64	1·52	1·40	1·24	1·00

Table E—Poisson Probabilities

The quantity tabulated is the probability that r occurrences will be observed in a Poisson distribution mean $= m$

$m \backslash r =$	0	1	2	3	4	5	6	7	8	9	10	11	12	13	14	15
0·02	·9802	·0196	·0002													
0·04	·9608	·0384	·0008													
0·06	·9418	·0565	·0017													
0·08	·9231	·0738	·0030	·0001												
0·1	·9048	·0905	·0045	·0002												
0·2	·8187	·1637	·0164	·0011	·0001											
0·3	·7408	·2222	·0333	·0033	·0002											
0·4	·6703	·2681	·0536	·0072	·0007	·0001										
0·5	·6065	·3033	·0758	·0126	·0016	·0002										
0·6	·5488	·3293	·0988	·0198	·0030	·0004										
0·7	·4966	·3476	·1217	·0284	·0050	·0007	·0001									
0·8	·4493	·3595	·1438	·0383	·0077	·0012	·0002									
0·9	·4066	·3659	·1647	·0494	·0111	·0020	·0003									
1·0	·3679	·3679	·1839	·0613	·0153	·0031	·0005	·0001								
1·1	·3329	·3662	·2014	·0738	·0203	·0045	·0008	·0001								
1·2	·3012	·3614	·2169	·0867	·0260	·0062	·0012	·0002								
1·3	·2725	·3543	·2303	·0998	·0324	·0084	·0018	·0003	·0001							
1·4	·2466	·3452	·2417	·1128	·0395	·0111	·0026	·0005	·0001							
1·5	·2231	·3347	·2510	·1255	·0471	·0141	·0035	·0008	·0001							
1·6	·2019	·3230	·2584	·1378	·0551	·0176	·0047	·0011	·0002							
1·7	·1827	·3106	·2640	·1496	·0636	·0216	·0061	·0015	·0003	·0001						
1·8	·1653	·2975	·2678	·1607	·0723	·0260	·0078	·0020	·0005	·0001						
1·9	·1496	·2842	·2700	·1710	·0812	·0309	·0098	·0027	·0006	·0001						
2·0	·1353	·2707	·2707	·1804	·0902	·0361	·0120	·0034	·0009	·0002						
2·1	·1225	·2572	·2700	·1890	·0992	·0417	·0146	·0044	·0011	·0003	·0001					
2·2	·1108	·2438	·2681	·1966	·1082	·0476	·0174	·0055	·0015	·0004	·0001					

m r =	0	1	2	3	4	5	6	7	8	9	10	11	12	13	14	15
2·3	·1003	·2306	·2652	·2033	·1169	·0538	·0206	·0068	·0019	·0005	·0001					
2·4	·0907	·2177	·2613	·2090	·1254	·0602	·0241	·0083	·0025	·0007	·0002					
2·5	·0821	·2052	·2565	·2138	·1336	·0668	·0278	·0099	·0031	·0009	·0002					
2·6	·0743	·1931	·2510	·2176	·1414	·0735	·0319	·0118	·0038	·0011	·0003					
2·7	·0672	·1815	·2450	·2205	·1488	·0804	·0362	·0139	·0047	·0014	·0004	·0001				
2·8	·0608	·1703	·2384	·2225	·1557	·0872	·0407	·0163	·0057	·0018	·0005	·0001				
2·9	·0550	·1596	·2314	·2237	·1622	·0940	·0455	·0188	·0068	·0022	·0006	·0002				
3·0	·0498	·1494	·2240	·2240	·1680	·1008	·0504	·0216	·0081	·0027	·0008	·0002				
3·1	·0450	·1397	·2165	·2237	·1734	·1075	·0555	·0246	·0095	·0033	·0010	·0003	·0001			
3·2	·0408	·1304	·2087	·2226	·1781	·1140	·0608	·0278	·0111	·0040	·0013	·0004	·0001			
3·3	·0369	·1217	·2008	·2209	·1823	·1203	·0662	·0312	·0129	·0047	·0016	·0005	·0001			
3·4	·0334	·1135	·1929	·2186	·1858	·1264	·0716	·0348	·0148	·0056	·0019	·0006	·0002			
3·5	·0302	·1057	·1850	·2158	·1888	·1322	·0771	·0385	·0169	·0066	·0023	·0007	·0002	·0001		
3·6	·0273	·0984	·1771	·2125	·1912	·1377	·0826	·0425	·0191	·0076	·0028	·0009	·0003	·0001		
3·7	·0247	·0915	·1692	·2087	·1931	·1429	·0881	·0466	·0215	·0089	·0033	·0011	·0003	·0001		
3·8	·0224	·0850	·1615	·2046	·1944	·1477	·0936	·0508	·0241	·0102	·0039	·0013	·0004	·0001		
3·9	·0202	·0789	·1539	·2001	·1951	·1522	·0989	·0551	·0269	·0116	·0045	·0016	·0005	·0002		
4·0	·0183	·0733	·1465	·1954	·1954	·1563	·1042	·0595	·0298	·0132	·0053	·0019	·0006	·0002	·0001	
4·1	·0166	·0679	·1393	·1904	·1951	·1600	·1093	·0640	·0328	·0150	·0061	·0023	·0008	·0002	·0001	
4·2	·0150	·0630	·1323	·1852	·1944	·1633	·1143	·0686	·0360	·0168	·0071	·0027	·0009	·0003	·0001	
4·3	·0136	·0583	·1254	·1798	·1933	·1662	·1191	·0732	·0393	·0188	·0081	·0032	·0011	·0004	·0001	
4·4	·0123	·0540	·1188	·1743	·1917	·1687	·1237	·0778	·0428	·0209	·0092	·0037	·0014	·0005	·0001	
4·5	·0111	·0500	·1125	·1687	·1898	·1708	·1281	·0824	·0463	·0232	·0104	·0043	·0016	·0006	·0002	·0001
4·6	·0101	·0462	·1063	·1631	·1875	·1725	·1323	·0869	·0500	·0255	·0118	·0049	·0019	·0007	·0002	·0001
4·7	·0091	·0427	·1005	·1574	·1849	·1738	·1362	·0914	·0537	·0280	·0132	·0056	·0022	·0008	·0003	·0001
4·8	·0082	·0395	·0948	·1517	·1820	·1747	·1398	·0959	·0575	·0307	·0147	·0064	·0026	·0009	·0003	·0001
4·9	·0074	·0365	·0894	·1460	·1789	·1753	·1432	·1002	·0614	·0334	·0164	·0073	·0030	·0011	·0004	·0001
5·0	·0067	·0337	·0842	·1404	·1755	·1755	·1462	·1044	·0653	·0363	·0181	·0082	·0034	·0013	·0005	·0002

Table F—Random Sampling Numbers

23 67 99 62 17   21 02 17 20 27   53 61 49 22 69   42 68 76 17 01   87 49 65 30 12   25 95 36 18 82
86 11 85 65 53   39 71 11 65 71   60 87 84 01 43   78 25 64 77 62   91 85 16 04 88   92 35 08 58 48
38 02 43 54 90   90 00 42 37 75   74 31 07 18 78   36 15 07 06 72   62 14 82 36 74   34 99 77 15 40
46 20 13 15 57   93 88 14 21 80   51 67 90 02 76   26 64 84 03 92   32 96 59 06 14   60 59 29 97 79
33 88 96 94 65   21 90 31 30 87   40 48 19 08 98   01 54 48 04 88   30 31 43 40 75   50 88 11 38 80

26 91 16 22 71   07 79 49 04 71   46 06 81 98 67   03 81 98 07 14   36 94 08 08 92   90 36 24 02 51
11 15 97 58 15   60 33 86 86   56 99 26 01 16   04 26 01 94 81   33 53 52 55 50   36 33 70 24 95
01 38 89 63 92   45 09 01 52 61   98 98 08 60 33   46 80 60 56 59   70 30 08 98 65   07 94 56 38 13
91 28 39 56 53   15 16 80 40 91   18 87 40 38 20   24 13 83 77 71   14 81 59 20 46
26 89 39 56 92   06 89 35 79 99   54 60 79 13 46   95 17 36 16 82   08 52 08 83 36

20 08 86 25 03   58 86 93 82 69   06 08 86 26 74   24 89 94 19 57   01 81 28 89 47   90 36 24 02 51
34 81 20 39 74   58 03 19 74 86   40 56 62 31 15   57 30 00 40 95   13 32 53 12 31   36 33 70 24 95
75 28 65 83 28   21 26 80 99 83   33 72 62 05 04   77 50 58 10 00   67 21 20 34 60   07 94 56 38 13
18 68 11 22 33   44 68 81 18 43   34 32 39 22 27   32 04 85 32 46   06 49 47 39 10   14 81 59 20 46
79 51 41 85 58   08 56 50 88 95   57 88 13 13 99   62 42 36 91 13   05 07 92 56 91   08 52 08 83 36

12 23 55 58 97   87 74 95 15 09   72 63 86 18 93   33 11 44 82 68   02 10 89 87 74   45 05 23 95 19
95 34 85 95 84   57 36 75 75 55   23 30 69 71 63   65 69 78 38 51   80 99 52 81 61   94 72 86 55 71
94 09 87 52 11   42 92 29 62 84   06 78 95 29 05   70 63 81 41 98   22 08 43 08 55   94 03 94 32 07
10 97 94 69 38   80 07 70 25 79   89 90 29 04 30   53 01 44 44 08   16 15 47 38 44   20 59 58 35 10
41 33 36 99 23   27 52 91 10 40   46 42 83 50 75   09 82 30 92 17   57 68 97 45 12   25 08 34 99 62

APPENDIX III
Worked Answers

CHAPTER 2

Question 1.

(a) $35 \times 20 + 5$ $\qquad = \underline{\underline{705}}.$

(b) $|35 - 20|$ $\qquad = \underline{\underline{15}}.$

(c) $|20 - 35| = |-15|$ $\qquad = \underline{\underline{15}}.$

(d) $5! = 5 \times 4 \times 3 \times 2 \times 1 = \underline{\underline{120}}.$

Question 2.

(a) $x + z \leqslant 10, x = 4$
$\quad 4 + z \leqslant 10, z \leqslant 6$ $\qquad \underline{\underline{\text{Ans.} = 6.}}$

(b) $y/z > 1\cdot4, y = 7$
$\quad 7/z > 1\cdot4, 7 > 1\cdot4z$
$\quad z < \dfrac{7}{1\cdot4}, z < 5$ $\qquad \underline{\underline{\text{Ans.} = 4.}}$

(c) $y - z \geqslant x, y = 7, x = 4$
$\quad 7 - z \geqslant 4, -z \geqslant 4 - 7$
$\quad z \leqslant 7 - 4, z \leqslant 3$ $\qquad \underline{\underline{\text{Ans.} = 3.}}$

Question 3.

(a) $\dbinom{20}{0} = 1$ (only one way of not choosing any).

(b) $\dbinom{20}{3} = \dfrac{20 \cdot 19 \cdot 18}{3 \cdot 2 \cdot 1} = 20 \cdot 19 \cdot 3 = \underline{\underline{1140}}.$

(c) $\dbinom{20}{5} = \dfrac{20 \cdot 19 \cdot 18 \cdot 17 \cdot 16}{5 \cdot 4 \cdot 3 \cdot 2 \cdot 1} = 19 \cdot 3 \cdot 17 \cdot 16 = \underline{\underline{15\,504}}.$

(d) $\dbinom{20}{17} = \dbinom{20}{20-17} = \dbinom{20}{3} = \underline{\underline{1140}}$ (as above).

Question 4.

	x	y	x^2	xy	$\lvert x - y \rvert$
	1	12	1	12	11
	3	10	9	30	7
	4	6	16	24	2
	5	9	25	45	4
	7	4	49	28	3
	9	0	81	0	9
	12	−1	144	−12	13
	14	−5	196	−70	19
Sums	55	35	521	57	68

(a) $\Sigma x = \underline{\underline{55}}$, $\Sigma y = \underline{\underline{35}}$.

(b) $\Sigma x^2 = \underline{\underline{521}}$, $(\Sigma x)^2 = (55)^2 = \underline{\underline{3025}}$.

(c) $\Sigma xy = \underline{\underline{57}}$, $\Sigma x \cdot \Sigma y = 55 \times 35 = \underline{\underline{1925}}$.

(d) $\Sigma \lvert x - y \rvert = \underline{\underline{68}}$.

Question 5.
(a) 6.479.
(b) 1·982.
(c) 0·06648.
(d) 0·3223.
(e) 7·974.

Question 6.
(a) 430.   (b) 3040.
(c) 0·00590.   (d) 0·00580.
(e) 3880.   (f) 3910.
(g) 3000 (3 sig. figs.).   (h) 4·32.

Question 7.
(a) 8·366600.
(b) 0·0221359.
(c) 18·4391.

Question 8.

8. $\Sigma x = 55 \quad \Sigma x^2 = 521 \quad N = 8$.

$$\left[\Sigma x^2 - \frac{(\Sigma x)^2}{N} \right] = 521 - \frac{(55)^2}{8}$$
$$= 521 - 378 \cdot 125$$
$$= 142 \cdot 875.$$

(a) $\sqrt{\dfrac{1}{N}\left[\Sigma x^2 - \dfrac{(\Sigma x)^2}{N}\right]} = \sqrt{142\cdot875/8}$

$\qquad = \sqrt{17\cdot86} = 4\cdot226.$

(b) $\sqrt{\dfrac{1}{N-1}\left[\Sigma x^2 - \dfrac{(\Sigma x)^2}{N}\right]} = \sqrt{142\cdot875/7}$

$\qquad = \sqrt{20\cdot41} = 4\cdot518.$

Question 9.

$P(r) = \dbinom{n}{r} p^r \cdot (1-p)^{n-r}.$

(a) $n = 10,\ p = 0\cdot3,\ r = 0.$

$\qquad P(0) = \dbinom{10}{0} 0\cdot3^0 \cdot 0\cdot7^{10}.$

Note: $\dbinom{10}{0} = 1,\ 0\cdot3^0 = 1$

$\qquad \therefore P(0) = 0\cdot7^{10}$

$\qquad \log. \ 0\cdot7 = \bar{1}\cdot84510$

$\quad 10 \log. \ 0\cdot7 = \overline{10}. + 8\cdot4510 = \bar{2}\cdot4510$

$\qquad 0\cdot7^{10} = \underline{\underline{0\cdot02825}}.$

(b) $n = 10,\ p = 0\cdot3,\ r = 3.$

$\qquad P(3) = \dbinom{10}{3} 0\cdot3^3 \cdot 0\cdot7^7$

$\qquad \dbinom{10}{3} = \dfrac{10 \times 9 \times 8}{3 \times 2} = 120$

$\qquad 0\cdot3^3 = 0\cdot027$

$\qquad \log. \ 0\cdot7 = \bar{1}\cdot84510$

$\quad 7 \log. \ 0\cdot7 = \bar{7} + 5\cdot91570 = \bar{2}\cdot91570$

$\qquad 0\cdot7^7 = 0\cdot08235$

$\qquad \therefore P(3) = 120 \times 0\cdot027 \times 0\cdot08235$

$\qquad\qquad = \underline{\underline{0\cdot2668}}.$

Question 10.

$10.\ P(r) = \dfrac{e^{-m} \cdot m^r}{r!}$

(a) $m = 1,\ r = 2.$

$\qquad P(2) = \dfrac{e^{-1} \cdot 1^2}{2 \cdot 1.} = e^{-1}/2$

From tables $e^{-1} = 0\cdot3679.$

$P(2) = 0\cdot3679/2 = \underline{\underline{0\cdot1839}}.$

(b) $m = 1\cdot4,\ r = 1.$

$\qquad P(1) = \dfrac{e^{-1\cdot4} \cdot 1\cdot4^1}{1} = e^{-1\cdot4} \times 1\cdot4$

From tables $e^{-1\cdot4} = 0\cdot2466.$

$P(1) = 0\cdot2466 \times 1\cdot4 = \underline{\underline{0\cdot3452}}.$

(c) $m = 2, r = 0$.

$$P(0) = \frac{e^{-2} \cdot 2^0}{0!} = e^{-2}$$

From tables $e^{-2} = 0.1353$.

$P(0) = \underline{\underline{0.1353}}$.

CHAPTER 7

Question 5.

Calculation for Mode.

Class	Class width	Frequency	Frequency Density
150–	8	103	12·9
158–	4	98	24·5
162–	4	190	47·5
166–	2	140	70·0
168–	2	116	58·0
170–	4	138	34·5
174–	4	62	15·5
178–	4	24	6·0
182–190	8	22	2·8

Modal class = 166–168.
Using estimation from part of histogram as in Fig. 60,
Mode   = 167·3.

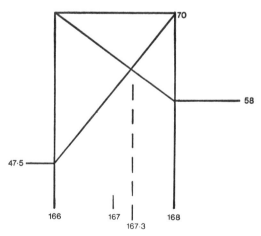

FIG. 60.—*Estimation of mode*

Calculation for Median.

Class	Frequency	Cumulative Frequency
150–	103	103
158–	98	201
162–	190	391
166–	140	531
168–	116	647
170–	138	785
174–	62	847
178–	24	871
182–190	22	893

893

Median rank = 893/2 = 446·5.
Median class = 166 — 168.
Estimating through the class,

$$\text{Median} = 166 + 2 \times \frac{(446 \cdot 5 - 391)}{(531 - 391)}$$
$$= 166 + 2 \times 55 \cdot 5 / 140$$
$$= 166 + 0 \cdot 79 = \underline{\underline{166 \cdot 8}}.$$

Calculation of Mean.

Class	Midpt = x	x = X — 167	f	fx
150–	154	—13	103	—1339
158–	160	—7	98	—686
162–	164	—3	190	—570
166–	167	0	140	—2595
168–	169	2	116	232
170–	172	5	138	690
174–	176	9	62	558
178–	180	13	24	312
182–190	186	19	22	418
			893	2210
				—2595
				—385

$$\bar{x} = \frac{-385}{893} = -0 \cdot 43.$$
$$\bar{X} = \bar{x} + 167 = 166 \cdot 57.$$

Note: Coding factor h not used in this case.

Question 6.

$$N = 893.$$
$$Q_1 \text{ rank} \quad = \quad N/4 = 223 \cdot 25.$$
$$\text{Median rank} = \quad N/2 = 446 \cdot 5.$$
$$Q_3 \text{ rank} \quad = \quad 3N/4 = 669 \cdot 75.$$

From the cumulative distribution curve as in Fig. 61.

$$Q_1 \text{ value} \quad = 163 \cdot 0.$$
$$\text{Median value} = 166 \cdot 6.$$
$$Q_3 \text{ value} \quad = 170 \cdot 4.$$

$$\text{Quartile deviation} = \frac{Q_3 - Q_1}{2} = \frac{170 \cdot 4 - 163}{2}$$

$$= \underline{\underline{3 \cdot 7.}}$$

Quartile measure of skewness

$$= \frac{(Q_3 - Med.) - (Med. - Q_1)}{Q.D.} = \frac{(170 \cdot 4 - 166 \cdot 6) - (166 \cdot 6 - 170 \cdot 4)}{3 \cdot 7}$$

$$= \frac{3 \cdot 8 - 3 \cdot 6}{3 \cdot 7} = \underline{\underline{0 \cdot 05.}}$$

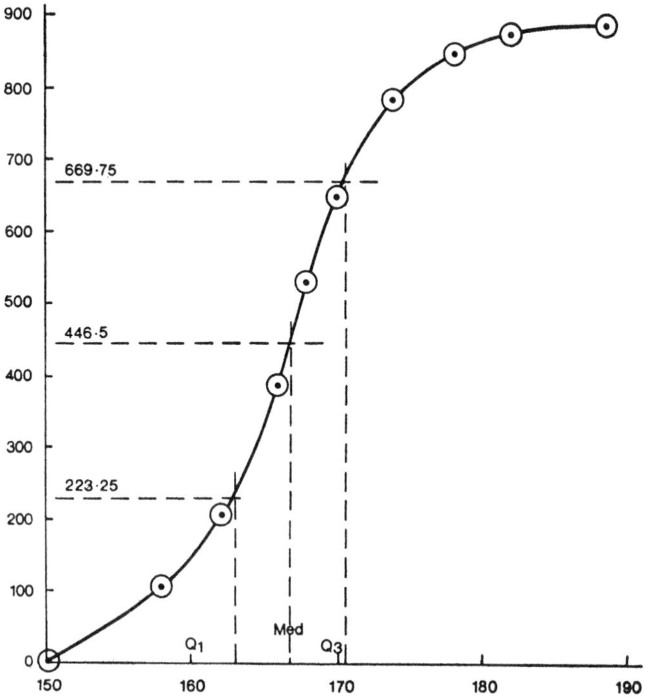

FIG. 61.—*Estimation of quantities*

Question 7.

Extending the table used in Question 5.

X	x	f	fx	fx^2
154	−13	103	−1339	17407
160	−7	98	−686	4802
164	−3	190	−570	1710
167	0	140	−2595	0
169	2	116	232	464
172	5	138	690	3450
176	9	62	558	5022
180	13	24	312	4056
186	19	22	418	7942
		893	2210	44 853

$$\frac{-2595}{-385}$$

$$Var._x = \frac{1}{n}[\Sigma fx^2 - (\Sigma fx)^2/n]$$

$$= \frac{1}{893}\left[44853 - \frac{(-385)^2}{893}\right]$$

$$= \frac{1}{893}[44853 - 165\cdot98]$$

$$= 50\cdot04$$

$$\text{s.d.}_x = \sqrt{50\cdot04} = 7\cdot074.$$

Note: Coding factor h not used, so $Var._X = Var._x$, s.d.$_X$ = s.d.$\bar{x}$,
i.e. $Var._X = \underline{50\cdot04}$, $s.d._X = \underline{7\cdot074}$.

Question 8.

X	$x = \dfrac{X - 18\cdot5}{0\cdot1}$	x^2
18·3	−2	4
18·1	−4	16
19·2	7	49
18·8	3	9
18·5	0	0
19·0	5	25
18·6	1	1
18·7	2	4
18·3	−2	4
	10	112

$\Sigma x = 10$ $\Sigma x^2 = 112$ $n = 9$ $c = 18\cdot5$ $h = 0\cdot1$.
$\bar{x} = \Sigma x/n = 10/9 = 1\cdot11$.

$$\bar{X} = \bar{x} \cdot h + c = 1 \cdot 11 \times 0 \cdot 1 + 18 \cdot 5$$
$$= 18 \cdot 61.$$

$$\sigma_x{}^2 = 1/n - 1 \cdot [\Sigma x^2 - (\Sigma x)^2/n]$$
$$= 1/8 \cdot [112 - (10)^2/9]$$
$$= 1/8[112 - 11 \cdot 11]$$
$$= 12 \cdot 61$$

$$\hat{\sigma}_x = \sqrt{12 \cdot 61} = 3 \cdot 551.$$
$$\hat{\sigma}_X{}^2 = \hat{\sigma}_x{}^2 \cdot h^2 = 12 \cdot 61 \times 0 \cdot 1^2$$
$$= 0 \cdot 1261.$$

$$\hat{\sigma}_X = \sigma_x \cdot h = 3 \cdot 551 \times 0 \cdot 1 = 0 \cdot 36.$$

Question 9.
Coefficient of Variation   = s.d./mean;
for estimates from Question 8 = $0 \cdot 36/18 \cdot 61$
$$= 0 \cdot 019$$
$$\text{or} \quad 1 \cdot 9\%.$$
From data of this question   = $0 \cdot 21/25 \cdot 3$
$$= 0 \cdot 0083$$
$$\text{or} \quad 0 \cdot 8\%$$

i.e. the first sample shows over twice as much variability as the second relative to the mean size.

Question 10.

X	log. X		
9·3	0·9685	n	= 20.
9·1	0·9590		
10·5	1·0212	$\bar{X} = \dfrac{214 \cdot 7}{20} = 10 \cdot 735.$	
13·2	1·1206		
12·1	1·0828		
10·2	1·0086		
10·5	1·0212	$\overline{\log. X} = \dfrac{20 \cdot 5190}{20} = 1 \cdot 02595.$	
9·8	0·9912		
10·6	1·0253		
14·0	1·1461	$G.M_X = 10 \cdot 616.$	
10·6	1·0253		
10·1	1·0043		
10·1	1·0043		
9·0	0·9542		
9·8	0·9912		
9·7	0·9869		
16·0	1·2041		
10·2	1·0086		
10·0	1·0000		
9·9	0·9956		
214·7	20·5190		

CHAPTER 8

Question 1.

Man	Estimate	Weight	Est. × Wt.
A	75	1	75
B	120	8	960
C	140	4	560
		13	1595

$$\text{Best estimate} = \frac{\Sigma(Est. \times Wt.)}{\Sigma\ Wts.} = \frac{1595}{13} = \underline{\underline{122 \cdot 7}}.$$

Question 5.

Base weighted Index.

Item	Consumption 1980	Wt.
A	1200	3
B	800	2
C	2000	5
		10

Relatives

Item	1980	1982	Relative
A	5	6	120
B	7	6	85·7
C	5	9	180

Item	Relative	Wt.	Rel. × Wt.
A	120	3	360
B	85·7	2	171·4
C	180	5	900
		10	1431·4

$$\text{Index} = \frac{\Sigma(Rel. \times Wt.)}{\Sigma\ Wts.} = \frac{1431 \cdot 4}{10} = 143.$$

Current weighted Index.

Item	Consumption 1982	Wt.
A	1600	16
B	1500	15
C	800	8
		39

Item	Relative	Wt.	Rel. × Wt.
A	120	16	1920
B	85·7	15	1285·5
C	180	8	1440
		39	4645·5

$$\text{Index} = \frac{\Sigma(Rel. \times Wt.)}{\Sigma\ Wts.} = \frac{4645·5}{39} = \underline{\underline{119.}}$$

Question 6.

Category	Relative	Wt.	Rel. × Wt.
Housing	345·6	135	46 656
Fuel & Light	398·5	62	24 707
Durables	240·9	65	15 658·5
		262	87 021.5

$$\text{Overall Index} = \frac{(Rel. \times Wt.)}{Wts.} = \frac{87\ 021·5}{262} = \underline{\underline{332·1}}$$

Question 7.

Share	Issued Capital	Wt.	Price 1981	Price 1982	Rel.
A	500 000	25	71	78	109·9
B	120 000	6	53	75	141·5
C	1 300 000	65	45	55	122·2
D	400 000	20	94	85	90·4

Arithmetic weighted Index

Share	Relative	Wt.	Rel. × Wt.
A	109·9	25	2747·5
B	141·5	6	849
C	122·2	65	7943
D	90·4	20	1808
		116	13 347·5

$$\text{Index} = \frac{\Sigma(Rel. \times Wt.)}{\Sigma\ Wts.} = \frac{13347·5}{116} = \underline{\underline{115·1.}}$$

Geometric weighted Index.

Share	Relative	Log. Rel.	Wt.	log. Rel. × Wt.
A	109·9	2·0401	25	51·0025
B	141·5	2·1507	6	12·9042
C	122·2	2·0871	65	135·6615
D	90·4	1·9562	20	39·1240
			116	238·6922

$$\text{log. Index} = \frac{\Sigma(\text{log. Rel.} \times Wt.)}{\Sigma\,Wts.} = \frac{238·6922}{116} = 2·0577.$$

$$\text{Index} = \underline{\underline{114·2.}}$$

CHAPTER 9

Question 2.

Probability of different sales.

Sales	Prob. (*from Poisson tables*)
0	0·22
1	0·34
2	0·25
3	0·13
4	0·05
5	0·01

Pay-off Tables (Profit).

		Sales				
		0	1	2	3	4	5
	1	—0·3	0·65	0·65	0·65	0·65	0·65
	2	—0·6	0·35	1·30	1·30	1·30	1·30
Orders	3	—0·9	0·05	1·00	1·95	1·95	1·95
	4	—1·2	—0·25	0·70	1·65	2·60	2·60
	5	—1·5	—0·55	0·40	1·35	2·30	3·25

Expectations = Pay-off × Probability.

		Sales						
		0	1	2	3	4	5	Total
	1	—·066	·221	·1625	·0845	·0325	·0065	0·441
	2	—·132	·119	·325	·169	·065	·013	0·559
Orders	3	—·198	·017	·25	·2535	·0975	·0195	0·4395
	4	—·264	—·085	·175	·2145	·0825	·0260	0·149
	5	—·330	—·187	·1	·1755	·0675	·0325	—0·1415

For maximum expectation of profit, order 2 units/week.

Question 4.

$$P(r) = \binom{n}{r} p^r \cdot (1 - p)^{n-r}$$

We require $P(0) + P(1) + P(2)$,
i.e. $r = 0, 1, 2$.
$n = 20, p = 0.04$.

$$P(0) = \binom{20}{0} 0.04^0 \cdot 0.96^{20} = 0.96^{20}$$

log. $0.96 = \bar{1}.98227$
20 log. $0.96 = \overline{20} + 19.6454 = \bar{1}.6454$
$0.96^{20} = 0.4420$,
i.e. $P(0) = 0.4420$.

$$P(1) = \binom{20}{1} 0.04^1 \cdot 0.96^{19} = 20 \times 0.04 \times 0.96^{19}.$$

log. $0.96 = \bar{1}.98227$
19 log. $0.96 = 19 + 18.66313 = \bar{1}.66313$
$0.96^{19} = 0.4604$.
$P(1) = 0.8 \times 0.4604 = 0.3683$.

$$P(2) = \binom{20}{2} 0.04^2 \cdot 0.96^{18} = \frac{20 \times 19}{2} \times 0.04^2 \times 0.96^{18}.$$

log. $0.96 = \bar{1}.98227$
18 log. $0.96 = 18 + 17.68086 = \bar{1}.68086$
$0.96^{18} = 0.47959$.
$P(2) = 190 \times 0.0016 \times 0.47959$
$\qquad = 0.1458$.
Hence $P(0) + P(1) + P(2)$
$\qquad = 0.4420 + 0.3683 + 0.1458$
$\qquad = \underline{\underline{0.9561}}.$

Question 5.

$n = 10$, chance of success "by chance" $= 0.5 = p$.

$$P(r) = \binom{n}{r} p^r \cdot (1 - p)^{n-r}$$

$$P(8) = \binom{10}{8} 0.5^8 \cdot 0.5^2$$

$$= \binom{10}{2} 0.5^{10} = \frac{10 \times 9}{2} \cdot 0.5^{10}$$

log. $0.5 = \bar{1}.69897$
10 log. $0.5 = \overline{10} + 6.9897 = \bar{4}.9897$
$0.5^{10} = 0.0009765$.
$P(8) = 45 \times 0.0009765$
$\qquad = \underline{\underline{0.0439}}.$

Assuming the samples are arranged at random and that a probability of 0·05 of him winning by chance is acceptable, then we want r, such that

$$P(r) + P(r + 1) \dots P(n) \leqslant 0.05.$$

Starting with $P(n)$:

$$P(10) = \binom{10}{10} 0.5^{10} \quad = 1 \times 0.0009765 \text{ (from above).}$$

$$P(9) \; = \binom{10}{9} 0.5^9 . 0.5 = 10 \times 0.0009765$$

$$= 0.009765.$$

$$\therefore P(10) + P(9) = 0.0107.$$
$$P(8) = 0.0439 \text{ (as above);}$$
so $P(10) + P(9) + P(8) = 0.0546.$

Strictly, we should insist on at least 9 right. But since 0·5 is an arbitrary figure we would probably accept 8 or more correct as reasonable proof of his ability.

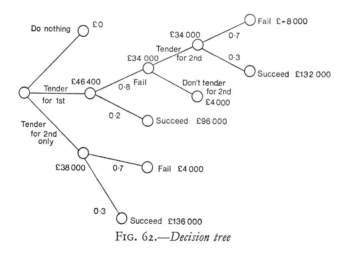

FIG. 62.—*Decision tree*

Question 7.

From the decision tree in Fig. 62 we see that at (A) we choose to tender for the second contract, and at (B) for the first, *i.e.* tender for first and if not successful tender for second. The average expectation of profit is £46 400.

Question 8.

From Poisson tables with $m = 1.8$ and $m = 1.2$

Goals	Prob. for C	Prob. for B	$P(B) \times P(C)$
0	0.165	0.301	0.050
1	0.298	0.361	0.108
2	0.268	0.217	0.058
3	0.161	0.087	0.014
4	0.072	0.026	0.002
5	0.026	0.006	
6	0.008	0.001	
7	0.002		

$$0.232$$

Prob. (draw) is given by $\Sigma(P(B) \times P(C)) = 0.232$.

Prob. (away win) $=$
$P(B = 1) \times P(C = 0) +$
$P(B = 2) \times P(C = 1 \text{ or less}) +$
$P(B = 3) \times P(C = 2 \text{ or less}), \text{ etc.}$
$= 0.361 \times 0.165 +$
$\quad 0.217 \times 0.463 +$
$\quad 0.087 \times 0.731 +$
$\quad 0.026 \times 0.892 +$
$\quad 0.006 \times 0.964 +$
$\quad 0.001 \times 0.990 = 0.254.$

Prob. (home win) $= 1 - P(\text{draw}) - P(\text{away win})$
$\qquad\qquad\qquad = 1 - 0.232 - 0.254$
$\qquad\qquad\qquad = 0.514.$
$P \text{ (home win)} = 0.514.$
$P \text{ (draw)} \quad\;\; = 0.232.$
$P \text{ (away win)} = 0.254.$

Question 9.

Ways of entering $\quad = 8 \times 7 \times 6 \times 5 \times 4 \times 3 \times 2 \times 1$
$\qquad\qquad\qquad\quad\; = 40320.$
$\therefore P \text{ (win by chance)} = 1/40320.$
Expectation of profit $= \dfrac{£1600}{40320} = 0.0397$
$\qquad\qquad\qquad\quad = 3.97\text{p}.$
Cost of entry $\qquad = 8.5\text{p}$
$\therefore$ on average it is not worth entering.

Question 10.

$P(\text{total failure}) = 1 - P(\text{no fail}) - P(1 \text{ fail})$
$= 1 - \binom{4}{0} 0.999^4 - \binom{4}{1} 0.999^3 . 0.001$
$= 1 - 0.996006 - 0.003988$

$= 1 - 0.999994$
$= 0.000006$ or 6×10^{-6}.

Note: this is greater than the allowed risk for a major function of an airliner per flight, and such equipment would need 5 or more control systems to meet safety requirements.

CHAPTER 10

Question 1.

$$\bar{x} = 85 \text{ kg} \quad \sigma_x = 4.5 \text{ kg}$$
95% confidence limits = mean $\pm$ 1.96 s.d.
$$= 85 \pm 1.96 \times 4.5$$
$$= 76.2 \text{ kg} - 93.8 \text{ kg}.$$
$$x = 92, z = (92 - 85)/4.5 = 1.56.$$
$$P(x > 92) = P(z > 1.56) = 0.0594,$$
i.e. <u>5.9%.</u>

Question 2.

From tables $P(z > z_1) = 0.25$,
when $z_1 = 0.6745$
and $P(x > 159) = 0.25$.

$z_1 = (x - \bar{x})/\sigma_x$, and taking $\bar{x} = \dfrac{147 + 159}{2} = 153$.

$0.6745 = (159 - 153)/\sigma_x$,
i.e. $\sigma_x = 6/0.6745 = 8.90$,
i.e. mean $= 153$ s.d. $= 8.9$.

Question 3.

$\bar{x} = 85 \text{ kg} \quad \sigma_x = 4.5 \text{ kg}.$
$P(x > 75) = 1 - P(x < 75);$
for $x = 75 \quad z = (75 - 85)/4.5 = -2.22,$
i.e. $P(x > 75) = 1 - P(z < -2.22)$
$\qquad\qquad = 1 - P(Z > 2.22)$
$\qquad\qquad = 1 - 0.0132$
$\qquad\qquad = 0.9868$
$\qquad$ or <u>98.7%.</u>

The value of z such that
$P(z > z_1) = 0.25$ is 0.6745.
Corresponding deviation from mean
$\quad = 0.6745 \times 4.5 = 3.0 \text{ kg},$
$\therefore$ central 50% in limits $= 85 \pm 3.0 \text{ kg},$
$\qquad$ *i.e.* <u>82.0 — 88.0 kg.</u>

Question 4.

Variance $= 300$ $\therefore$ s.d. $= 17 \cdot 32$.
For 90% confidence need 5% in tails.
For $P(z > z_1) = 0 \cdot 05$.
$\qquad z_1 = 1 \cdot 645$.
With 90% confidence number $= 340 \pm 1 \cdot 645 \times 17 \cdot 32$
$\qquad = 340 \pm 28 \cdot 5$,
i.e. $311 \cdot 5 - 368 \cdot 5$
(or, since we cannot have $0 \cdot 5$ of a person)
$\qquad\qquad 311 - 369$ (90% confidence).

For $x = 300$, $z = \dfrac{300 - 340}{17 \cdot 32} = -2 \cdot 31$.
$P(x < 300) = P(z < -2 \cdot 31) = P(z > 2 \cdot 31)$
$\qquad\qquad = 0 \cdot 0104$.
For $x = 400$, $z = \dfrac{400 - 340}{17 \cdot 32} = 3 \cdot 46$.
$P(x > 400) = P(z > 3 \cdot 46) = 0 \cdot 0002$.
$P(300 < x < 400) = 1 - P(x < 300) - P(x > 400)$
$\qquad\qquad\qquad = 1 - 0 \cdot 0104 - 0 \cdot 0002$
$\qquad\qquad\qquad = 0 \cdot 9894$
$\qquad\qquad\qquad$ or $98 \cdot 9\%$.

Question 5.

For quartiles need 25% in tails.
For $P(z > z_1) = 0 \cdot 25$, $z_1 = 0 \cdot 6745$,
$\therefore$ required deviation from mean
$\qquad = 0 \cdot 6745 \times 17 \cdot 32 = 11 \cdot 7$
$\therefore$ quartiles are at $340 \pm 11 \cdot 7$,
i.e. $328 \cdot 3 - 351 \cdot 7$.
Rounding $Q_1 = 328$, $Q_3 = 352$.

For $x = 320$, $z = (320 - 340)/17 \cdot 32 = -1 \cdot 15$.
$P(x > 320) = 1 - P(x < 320)$
$\qquad\qquad = 1 - P(z < -1 \cdot 15) = 1 - P(z > 1 \cdot 15)$
$\qquad\qquad = 1 - 0 \cdot 1251 = 0 \cdot 8749$
$\qquad\qquad$ or $87 \cdot 5\%$.

CHAPTER 11

Question 1.

Estimate of population variance.
$\bar{x} = (0 \cdot 95 + 0 \cdot 91 + 0 \cdot 93 + 0 \cdot 98)/4 = 0 \cdot 9425$.

x	$(x - \overline{x})$	$(x - \overline{x})^2$
0·95	0·0075	0·00005625
0·91	—0·0325	0·00105625
0·93	—0·0125	0·00015625
0·98	0·0375	0·00140625
		0·00267500

$\hat{\sigma}_x^2 = 0·002675/3 = 0·000892$

$\hat{\sigma}_x = 0·0299.$

Expect x in the range

   $0·9425 \pm 1·65 \times 0·0299$ (90% confidence),

   i.e. $0·9425 \pm 0·0493$

   or $\underline{\underline{0·8932 - 0·9918.}}$

Question 2.

Estimate of variance for 2nd sample.

$\overline{x} = (0·93 + 0·97 + 0·90 + 0·88 + 0·92)/5 = 0·92$

x	$(x - \overline{x})$	$(x - \overline{x})^2$
0·93	0·01	0·0001
0·97	0·05	0·0025
0·90	—0·02	0·0004
0·88	—0·04	0·0016
0·92	0	0
		0·0046

$\hat{\sigma}_x^2 = 0·0046/4 = 0·00115.$

Testing for a difference of means at the 5% significance level we have a two-tailed test with $3 + 4 = 7$ degrees of freedom. The critical values of "t" are $\pm 2·37$.

On the Null Hypothesis of no difference we expect

   difference of means $= 0$

s.d. of diff. of means $= \sqrt{\dfrac{·00115}{5} + \dfrac{0·000892}{4}}$

   $= \sqrt{0·000453} = 0·0213.$

"t" $= \dfrac{observed\ diff. - expected\ diff.}{s.d.\ of\ diff.} = \dfrac{(0·9425 - 0·92) - 0}{0·0213}$

   $= \dfrac{0·0225}{0·0213} = 1·06$ N.S.

The two sample means do not differ significantly.

Question 3.

Sample variance $= 6$

$\therefore$ estimate of population variance $= 6 \times \dfrac{10}{9} = 6·67.$

We do not know before we test which way the sample may differ from the population, so we have a two-tailed test, with 9 degrees of freedom and at the 5% significance level this gives a critical value for "t" of $\pm 2 \cdot 26$.

On the Null Hypothesis of no difference we expect

$$\text{mean of sample means} = 35$$

$$\text{s.d. of sample means} = \sqrt{\frac{6 \cdot 67}{10}} = 0 \cdot 816.$$

$$\text{"}t\text{"} = \frac{observed\ mean - expected\ mean}{s.d.\ of\ mean} = \frac{31 - 35}{0 \cdot 816}$$

$$= -4 \cdot 90^{***}.$$

We have a very highly significant difference and hence conclude that the sample is extremely unlikely to have come from a population, mean $= 35$.

Question 4.

$\hat{\pi} = p = 0 \cdot 38, n = 400$

$\therefore \sigma_p = \sqrt{(0 \cdot 38 \times 0 \cdot 62)/400}$

$\qquad = \sqrt{0 \cdot 000589} = 0 \cdot 0243$

$\therefore \pi = 0 \cdot 38 \pm 1 \cdot 65 \times 0 \cdot 0243$

$\qquad = 0 \cdot 38 \pm 0 \cdot 04,$

i.e. $\pi = 0 \cdot 34 - 0 \cdot 42$ (90% confidence).

Question 5.

Salesman	Before	After	d	d^2
1	48	53	5	25
2	41	40	-1	1
3	52	59	7	49
4	38	40	2	4
5	51	47	-4	16
6	44	48	4	16
7	52	54	2	4
			15	115

$\bar{d} = 15/7 = 2 \cdot 14.$

$\hat{\sigma}_d^2 = 1/6[\Sigma d^2 - (\Sigma d)^2/n] = 1/6[115 - (15)^2/7]$

$\qquad = 82 \cdot 86/6 = 13 \cdot 81.$

$\hat{\sigma}_{\bar{d}}^2 = 13 \cdot 81/7 = 1 \cdot 973.$

$\hat{\sigma}_{\bar{d}} = 1 \cdot 40.$

We are looking for an increase so we have a one-tailed test, and with 6 degrees of freedom and a 5% significance level we have the critical value of "t" = $1 \cdot 94$.

On the Null Hypothesis of no change we expect

$$\text{mean diff.} = 0$$
$$\text{s.d. of mean diff.} = 1\cdot40$$
$$\text{``}t\text{''} = \frac{\textit{obs. mean diff.} - \textit{exp. mean diff.}}{\textit{s.d. mean diff.}}$$
$$= \frac{2\cdot14}{1\cdot40} = 1\cdot53 \text{ N.S.}$$

We conclude that the consultant has not made good his claim on the basis of this test.

Question 6.

$$n = 2000 \quad \hat{\pi} = p = 300/2000 = 0\cdot15.$$
$$\text{s.d. of } p = \sqrt{\frac{0\cdot15 \times 0\cdot85}{2000}} = \sqrt{0\cdot00006375}$$
$$= 0\cdot00798.$$
$$\therefore \pi = 0\cdot15 \pm 1\cdot96 \times 0\cdot00798$$
$$= 0\cdot15 \pm 0\cdot0156,$$
$$\textit{i.e. } \pi = 0\cdot1344 - 0\cdot1656 \text{ (95\% confidence)}$$
$$\text{for } \pi = 0\cdot40$$
$$\hat{\sigma}_p = \sqrt{(0\cdot4 \times 0\cdot6)/n}$$
and we want $1\cdot96 . \hat{\sigma}_p \leqslant 0\cdot02$,
i.e. $1\cdot96\sqrt{(0\cdot4 \times 0\cdot6)/n} \leqslant 0\cdot02$
or $n \geqslant (0\cdot4 \times 0\cdot6 \times 1\cdot96^2)/(0\cdot02)^2$,
i.e. $n \geqslant \underline{\underline{2305}}$.

Question 7

Workman	Before	After	d	d^2
A	13	11	—2	4
B	5	5	0	0
C	7	5	—2	4
D	16	12	—4	16
E	11	10	—1	1
F	5	4	—1	1
G	8	7	—1	1
H	9	7	—2	4
I	16	14	—2	4
			—15	35

$$\hat{\sigma}_d^2 = \frac{1}{n-1}\left[\Sigma d^2 - \frac{(\Sigma d)^2}{n}\right] = \frac{1}{8}\left[35 - \frac{(-15)^2}{9}\right]$$
$$= \frac{10}{8} = 1\cdot25$$
$$\hat{\sigma}_{\bar{d}}^2 = 1\cdot25/9 = 0\cdot1389$$
$$\hat{\sigma}_{\bar{d}} = \sqrt{0\cdot1389} = 0\cdot37$$

We are looking specifically for a decrease so we have a one-tailed test, with 7 degrees of freedom and at the 5% significance level the critical value of "t" is $-2 \cdot 37$.

On the Null Hypothesis of no change, we expect

$$\text{mean diff.} = 0$$
$$\text{s.d. of mean diff.} = 0 \cdot 35.$$
$$"t" = \frac{obs.\ mean\ diff. - exp.\ mean\ diff.}{s.d.\ mean\ diff.} = \frac{-1 \cdot 875}{0 \cdot 37}$$
$$= -5 \cdot 07\ ^{***}.$$

We conclude that there is a negligible doubt that the training is effective.

Question 8.

$$n = 450, \quad p = 0 \cdot 52$$
Testing against $\pi = 0 \cdot 50$
$$\sigma_\pi = \sqrt{(0 \cdot 5 \times 0 \cdot 5)/450} = \sqrt{0 \cdot 000555}$$
$$= 0 \cdot 0236.$$

We are testing for a percentage greater than 50% so we have a one-tailed test, hence at the 5% significance level the critical value of $z = 1 \cdot 65$.

On the Null Hypothesis of no difference we expect

$$\text{sample proportion} = 0 \cdot 50$$
$$\text{s.d. of sample proportion} = 0 \cdot 0236$$
$$z = \frac{obs.\ prop. - exp.\ prop.}{s.d.\ prop.} = \frac{0 \cdot 52 - 0 \cdot 50}{0 \cdot 0236}$$
$$= 0 \cdot 85\ \text{N.S.}$$

On this evidence, Joe Bloggs cannot assume that he will win the election.

Question 9.

Estimating the variance.
$$\bar{x} = (104 + 121 + 110 + 115)/4 = 112 \cdot 5.$$

x	$(x - \bar{x})$	$(x - \bar{x})^2$
104	$-8 \cdot 5$	$72 \cdot 25$
121	$8 \cdot 5$	$72 \cdot 25$
110	$-2 \cdot 5$	$6 \cdot 25$
115	$2 \cdot 5$	$6 \cdot 25$
		$157 \cdot 00$

$$\hat{\sigma}_x^2 = 157/3 = 52 \cdot 33.$$
$$\hat{\sigma}_{\bar{x}}^2 = 52 \cdot 33/4 = 13 \cdot 08.$$
$$\hat{\sigma}_{\bar{x}} = 3 \cdot 62.$$

We have 3 degrees of freedom and for a two-tailed test the critical values for "t" for 5% significance are $\pm 3 \cdot 18$.

$\mu = \overline{x} = 112 \cdot 5$
$\therefore \mu = 112 \cdot 5 \pm 3 \cdot 18 \times 3 \cdot 62$
$\quad = 112 \cdot 5 \pm 11 \cdot 5,$
i.e. mean $= 101 - 124$ (95% confidence).

Question 10.

By examination 108 is in the 95% range for the population mean, so the data does not contradict the statement.

CHAPTER 14

Question 1.

From the table, total accidents $= 215$
mean rate $= 215/294 = 0 \cdot 73$.

Accidents	Employees	Prob.	Expected
0	169	0·482	141·71
1	67	0·352	103·49
2	32	0·128	37·63
3	20	0·031	9·11
4	6	0·006	1·76

294

(Prob. is calculated from $P(0) = e^{-0 \cdot 73}$
$$P(1) = (P(0) \times 0 \cdot 73)/1, \text{ etc.}).$$
Expected $=$ Prob. $\times 294$.
Calculation of χ^2

O	E	$O - E$	$(O - E)^2$	$(O - E)^2/E$
169	141·71	27·29	744·74	5·26
67	103·49	−36·49	1331·52	12·87
32	37·63	−5·63	31·70	0·84
20	9·11	10·89	118·59	13·02
6	1·76	4·24	17·98	10·21

$$\chi^2 = 42 \cdot 20^{***}$$

We have $5 - 2 = 3$ degrees of freedom, and for 5% significance level the critical value of $\chi^2 = 7 \cdot 81$.
The value found is very highly significant. We conclude that the Poisson distribution is not a good fit to this data.

Question 2.

Calculation of mean and variance.

Class	Mid pt. $= X$	$x = (X - 150)/20$	f	fx	fx^2
60–120	90	-3	15	-45	135
120–140	130	-1	20	-20	20
140–160	150	0	45	-65	0
160–180	170	1	25	25	25
180–200	190	2	15	30	60
200–260	230	4	15	60	240
			135	115	480
				-65	
				50	

$\bar{x}$ = 50/135 = 0·37.

X = 0·37 × 20 + 150 = 157·4.

$Var._x$ = 1/135[480 − (50)²/135]

= 3·4184

$s.d_x$ = 1·849.

$s.d_X$ = 1·849 × 20 = 36·98.

Fitting the Normal Curve.

Class bound	z	Prob. in tail	Prob. in class	Exp.
120	$-1·01$	0·156	0·156	21·06
140	$-0·47$	0·319	0·163	22·00
—			*0·209	28·22
160	0·07	0·472	0·201	27·14
180	0·61	0·271	0·146	19·14
200	1·15	0·125	0·125	16·87

* by difference.

Test of Fit by χ^2

O	E	$O - E$	$(O - E)^2$	$(O - E)^2/E$
15	21·06	$-6·06$	36·72	1·74
20	22·00	$-2·00$	4·00	0·18
45	28·22	16·78	281·57	9·98
25	27·14	$-2·14$	4·58	0·17
15	19·71	$-4·71$	22·18	1·13
15	16·87	$-1·87$	3·50	0·21

$$\chi^2 = 13·41**$$

We have 3 degrees of freedom, and for 5% significance level the critical value of $\chi^2 = 7·81$. This is exceeded and so the normal distribution is not a good fit.

Question 3.
Observed.

	W.	P.	M.	
Absent	15	15	10	40
Never absent	30	95	35	160
	45	110	45	200

On Null Hypothesis.

Expected.

	W.	P.	M.	
Absent	9	22	9	40
Never absent	36	88	36	160
	45	110	45	200

Calculation of χ^2.

O	E	$(O - E)$	$(O - E)^2$	$(O - E)^2/E$
15	9	6	36	4·00
15	22	−7	49	2·23
10	9	1	1	0·11
30	36	−6	36	1·00
95	88	7	49	0·57
35	36	−1	1	0·03

$$\chi^2 = 7\cdot94 \text{ N.S.}$$

We have $(3 - 1)(3 - 1) = 4$ degrees of freedom and for 5% significance level the critical value of $\chi^2 = 9\cdot49$.

We reject the null hypothesis and conclude that absenteeism does not differ significantly between the departments.

Question 4.

On the Null Hypothesis.

Expected.

	For	D.K.	Against	
Under 21	14	9·33	11·67	35
21–29	44	29·33	36·67	110
30–49	36	24	30	90
50 and over	26	17·33	21·67	65
	120	80	100	300

Calculation of χ^2.

O	E	$(O - E)$	$(O - E)^2$	$(O - E)^2/E$
20	14	6	36	2·57
40	44	−4	16	0·36
40	36	+4	16	0·44
20	26	−6	36	1·39
10	9·33	0·67	0·45	0·05
30	29·33	0·67	0·45	0·02
20	24	−4	16	0·67
20	17·33	2·67	7·13	0·41
5	11·67	−6·67	44·49	3·81
40	36·67	3·33	11·09	0·30
30	30	0	0	0
25	21·67	3·33	11·09	0·51

$$\chi^2 = 10\cdot53 \text{ N.S.}$$

We have $(3 - 1)(4 - 1) = 6$ degrees of freedom and for 5%
significance level the critical value of $\chi^2 = 12\cdot59$.
We conclude there is no dependence of opinion on age.

Question 5.

Test against expected value for an even split.

O	E	$(O - E)$	$(O - E)^*$	$(O - E)^{*2}$	$(O - E)^{*2}/E$
159	145	14	13·5	182·25	1·26
131	145	−14	−13·5	182·25	1·26

$$\chi^2 = 2\cdot52 \text{ N.S.}$$

With 1 degree of freedom at the 5% significance level, critical
value of $\chi^2 = 3\cdot84$. There is no evidence of a majority in favour.

Question 6.

On the Null Hypothesis of no effect.

Expected.

	Less headaches	Same	
drug	14	6	20
no drug	14	6	20
	28	12	40

Calculation of χ^2.

O	E	$(O-E)$	$(O-E)^*$	$(O-E)^{*2}$	$(O-E)^{*2}/E$
16	14	2	1·5	2·25	0·16
12	14	−2	−1·5	2·25	0·16
4	6	−2	−1·5	2·25	0·37
8	6	2	1·5	2·25	0·37

$$\chi^2 = 1\cdot06 \text{ N.S.}$$

We have $(2-1)(2-1) = 1$ degree of freedom and at the 5% significance level the critical value of $\chi^2 = 3\cdot84$.

The data does not show any significant effect for the drug.

Question 7.

On the Null Hypothesis of no difference.

Expected.

	A	B	
Above	43	43	86
Below	43	43	86
	86	86	172

Calculating χ^2.

O	E	$(O-E)$	$(O-E)^*$	$(O-E)^{*2}$	$(O-E)^{*2}/E$
49	43	6	5·5	30·25	0·70
37	43	−6	−5·5	30·25	0·70
49	43	6	5·5	30·25	0·70
37	43	−6	−5·5	30·25	0·70

$$\chi^2 = 2\cdot80 \text{ N.S.}$$

We have $(2-1)(2-1) = 1$ degree of freedom and for a 5% significance level the critical value of $\chi^2 = 3\cdot84$.

We conclude that the two samples do not differ significantly.

Question 8.

Assuming equal skill, average score

$$= (10 + 12 + 15 + 8 + 16)/5 = 12\cdot2$$

O	E	$(O-E)$	$(O-E)^2$	$(O-E)^2/E$
10	12·2	−2·2	4·84	0·40
12	12·2	−0·2	0·04	0
15	12·2	2·8	7·84	0·64
8	12·2	−4·2	17·64	1·45
16	12·2	3·8	14·44	1·18

$$\chi^2 = 3\cdot67 \text{ N.S.}$$

We have $5 - 2 = 3$ degrees of freedom and for a 5% significance level the critical value of $\chi^2 = 7 \cdot 82$.

We conclude that the archers do not differ significantly.

Question 9.

On the Null Hypothesis of no dependence.

Expected.

	Fat	*Normal*	*Thin*	
Normal	72·75	151·5	75·75	300
Neurotic	14·55	30·3	15·15	60
Psychotic	9·7	20·2	10·1	40
	97	202	101	400

Calculation of χ^2.

O	E	$(O - E)$	$(O - E)^2$	$(O - E)^2/E$
82	72·75	9·25	85·56	1·18
7	14·55	−7·55	57·00	3·92
8	9·7	−1·7	2·89	0·30
140	151·5	−11·5	132·25	0·87
34	30·3	3·7	13·69	0·45
28	20·2	7·8	60·84	3·01
78	75·75	2·25	5·06	0·07
19	15·15	3·85	14·82	0·98
4	10·1	−6·1	37·21	3·68

$$\chi^2 = 14 \cdot 46^{**}$$

We have $(3 - 1)(3 - 1) = 4$ degrees of freedom and for 5% significance level the critical value of $\chi^2 = 9 \cdot 49$.

We conclude that there is a significant relationship between mental state and physical build.

CHAPTER 15

Question 1.

	A	B	C
	5	8	3
	7	5	5
	4	12	4
	9	7	9
	6	7	5
Sum	31	39	26 = 96
Sum²	961	1521	676 = 3158/5 = 631·6.

$C.F.\ = 96^2/15 = 614\cdot4.$
Total Squares $= 694.$
$C_{TOT} = 694 - 614\cdot4\ \ = 79\cdot6.$
$C_{COL} = 631\cdot6 - 614\cdot4 = 17\cdot2.$

Source	S.Sq.	d.f.	M.S.	F.
Between cols.	17·2	2	8·6	1·65 N.S.
Within-cols.	62·4	12	5·2	
Total	79·6	14		

At the 5% level with (2, 12) degrees of freedom, critical value of $F = 3\cdot89.$
We conclude that the levels do not differ significantly.

Question 2.

Coding the data by subtracting 160.

		\multicolumn{5}{c}{A}			Sum	Sum²
		1	2	3	4	5	Sum	Sum²
	1	−3	−1	4	28	1	29	841
	2	7	−3	4	19	−3	24	576
B	3	−11	−13	−7	0	−13	−44	1936
	4	25	3	22	31	27	108	11 664
	5	9	13	−1	25	11	57	3249
Sum		27	−1	22	103	23 =	174	18 266/5 = 3653·2.
Sum²		729	1	484	10 609	529 =		

$529 = \dfrac{12\ 352}{4} = 2470\cdot4.$

$C.F.\ = 174^2/25 = 1211\cdot04.$
Total Squares $= 5568.$
$C_{TOT} = 5568 - 1211\cdot04 = 4356\cdot96.$
$C_{COL} = 2470\cdot4 - 1211\cdot04 = 1259\cdot36.$
$C_{ROW} = 3653\cdot2 - 1211\cdot04 = 2442\cdot16.$

Source	S. Sq.	d.f.	M.S.	F.
Main A	1259·36	4	314·8	7·7**
Main B	2442·16	4	610·5	14·9***
Residual	655·44	16	40·96	
Total	4356·96	24		

For 5% significance level and (4, 16) degrees of freedom the critical value of $F = 3\cdot01.$
We conclude that both factors are significant.

Question 6.

Coding by $x = (X - 18\cdot0)/0\cdot1$.

Tester

		A	B	C	D	Sum	Sum^2
	1	4	1	2	2	9	81
Procedure	2	2	0	2	0	4	16
	3	6	3	5	3	17	289
Sum		12	4	9	5 = 30		386/4 = 96·5.
Sum^2		144	16	81	25 = 266/3 =		88·67.

$C.F. = 30^2/12 = 75.$
Total Squares $= 112.$
$C_{TOT} = 112 - 75 = 37.$
$C_{COL} = 88\cdot67 - 75 = 13\cdot67.$
$C_{ROW} = 96\cdot5 - 75 = 21\cdot5.$

Source	S. Sq.	d.f.	M.S.	F
Main A	13·67	3	4·56	14·9**
Main B	21·50	2	10·75	35·2***
Residual	1·83	6	0·305	
Total	37	11		

At the 5% significance level and for $(3, 6)$ and $(2, 6)$ degrees of freedom the critical values of F are 4·76 and 5·14.
We conclude that there are significant effects due to both testers and procedures.

Question 10.

Source	S. Sq.	d.f.	M.S.	F	
Main A	39·41	3	13·14	<1	N.S.
Main B	108·23	2	54·11	4·09	N.S.
A × B	79·32	6	13·22	7·15**	
Residual	22·18	12	1·85		
Total	249·14	23			

For 5% significance level the critical values for $(6, 12)$, $(3, 6)$ and $(2, 6)$ degrees of freedom are 3·00, 4·76 and 5·14.
We conclude that the highly significant interaction may be "swamping" the main effects, which are not significant on the basis of this data.

CHAPTER 16

Question 1.

Let $X =$ Temp. $x = X - 15$.
$Y =$ Sales, $y = (Y - 1500)/50$.

X	Y	x	y	x^2	y^2	xy
10	1100	-5	-8	25	64	40
12	1050	-3	-9	9	81	27
15	1250	0	-5	0	25	0
18	1500	3	0	9	0	0
20	1550	5	1	25	1	5
17	1600	2	2	4	4	4
21	1650	6	3	36	9	18
22	1800	7	6	49	36	42
21	1850	6	7	36	49	42
18	1700	3	4	9	16	12
17	1600	2	2	4	4	4
15	1200	0	-6	0	24	0
18	1800	3	6	9	24	18
20	1850	5	7	25	49	35
20	1750	5	5	25	25	25
22	1950	7	9	49	81	63
17	1800	2	6	4	36	12
14	1500	-1	0	1	0	0
13	1300	-2	-4	4	16	8
9	1000	-6	-10	36	100	60
		39	16	359	644	416

$n \quad = 20, \quad \Sigma_x = 39, \quad \Sigma_y = 16.$
$\Sigma_x^2 = 359, \quad \Sigma_y^2 = 644, \quad \Sigma_{xy} = 416.$
$C_{xx} = 359 - (39)^2/20 \quad = 282 \cdot 95.$
$C_{yy} = 644 - (16)^2/20 \quad = 631 \cdot 20.$
$C_{xy} = 416 - (39 \times 16)/20 = 384 \cdot 8.$
$\sqrt{C_{xx}} = 16 \cdot 82.$
$\sqrt{C_{yy}} = 25 \cdot 12.$
$r = \dfrac{C_{xy}}{\sqrt{C_{xx}} \cdot \sqrt{C_{yy}}} = \dfrac{384 \cdot 8}{16 \cdot 82 \times 25 \cdot 12} = 0 \cdot 91.$

Proportion of variability explained $= 0 \cdot 91^2 = 0 \cdot 83$.
Calculation of regression line:

$x = 39/20 = 1 \cdot 95.$
$\bar{X} = 15 + 1 \cdot 95 = 16 \cdot 95.$
$\hat{y} = 16/20 = 0 \cdot 8.$
$\bar{Y} = 0 \cdot 8 \times 50 + 1500 = 1540.$
$b = \dfrac{C_{xy}}{C_{xx}} \times hy \quad (hx \text{ not used}).$

$$= \frac{384 \cdot 8 \times 50}{282 \cdot 95} = 68 \cdot 00.$$

$$a = \bar{Y} - b\bar{X} = 1540 - 68 \times 16 \cdot 95$$
$$= 387 \cdot 4.$$

Regression line is
$$\hat{Y}_i = 387 \cdot 4 + 68X_i.$$

Variability due to regression
$$= b, C_X = 68 \times 384 \cdot 8 \times 50$$
$$= 1\ 308\ 320.$$

Total Variability.
$$= C_{YY} = 631 \cdot 20 \times 50^2 = 1\ 578\ 000.$$

Variability around regression $= 269\ 680.$
Degrees of freedom $= 20 - 2 = 18.$
$\therefore$ Variance around regression $= 269\ 680/18$
$$= 14\ 982.$$
s.d. around regression $= 122 \cdot 4.$

$$Y_i = \hat{Y}_i \pm t_{00 \cdot 5} \cdot s \cdot \sqrt{1 + \frac{1}{n} + \frac{(x_i - \bar{x})^2}{C_{xx}}}.$$

For $X_i = 21$
$$\hat{Y}_i = 387 \cdot 4 + 68 \times 21$$
$$= 1815 \cdot 4.$$

$t_{00 \cdot 5}$ with 18 degrees of freedom $= 2 \cdot 10.$

$$Y_i = 1815 \cdot 4 \pm 1 \cdot 734 \times 122 \cdot 4 \cdot \sqrt{1 + \frac{1}{20} + \frac{(21 - 16 \cdot 95)^2}{282 \cdot 95}}$$

$$= 1815 \cdot 4 \pm 212 \cdot 24\sqrt{1 \cdot 108}$$
$$= 1815 \cdot 4 \pm 222 \cdot 9,$$

i.e. $1592 \cdot 5 - 2038 \cdot 3$ (90% confidence).

At the 5% significance level, the critical value for

$$r_{sp} = \frac{2}{\sqrt{n - 1}}$$
$$= \frac{2}{\sqrt{19}} = 0 \cdot 46.$$

The value we have is significant.

Question 5.

The critical value for r with 26 sets of measurements at the 5%
significance level is $\dfrac{2}{\sqrt{25}} = 0 \cdot 4.$

All three correlations are significant.
Removing the effect of time, if the two quantities are 1 and 2:

Then

$$r_{12 \cdot t} = \frac{r_{12} - r_{1t} \cdot r_{2t}}{\sqrt{(1 - r_{1t}{}^2)} \cdot \sqrt{(1 - r_{2t}{}^2)}}$$

$$= \frac{0 \cdot 83 - 0 \cdot 91 \times 0 \cdot 75}{\sqrt{(1 - 0 \cdot 91^2)} \cdot \sqrt{(1 - 0 \cdot 75^2)}}$$

$$= \frac{0 \cdot 1475}{\sqrt{0 \cdot 1719 \times 0 \cdot 4375}} = \frac{0 \cdot 1475}{0 \cdot 2742}$$

$$= 0 \cdot 54.$$

The critical value is now $\dfrac{2}{\sqrt{n-2}} = \dfrac{2}{\sqrt{24}} \backsimeq 0 \cdot 4.$

The correlation, although smaller, is still significant without the effect of time.

APPENDIX IV
List of Symbols

α	Smoothing constant.
α	Population regression coefficient.
a	Sample regression coefficient.
A	Factor in quality control chart construction.
β	Population regression coefficient.
b	Sample regression coefficient.
c	Coding constant.
c	Number of columns.
c	Allowed number of defectives in acceptance sampling.
C	Coefficient of variation.
C	(subscripted) Corrected sum of squares.
d	Difference of matched figures.
d_n	Factor for calculation of standard deviation.
D	Factor in quality control chart construction.
e	Base of natural logarithms $= 2 \cdot 718$.
f	Class frequency.
F	Variance ratio.
$G.M.$	Geometric mean.
h	Coding factor.
k	General purpose constant.
χ^2	Chi-squared (*see* text).
μ	Population mean.
m	Sample mean.
n	Number in sample.
N	Number in population.
π	Natural constant $= 3 \cdot 146$.
π	Population proportion.
p	Sample proportion.
Π	Product operator.
$P(r)$	Probability that event (r) will occur.
q	General constant.
Q	Quartile.
QD	Quartile deviation.
r	Number of rows.
r	Required result in sampling.
r	Coefficient of correlation.
R	Coefficient of multiple correlation.
σ	Population standard deviation.
σ^2	Population variance.
s	Sample standard deviation.
s^2	Sample variance.
Σ	Summation operator.

S	Smoothed figures in exponential smoothing.
Sk_p	Pearson's measure of skewness.
t	Constant, time.
"t"	Students' "t."
T	Smoothed trend in exponential smoothing.
w	Weighting factor.
w	Sample range.
x	General variable.
x	Coded value of data.
X	Original value of data.
y	General variable.
y	Coded value of data.
Y	Original value of data.
z	Standardised deviation (normal curve).

The use of the bar, *e.g.* $\bar{x}$,
　　　　the circumflex, *e.g.* $\hat{x}$,
　and of sub-scripts, *e.g.* x_t,
will be explained as they occur in the text.

INDEX